Studies in Deprivation and Disadvantage 10

Parents and Children

Incomes in Two Generations

SSRC
DHSS

Studies in Deprivation and Disadvantage 10

DHSS

Studies in Deprivation and Disadvantage 10

Parents and Children

Incomes in Two Generations

A. B. Atkinson
A. K. Maynard
C. G. Trinder

in conjunction with

J. Corlyon
S. P. Jenkins
H. Sutherland

Heinemann Educational Books · London

Heinemann Educational Books Ltd
22 Bedford Square, London WC1B 3HH

LONDON EDINBURGH MELBOURNE AUCKLAND
HONG KONG SINGAPORE KUALA LUMPUR NEW DELHI
IBADAN NAIROBI JOHANNESBURG
EXETER (NH) KINGSTON PORT OF SPAIN

First published 1983

British Library Cataloguing in Publication Data

Atkinson, A.B.
   Parents and children: incomes in two generations.—
(Studies in deprivation and disadvantage; 10)
   1. Socially handicapped—Great Britain—Income
   2. Socially handicapped children—Great Britain—
Income
I. Title   II. Maynard, A.K.   III. Trinder,
C.G.   IV. Series
362.8   HN400

ISBN 0–435–82097–4

Typeset by Inforum Ltd, Portsmouth
Printed in Great Britain by Biddles Ltd, Guildford, Surrey

Contents

Preface

This book reports the results of a study of intergenerational income mobility in Britain, based on a follow-up survey of the families interviewed in Seebohm Rowntree's investigation of poverty in York in 1950. The research was supported by the DHSS/SSRC Contract for Research on Transmitted Deprivation. The first stage was a pilot project carried out by Atkinson and Trinder from 1 January 1974 to 30 September 1975. This reviewed the existing literature on the association of economic advantage and disadvantage across generations and explored the feasibility of using a follow-up survey to provide new evidence. On the basis of this experience, Atkinson, Maynard and Trinder put forward a proposal for a full-scale follow-up of the Rowntree families. This received support from the DHSS/SSRC Contract from December 1975 to December 1978. It is this research which is described in this book. Subsequent to the end of the grant from the DHSS/SSRC Contract, we have received financial help from the Joseph Rowntree Memorial Trust and from the Nuffield Foundation, which has allowed us to develop the work. The results are in part incorporated in this book and have in part appeared in articles (see the References).

The book appears some years after the follow-up survey was carried out. To a certain extent this reflects the usual time needed to digest and analyse survey findings, but it also reflects the fact that we have written two reports on this study. In the first report, written in summer 1980 (and revised a year later), we attempted to provide a full account of the methodology and details of the survey. This we felt to be necessary in view of the novel nature of the method and of the material. This report, entitled 'From Parents to Children: Living Standards in Two Generations', is unpublished, but copies are lodged in the British Library of Political and Economic Science, at the Social Science Research Council, at the University of York, and at the National Institute of Economic and Social Research. At the same time, it has been urged on us by the Organising Group of the DHSS/SSRC Joint Working Party that we should, in addition, prepare a shorter version, excluding much of the technical detail. We share their view that this will help make the findings more accessible to the general reader, and this is the reason for the second report, which is contained in this volume.

The research has involved a great many people, and we should like to take this opportunity to thank them. The DHSS/SSRC grant allowed for the appointment, in addition to Christopher Trinder, of Judy Corlyon, who has been associated with the project throughout its existence. Under the Nuffield Foundation grant, we were able to employ Stephen Jenkins at the University of York. Holly Sutherland, of the Department of Political Economy, University College London, played a large role in the computer analysis of the data. All three have contributed in a major way to the success of the research, which, as we have tried to indicate on the title-page, is very much a joint product.

In the course of the project, we have received a great deal of help. Mr T. J. Brooke provided valuable information about the original 1950 inquiry. Paul Shanahan worked on the initial tracing of the sample; Martin Gannon carried out research in York Public Library on the more difficult-to-trace families; and Peter Arnold followed up these leads in the York streets. Chris Gray and Paul O'Riordan spent many evenings assisting with the computing work. Karen Trinder helped with the reanalysis of Rowntree's 1950 data and with the collating of the 1975–8 schedules. Sarah Harrison spent many weeks photo-copying. Carolyn Slingsby was a full-time interviewer until October 1976, and Mary Atherley, Helen Sills and Mary Cole worked as part-time interviewers. Their conscientious and skilful work were essential to the success of the project.

Many people offered advice and encouragement. The design of the questionnaire was improved by Peter Townsend, Adrian Sinfield and Dennis Marsden of the University of Essex, and by Peter Willmott, Linda McDowell and Lucy Syson of the Institute of Community Studies, London. We have drawn on an undergraduate finals project by Stuart Allcock (University of York, 1977). Arthur Walker was a continuous source of encouragement. We are very grateful to Anne Robinson for typing and retyping much of the material – and for her suggestions to make the report more readable – and to Jane Dickson for typing most of the final report. Judith Atkinson, John Goldthorpe, Richard Layard, Lee Rainwater, Michael Wagner, the Joint Working Party and two referees provided most helpful criticism of earlier versions. The project was administered by the Institute of Social and Economic Research at the University of York, and we should like to acknowledge the assistance of Professor Jack Wiseman and John Nash.

The Joseph Rowntree Memorial Trust very kindly made available to us, under conditions of confidentiality, the survey returns from the original 1950 inquiry. Without access to these, our follow-up study would have been impossible.

Finally, we should thank the families who took part in our follow-up survey. We very much appreciated their co-operation and – in a number of cases – enthusiasm. The families took great trouble to answer our questions and we, in turn, have taken every care to ensure that the confidentiality of what they told us is preserved. When referring to individual families, we have used fictitious names and changed details to avoid any possible clue being given to the identity of our respondents.

Note for the Reader

In order to ease the flow of the text, references have been kept to a minimum. However, the notes for each chapter at the end of the book provide information about sources and further references. References in the text are indicated by the author's name and the date of publication: for example, Smith (1982). Where there are two works by the same author in one year, they are referred to as Smith (1982a and 1982b). The full citation is given in the References at the end of the book.

We have tried in this book to employ only the simplest statistical tools. However, there are places in which we could not avoid using statistical methods or terms which may not be familiar. We have therefore included a note at the end of the book giving a brief explanation.

In certain tables, the figures have been rounded and do not necessarily sum exactly to the totals shown.

1 Intergenerational Income Mobility – the Issues

Introduction

This book reports the results of a study of intergenerational income mobility in Britain, based on a follow-up of the investigation organised by Seebohm Rowntree in York in 1950. The study aims to provide factual evidence in a field where little is at present known and to interpret this evidence, with particular reference to continuities in low incomes across generations. The kinds of question we have been seeking to answer are these: How much continuity is there in economic status across generations? Do the children of poor parents tend themselves to have low incomes? To the extent that economic advantage tends to be associated across generations, what are the mechanisms that lead to continuity? What, for example, is the role of education? How is mobility influenced by the structure of the labour-market?

To answer these questions we had to collect new data, and the first part of the book is concerned with describing the procedures adopted. The problems we faced, notably in tracing the children of the original Rowntree families, are rather different from those usually encountered in social science research and the evidence needs to be interpreted with care. Nevertheless, we feel that the findings, the first on income mobility across generations in Britain, go some way towards filling an important gap in our knowledge and provide a valuable basis for examining the determinants of earnings and income.

In seeking to interpret the evidence, we have had to become acquainted with the approaches adopted in a number of different subjects. There is an obvious parallel between our work and the more fully developed field of occupational mobility. Our investigation of family background has led us into territory explored in the longitudinal studies of J. W. B. Douglas (for example, Douglas, Ross and Simpson, 1968) and the National Child Development Study (for example, Davie, Butler and Goldstein, 1972). The issues raised by the role of education are similar to those discussed by sociologists (for example, Halsey, Heath and Ridge, 1980) and psychologists (such as Rutter *et al.*, 1979). The study of the labour-market brings us into the field of industrial relations, job recruitment and employment practices. In the analysis of our data, we have tried to learn from these different approaches and to draw on their findings. At the same time, we have been conscious of our limited expertise in these different disciplines and of the restrictions of both our research budget and time. We have tended therefore to focus on those issues which have attracted most attention from economists.

Outline of the book

The project grew out of the realisation that very little is known about intergenerational income mobility. Although research on occupational mobility has been pioneering and fruitful, there was, when we began our study, no comparable evidence on intergenerational income mobility in Britain. In Chapter 2, we outline the possible approaches to collecting such evidence, drawing on the experience of occupational mobility studies. We explain why the latter evidence cannot be directly applied to earnings or income. After describing the limited information about income mobility in other countries, we assess the potential of different sources in Britain. By a process of elimination, we were led to the idea of a follow-up survey to the 1950 Rowntree inquiry in York.

The Rowntree survey is described in Chapter 3, where we examine its adequacy as the base for a follow-up investigation. We discuss the problem of tracing the children of the original respondents after more than a quarter of a century, and give an account of the methods and detective work involved. The interviews with the second generation in 1975–8 are the subject of Chapter 4, where we describe the main chracteristics of our respondents. It should be stressed that neither generation is a nationally representative sample. Rowntree's original survey related to the 'working-class population' in one city. Our follow-up survey was not confined to families who stayed in York, but the majority of the children interviewed still lived in the city.

In our analysis of the evidence collected in the follow-up study, the main focus is on the association of economic status, measured in terms of income or earnings. We first present the findings about the extent of continuity across generations and then seek to examine some of the mechanisms lying behind the observed association. Chapter 5 is concerned with income mobility; in each case, income is expressed relative to the Supplementary Benefit (in 1950 National Assistance) scale. We study the mobility between income-groups of parents and children, and the extent to which advantage or disadvantage tends to be associated. Particular attention is paid to the position of low-income families, defined as those below 140 per cent of the Supplementary Benefit scale. In Chapter 6, we turn to the degree of intergenerational earnings mobility where the father was in work in 1950 and the child was employed in 1975–8. We consider a number of different indicators of the extent of mobility, and examine how far they are influenced by different adjustments to the data: for example, to allow for temporary variations in earnings or for life-cycle differences.

The mechanisms lying behind the pattern of earnings mobility are taken up in Chapter 7, where we concentrate on the role played by family background, with especial reference to family income. Does family advantage, in terms of the earnings position of the father, influence access to education (staying on at school, attending a selective school, etc.)? Family background and education may, in turn, affect entry into the labour-market: for example, whether the child gets an apprenticeship. In considering the role of family advantage, the relative significance of 'direct' and 'indirect' effects is of particular interest. For example, do children from better-off homes enjoy higher earnings because their parents are able to provide them with a better education (an indirect effect), or do they obtain access directly to better-paying jobs?

In Chapters 8 and 9 we investigate more specifically two particular aspects – education (Chapter 8) and the labour-market (Chapter 9). These chapters aim to exploit the rich qualitative information contained in our survey and to explore more deeply some of the links suggested by the statistical analysis of Chapter 7. Thus, among other aspects, in Chapter 8 we consider the educational experiences of the children from low-income families. In Chapter 9 we concentrate on the labour-market, with particular reference to conditions in York. We explore the industrial pattern of employment, the extent of continuities in jobs across generations, and factors which appear to be associated with unusually high or low earnings (allowing for age, education and location). In this analysis, particular attention is paid to the role of two major employers – British Rail and Rowntree – and to their rather different employment patterns.

Finally, in Chapter 10 we summarise the research and draw together the main findings. These findings are directed at the questions listed above, but these questions themselves are related to major policy issues which the reader will doubtless be bearing in mind. The investigation may also serve to illustrate a number of features of social science research. This project, perhaps more than most, has involved a high degree of vertical integration. We have gone from the problem of securing the original data and the Rowntree records (really the province of the economic or social historian), through the stage of collecting our own data (more commonly today the responsibility of the statistician), to the analysis and interpretation of the findings (where the economist usually comes in). In seeking to cover this wide range of activities, we have no doubt done less than justice to important problems, but the history of our project may help students, in particular, to take a broader view of research methods and approaches.

Questions of Fact

Few people would be surprised to learn that economic advantage, or disadvantage, tends to be associated across generations. Everyday observation suggests that the children of low-income parents are more likely, and that those from well-off homes are less likely, to fall below the poverty line. What is much less clear, however, is the *extent* of the association. *How much* more likely is it that we would find continuity rather than discontinuity of deprivation?

This is the basic factual question with which we are concerned. It may be helpful to begin with an analogy – the association of heights across generations.

An analogy with heights

Tall fathers tend to have sons whose height is above the average, but we want to know the strength of the association. Suppose, then, that we collect (hypothetical) data on the stature of fathers and sons, as illustrated in Figure 1.1. It turns out that the mean, or average, height is the same for both (5 feet 10 inches), as is the standard deviation (2½ inches). By eye, it is clear that there is a tendency to move ('regress') towards the mean, but we want to measure its extent. One method is to take the coefficient of correlation (this and other statistical terms are defined in the section entitled 'Statistical Terms: an Explanatory Note', at the end of the book). In the classic work by Galton and Pearson at University College London, the correlation of stature for fathers and sons was found to be about 0.5 (see Carter, 1962, who comments that 'it is regrettable that no similar study has been made in the last fifty years' – p. 103).

The statement that the correlation coefficient for heights is 0.5 may not in itself be very meaningful. We may note, however, that in this case 0.5 is also the coefficient in a simple linear regression of the son's height on that of the father. Such a regression (see the explanatory note at the end of the book) involves fitting a straight line such as the broken line shown in Figure 1.1. From this we can read off the predicted height of the son, given the height of the father. The coefficient of 0.5 means, in effect, that the expected height of the son is half-way between that of his father and the mean (5 feet 10 inches). So the expected height of the son of a man 6 feet 2 inches tall is 6 feet. Alternatively, we may compare the correlation coefficient for heights with those for other variables. The correlation for the length of forearm, for instance, taken from the same source, is 0.42 (Falconer, 1977), which is rather lower. On the other hand, the correlations for heights in the same generation go from 0.53 for siblings to 0.64 for fraternal twins and 0.93 for identical twins (Falconer, 1977).

The regression coefficient is a convenient method of summarising the extent of the association, and it is one that we shall use for income and earnings. The use of a single statistic to encompass all the information collected is, however, open to question. An alternative, and

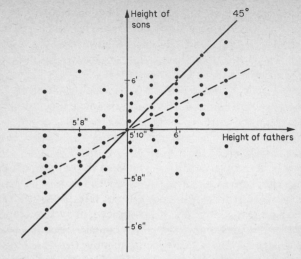

Figure 1.1   Illustrative example of heights of fathers and sons

richer, representation is shown – again taking hypothetical data for heights – in Table 1.1, which gives the precentages making the transition from one range to another. The heights which divide the sample of fathers into fifths (the 'quintiles') are approximately 5 feet 8 inches, 5 feet 9½ inches, 5 feet 10½ inches, and 6 feet. If we take fathers over 6 feet then Table 1.1 indicates that 45 per cent of the sons were also over 6 feet, and that only 5 per cent were under 5 feet 8 inches. Conversely, 45 per cent of the sons of fathers in the bottom 20 per cent, below 173 cm, were themselves 5 feet 8 inches below. Put another way, the 'odds' on being in the bottom 20 per cent were nine times greater if

Table 1.1   Transition matrix: heights of fathers and sons (illustrative example)

Percentage of fathers (by fifths)	Percentage of sons (by fifths)				
	Top 20%	Second 20%	Third 20%	Fourth 20%	Bottom 20%
Top 20%	45	25	16	9	5
Second 20%	25	26	22	18	9
Third 20%	17	21	24	23	15
Fourth 20%	9	18	22	25	26
Bottom 20%	4	10	16	25	45

your father was in the bottom 20 per cent, than if he was in the top 20 per cent.

The example of heights also illustrates some of the difficulties which are likely to arise in the collection and analysis of the data. The first obvious – but often overlooked – point is that there may be inaccuracy in recording. In the analysis we need to allow for the fact that the observations are measured with error; some of the apparent mobility may be due to misrecording or misreporting. The second point concerns the age at which height is observed. Suppose that we are comparing the heights of the fathers with those of their sons at the same calendar date. If both generations have by this time reached adulthood, then no serious error may result. However, if the sons are measured at school at the age of 13, this does not necessarily provide a reliable guide to their subsequent adult height. Some may be close to their final stature; others may shoot up later. The 'life-cycle' difference induces in effect an error of measurement in the height of the sons.

The life-cycle factor may indeed lead to serious bias in the estimation of the degree of association. A careful experimenter would not *choose* a sample of fathers aged 40 years old and then measure the height of their sons, of whatever age, but if these were the only data available, then it might be tempting to use them. However, the potential for bias is evident. Suppose that taller fathers tend to have higher incomes, and higher income men tend to marry later and have, at any given age, younger children. The age difference between their children and those of shorter men will tend to mask the true correlation between the heights of the two generations. The measured regression coefficient will on this account understate the true degree of association.

Incomes across generations

The analogy with heights serves to bring out the kind of question we want to ask here about income and some of the methods employed. We shall, for example, be seeking to measure the correlation coefficient, or the regression coefficient. What is the expected advantage of the son of a father who has double the average income? We shall be interested in comparing the correlation with other yardsticks. For example, Nickell (1982) reports that the correlation between a person's occupational position on entry into the labour-market and at age 60 is 0.62. Evidence in the United States (Lillard and Willis, 1978) suggests that the correlation of the logarithm of earnings in one year with that six years later is around 0.7. We should not expect the correlation *across* generations to be nearly so high, but we want to know in what range it is likely to be.

In the same way, we shall be concerned with the transitions between income-ranges, particularly if the transition matrix is asymmetric (unlike Table 1.1). The movements between ranges take on special significance if the lowest income-range consists of those below an (appropriately defined) poverty line. Suppose that we define a poverty standard for one generation and indentify the families which fall below this level. If we then take a corresponding poverty line for the next generation (suitably adjusted for changes in prices, etc.), how many of the children of the first-generation poor will themselves be in poverty? On a strictly random basis, we should expect the proportion of the children of the poor to be no different from that in any subsample of the population. On the other hand, if there were a perfect correlation of incomes then all the children of the poor would themselves be below the line. In reality, we expect the situation to lie between these two cases, but we should like to know which it more closely approximates.

The example of heights is useful in bringing out some of the difficulties which we are likely to encounter; however, in some respects it is misleading, and suggests that our task is easier than it really is. Height is a relatively stable characteristic. Although people are reputed to stretch slightly during the day, it is not likely to matter very much when the measurement is made. There is not a great deal of transitory variation in height (for weight this may be more significant). Incomes or earnings, however, can exhibit considerable variation. Mr Allen (all names are fictitious) is on piece-work, and his take-home pay depends on production that week; Mr Bedford works a regular cycle of shifts, getting more when he is on nights; Mrs Campbell is a school dinner lady, receiving part-pay during the school holidays; Mr Davidson is an actor and is frequently 'between jobs'. In these situations, there may be substantial difficulties in separating the 'transitory' from the 'permanent' elements of income. It is the latter which we are seeking to measure as an indicator of long-run economic status, but it may be hard to identify this from the observations.

The life-cycle factor, relevant when comparing the heights of adults and children, is of much wider significance for incomes. For most people, earnings tend to rise with age, reaching a peak, and then fall towards the end of the working lifetime. The observed degree of association across generations will depend on the points in the life cycle at which the earnings of fathers and sons are recorded. In this case, it is no longer sufficient to take father and sons who are both adults. Moreover, the profile of earnings varies considerably across occupations, and typically the peak shifts to older ages as one considers higher-paying jobs. For incomes, the life cycle is even more pronounced, with income in retirement typically being much below that when at work.

There are factors influencing economic status which have no parallel in the case of heights. Career changes are an example. A person may move up or down the earnings ladder. This is particularly likely in the early stages of a career; and this suggests that observations in, say, the first decade of the working life should be avoided. Similarly, income from investment may change overnight as the result of inheritance.

Perhaps the most important difference is that height is a single, relatively well-defined variable, whereas economic status is more complex. We have referred to the variation over the life cycle, and there are evident problems in seeking to reduce lifetime experiences to a single indicator of economic well-being. Even at a point in time, a single number may have limited meaning. To know that a person earns £100 a week as a labourer is not sufficient to tell us whether or not he is below the poverty line. It depends on whether there are other benefits from work, such as free housing. It depends on other sources of income. Does he receive state benefits such as Family Income Supplement? It depends on whether he is married and on whether his wife works. It depends on whether he has children and on their needs. The analogy with height is deceptive in giving the impression that, if one sees father and son together, one can tell at a glance how close their resemblance is. Even with the aid of a detailed and lengthy questionnaire, determining economic status is an elusive and intricate task.

Interpreting the Evidence

Establishing the facts about the degree of intergenerational mobility is a major objective of our research, but a second important aim is to throw light on the mechanisms at work. To continue our analogy with heights, we observe the distribution of heights among the sons and are interested in the factors governing this distribution. Why is Mr Foster 5 feet 11 inches? Why are a fifth of the sons less than 5 feet 8 inches? The association across generations directs attention to the role of the father's height in influencing the height of his son, via genetic inheritance, but there may be other determinants. Height may be affected by whether or not his mother smoked during pregnancy. Physical development may reflect family living standards, with children from poorer homes tending to be smaller. Children with fewer siblings may have an advantage in terms of development. Understanding the relative importance of these different elements is important, if we are concerned either to raise the average level of stature or to reduce the proportion too small to qualify to be policemen.

In the case of earnings and incomes, the cross-generation link has tended in fact to attract relatively little attention. There has been an extensive literature on the causes of economic success, but this has tended to concentrate on the characteristics of the individual rather than on the relation to his family background. Yet these are interlinked, and knowledge about the degree of intergenerational association is essential in any assessment of the relative importance of different factors.

Determinants of earnings

In order to illustrate the main issues, we focus for the present on the determinants of earnings, that is, a person's potential earnings when employed, disregarding other sources of income such as benefits or investment income.

The dominant strand in recent writing by economists on the determinants of earnings has been that based on human-capital formation, pioneered by Mincer (1958) and Becker (1964). The concept of human capital is extremely broad, involving the acquisition of earning capacities via either formal or informal education, and encompassing on-the-job training and child care as well as the more obvious investment in school education. The breadth of the concept poses problems for the implementation and testing of the human-capital theory, and much of the empirical research concentrates on the relation between education, work experience and earnings – see the bold lines in Figure 1.2. Thus Mincer (1979) reports that the average return to a year of education in the United States is an increase in earnings of between 7 per cent and 11 per cent. In the United Kingdom, Psacharopoulos and Layard state that the private rate of return to an additional year's schooling is estimated at about 10 per cent (1979, p. 492). Analyses of this kind have been highly influential, especially in the United States; for example, Thurow (1976, p. 188).

Equalizing human-capital investments, especially educational investments, is at the heart of many of the economic and social policies that have been adopted over the past fifteen years . . . the left, the center, and the right all affirm the central importance of education (human investment) as a means of solving our social problems, especially poverty.

However, the human-capital approach has been criticised. It has been asserted that education and earnings may both be related to other 'left out' variables, and there is no causal significance to the estimated relationship.

An omitted variable which has received much attention is 'ability', typically measured by performance in intelligence (IQ) tests. Critics of compensatory education policies, such as Jensen (1969) in the United States, argued that there is a strong association between IQ and earnings – see the broken line in Figure 1.2. If education is positively correlated with IQ, as seems plausible, then the estimated relationship between education and earnings may overstate the true effect. Policy measures based on an estimated human-capital model leaving out IQ (the bold lines in Figures 1.2) would, on this argument, lead to disappointing results in terms of raising earnings.

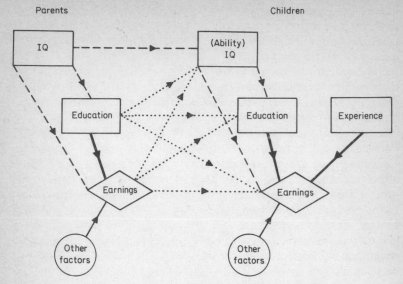

Figure 1.2   Some of the factors determining earnings

Ability is not, however, the only variable that can be omitted. In this book we are primarily concerned with another – the influence of family background – which has been stressed by other critics of the human-capital approach. To explore this, we have to bring in the preceding generation, as in the left-hand side of Figure 1.2. The links across generations are, of course, manifold, and only some of the connections are shown in the diagram. Moreover, 'family background' is a term which covers a variety of factors. Here we use it to denote the advantages conveyed by parental education, parental income and earnings. Thus the children of highly educated parents may be better informed about educational openings or better motivated to acquire educational qualifications, both of which give rise to a direct link: Education → Education in Figure 1.2. It may be the case that the children of more educated parents perform better on IQ tests, giving rise to an indirect link: Education → IQ → Education.

Of particular interest here is the relationship between earnings in the two generations. The link may be direct or indirect. A direct link arises, for instance, where parents are able to secure favoured jobs for their children, and in certain occupations (for example, medicine) this is reputed to happen. Or it may be that the parents play no active role and that it is simply that children from better-off homes have an advantage when applying for jobs. The recruitment criteria applied by employers may be consciously or subconsciously biased against children living in certain neighbourhoods or whose parents are not telephone subscribers. Indirect effects may occur via the dependence of education on parental earnings. High-income parents may be able to secure better-quality education for their children, either by their choice of school or merely by living in the right neighbourhood. In low-income families there may be pressure on children to leave school at the earliest opportunity. Or, with a more complicated indirect effect, the children of high-earning parents may score better on IQ tests, hence securing access to selective schools, and hence obtaining higher earnings (a link: Earnings → IQ → Education → Earnings).

Evidence on the cross-generation earnings pattern is therefore important in understanding the determinants of earnings. At the same time, it needs careful handling. A positive correlation between earnings in the two generations does not necessarily imply a causal link from parents to children. The correlation may be observed because earnings in each generation are associated with another variable correlated across generations. It is theoretically possible to observe a substantial positive correlation between the earnings of fathers and sons without there being any causal relationship. It is also conceivable that there is a causal link, but in the reverse direction, from children to parents. For example, the son who has done well in business may find a job for his father or father-in-law.

Social and economic framework
The quantification of the strength of association between family background and the variables outlined earlier (for example, education and earnings) represents a significant addition to the state of knowledge about this subject in Britain. We should not lose sight, however, of the wider social and economic framework within which the individual process is embedded.

The need for this wider perspective is well illustrated by the example of compensatory educational policy. Suppose – for the sake of argument – that investigation of low pay reveals that the children from low-income families leave school without educational qualifications and that this lack of marketable qualifications leads them, in turn, to be low paid. If the government, through special measures, could ensure that no one left school without the equivalent of five O levels, then this would – on a straightforward interpretation of the human-capital approach – reduce the incidence of low pay. However, this takes one particular view of the working of the labour-market. It assumes that the earnings distribution is determined by the pattern of individual characteristics. It is a supply rather than a demand theory. Better pay is like the award of swimming certificates: everyone who swims the required distance can get one and it does not matter how many others have qualified. If, however, it is a question of people competing for jobs, then possession of qualifications may not be sufficient. In terms of the swimming analogy, we may at the other extreme have a race with a fixed structure of prizes. In this case, improving swimming performance is of no value in its own right; it is a question of swimming faster than the others. If the general level of educational qualifications is raised, a person may still come last even if he now has five O levels rather than two CSE awards. Where the structure of jobs is fixed, compensatory policy may have little or no impact on the distribution of earnings. It may affect *who* gets better-paid positions, but it will not eliminate low-paying jobs.

This example illustrates the need to consider the wider economic context – in this case the working of the labour-market. The implications of a policy may be quite different, depending on the view one takes, and different views may lead one into different areas of research. The human-capital approach minimises the significance of the demand for labour. The job-structure approach, in contrast, directs attention to the nature of employment and the role of different types of job in the economy. What is the function of low-paid jobs and what are the structural forces which lead to their being preserved?

The same applies to the social and political context. Again, an example may be helpful. Suppose that we were to find that one reason for continuities in low income across generations is that the children of one-parent families are themselves more likely to be single parents. This observation, and the factors leading to continuity at the family level, would be of considerable interest. But one must not lose sight of the fact that one-parent families would not fall below the poverty line if there were an adequate system of social-security benefits. It would still be the case that the other disadvantages of one-parent families were associated across generations, but the continuity of economic status, which is our primary concern here, would be broken. In seeking to understand the reasons for continuity, we must therefore consider the broader social question as to why income maintenance provisions for single parents have remained insufficient. To explain this, one needs to look not at individual families, but at the behaviour of governments, politicians, and the pressures to which they are subject. One has to examine the role of social security in the functioning of society as a whole.

In this book, our research deals with individual families and their history. The reader should, however, bear in mind that our findings can only be properly interpreted in a wider context. This is a theme to which we return in Chapter 10.

Mobility and Inequality

There are a number of reasons why we may be concerned about the extent of intergenerational income mobility. It has been argued that barriers to mobility are a factor leading to poor economic performance. In his *Essays in Persuasion*, Keynes (1931, p. 299) wrote that:

The hereditary principle in the transmission of wealth and the control of business is the reason why the leadership of the capitalist cause is weak and stupid. It is too much dominated by third-generation men.

According to *The Economist* (20 March 1965):

It is management consultants and foreign bankers, more even than socialist doctrinaires, who nowadays can be heard to bewail the effects of Britain's encrusted social structure.

The former West German Chancellor, Helmut Schmidt, has suggested that:

As long as you maintain that damn class-ridden society of yours, you will never get out of your mess [quoted by Bauer, 1981].

One can indeed see how there may be an efficiency case for encouraging mobility. If, for instance, family background is as important as education in determining earnings, then this suggests that the allocation of people to jobs could be improved.

It is, however, the equity issues which have received most attention. In particular, intergenerational immobility is frequently taken to be a sign of unequal opportunity. 'Equality of opportunity' is a phrase which occurs often in public debate, appearing in party manifestos, political speeches and tracts on educational and social reform. It has been widely accepted as a goal of government policy – in contrast to equality of outcome – and many writers treat it as of self-evident merit. It is, however, a concept that needs closer examination. What exactly is meant by equality of opportunity and how can it be related to our analysis?

Equality of opportunity

There have been a variety of definitions of equality of opportunity, but the following may serve to illustrate the general concept. According to the classic essay by Tawney (1964, pp. 103–4), equality of opportunity obtains:

in so far as, and only in so far as, each member of a community, whatever his birth, or occupation, or social position, possesses in fact, and not merely in form, equal chances of using to the full his natural endowments of physique, of character, and of intelligence.

Or, to take a more recent definition, we may quote Taubman (1978, p. 6), who sees equality of opportunity as eliminating:

all the barriers that prevent individuals from obtaining the training necessary to convert the potential talents implicit in their genetic endowments into capabilities.

These statements can be interpreted in the light of the earlier illustration of the determinants of earnings. In terms of Figure 1.2, equality of opportunity requires that earnings be determined solely by ability, education and experience, and that education depends solely on ability. The dotted lines in Figure 1.2, which denote sources of inequality of opportunity, should not be present. If family background conveys an advantage, for example, in terms of superior access to education, then people do not have equal chances of realising their abilities.

Seen in this way, the concept appears straightforward; however, there are difficulties lurking beneath the surface. First, some writers regard the principle of equality of opportunity as one that can be accepted without question. According to Joseph and Sumption (1979, pp. 28–9):

It is a commanding rallying cry. No one would overtly deny that it is just . . . Equality of opportunity is an attack on privilege in the name of liberty.

This last claim is, however, open to challenge. To eliminate inequality of opportunity requires, for example, that parents should not be able to purchase superior education for their children, which is in itself a restriction of liberty. There is an undoubted tension between the liberty of the donors and the unequal advantage provided to the recipients: 'an inevitable conflict between the pursuit of competitive equality of opportunity and the exercise of autonomous choice.' (Lloyd Thomas, 1977). The principles of equality of opportunity and of liberty may be in conflict, and not everyone would agree that the former should take priority. Nozick, for instance, argues that 'holdings to which . . . people are entitled may not be seized, even to provide equality of opportunity to others' (1974, p. 235).

A second difficulty is that the interpretation of equality of opportunity draws a sharp distinction between genetic and material advantage, and it is not clear why this should be. Why are the broken lines in Figure 1.2 more acceptable than the dotted lines? Knight, for example, argued that (1947, p. 151):

there is no visible reason why anyone is more or less entitled to the earnings [resulting from] inherited personal capacities than to those of inherited property in any other form.

The same point is made by Johnson (1973, p. 60), who notes the vested interest of intellectuals in drawing the distinction. Suppose, however, that we regard differences in abilities as a source of unequal opportunities. In a world of equal opportunity, we are then left with only the continuous lines in Figure 1.2. Differences in earnings arise only from 'other factors', which, at least *ex ante*, are the same for everyone. The difference between the principles of equality of opportunity and equality of results reduces in this case to the distinction between *ex ante* and *ex post*. This is a valid distinction, but rather different from what might be expected.

The concept of equality of opportunity needs therefore to be treated with care. It is not necessarily more straightforward or self-evident than equality of results. Moreover, the relationship between opportunity and outcome is not clear cut. If compensatory educational policy reduces the strength of the link between family income and schooling, will this reduce inequality of earnings? Okun is 'confident that greater equality of opportunity would produce greater equality of income' (1975, p. 83), but Herrnstein argues (1973, p. 151):

Greater wealth, health, freedom, fairness, and educational opportunity are *not* going to give us automatically the egalitarian society of our philosophical heritage. They will instead give us a society sharply graduated, with even greater innate separation between the top and the bottom.

Equality of results

It should be clear from our earlier discussion that either Okun or Herrnstein may be correct – or neither – depending on the assumptions made. Suppose the simple human-capital view of the labour-market is correct. Then a policy of equalising educational attainment will, other things being equal, reduce earnings differences, as predicted by Okun. But imagine that the influence of family background is eliminated by redistributing schooling so that it is more closely related to ability. This reinforcement of the direct effect of ability on earnings may lead to an *increase* in earnings differentials, as claimed by Herrnstein. Finally, if we take the opposite extreme view of the labour-market, and assume a fixed structure of jobs and associated earnings, then policies to equalise opportunity are precluded by assumption from having any impact on the distribution of outcomes.

This last example raises the question as to whether the study of intergenerational mobility has any relevance for those whose concern is solely with equality of outcome. To pose the issue in its starkest form, if the problem of poverty is one of inadequate incomes today, then the fact that a person's parents were also poor is irrelevant (although it may, of course, aid in understanding the causes of poverty). For this reason, many people quite understandably feel that issues of mobility are secondary to those of current deprivation.

Mobility may become of significance for the equality of results when we take a longer time perspective. If our view of the distribution is widened to that of lifetime economic status, then each person's lifetime welfare typically depends on the income of more than one generation. Through the family and other social institutions, there is a degree of income-sharing between generations. To take a simple illustration, we may divide a person's life into three stages. In the first, as a child, he enjoys consumption related to the income of his parents; in the second, at work, his standard of living depends primarily on his own income; in the third he is retired, and his consumption is related to his own income and to that of his children. The lifetime welfare of each person depends therefore on the incomes of three successive generations; depending on how these are aggregated into an index of well-being, social judgements about the extent of inequality may be affected by the degree of correlation between them. There will be more lifetime inequality, if childhood advantage is compounded in higher earning power and if the advantage is reproduced in the next generation.

The example just given shows how the degree of intergenerational mobility may enter the measurement of the extent of inequality between individuals, when their economic status is assessed on a lifetime basis. This approach may be extended further to a 'dynastic' view of inequality, where the welfare of a dynasty depends on the incomes of successive generations. On this basis, we take account of the fact, for example, that earlier Marquesses of Salisbury have also been well-to-do.

To sum up, there are indeed important links between the degree of mobility and economic inequality. The investigation on which we have embarked is of definite relevance to issues of justice and fairness. But the nature of the underlying social judgements is worthy of more careful consideration than it is usually given.

Concluding Comments

In this chapter we have described the principal aims of our research and sought to provide some of the necessary background. It is perhaps inevitable that, in seeking to cast light on a neglected subject, we have raised more questions than we can hope to answer. A number of the issues cannot be resolved with the empirical material we have been able to collect, and some may be insoluble. The application of the findings depends both on the wider economic and social framework and on the social judgements on which policy recommendations are based. These are considerations which the reader should bear in mind throughout the chapters which follow.

2 Incomes and Mobility – a Survey

Introduction: Possible Approaches
In this chapter, we survey the evidence about intergenerational income mobility which was available when we embarked upon this study. Ideally, we should like observations for two generations of an accurately measured indicator of economic status, such as earnings or income, at comparable stages of the life cycle, for a random national sample of the first generation, and with sufficient additional evidence to allow us to investigate the factors influencing mobility. Such an 'ideal' is clearly exacting and any actual empirical study is likely to fall short in a number of respects (our own inquiry certainly does). In what follows, we first outline the possible approaches to collecting such evidence, then discuss briefly the results from the more thoroughly investigated field of occupational mobility, and finally describe the handful of studies of income mobility which have been carried out in the United States and Scandinavia.

There are three main methods which could be employed to collect intergenerational data.

(1) Longitudinal studies: data are collected on a prospective basis for a sample of parents and children who are continually monitored or regularly traced until a generation is completed.
(2) Retrospective surveys: data are collected from present-day respondents about past history; parents or children are questioned about incomes a generation ago.
(3) Record linkage: the respondents to an earlier survey, or administrative source, are traced, or data are collected from children where records on parents can be traced.

These are considered in turn.

Longitudinal studies
The term 'longitudinal', or 'panel', is applied to studies based on repeated measurements of the same individuals or families (Wall and Williams, 1970). In recent years there has been a rapid growth of interest in the collection of such panel data on incomes; a leading example in the United States is the University of Michigan Panel Study of Income Dynamics (Morgan, *et al.*, 1974), which collected income information for successive years for 5000 families. These studies differ,

however, from the data we are seeking since they are concerned essentially with *intra*generational, rather than *inter*generational, income mobility. We need data spanning two generations of the same family.

The potential of the longitudinal approach may be illustrated by reference to two well-known studies in Britain. The first is the Douglas (Population Investigation Committee) cohort of all children born in Great Britain in one week in 1946. This began as a perinatal survey, with no express intention of a long-term follow-up, but it has subsequently been the base for following the life history of the children, with periodic re-interviews. The second, the National Child Development Study, was planned from the outset as a longitudinal investigation. This study began with some 17 000 children born in one week in 1958, and their progress has been monitored at subsequent interviews. If, in each of these studies, income information had been collected from the parents at the outset, then by the mid-1970s (mid-1980s in the case of the later study) we would have had data from the children which could have been compared with those from the parents at a broadly similar stage of the life cycle. The source would have been richer still, if contact had been maintained with the parents and income data collected on a regular basis. Unfortunately, although both studies collected a considerable amount of information on home background, including education and occupation of the father, in neither study were the participants asked about income or earnings.

The attractions of the longitudinal approach are evident. Information collected on the earnings and income of parents at a particular age, coupled with a thirty-year follow-up of the children (and if possible the parents), would be very valuable. At the same time, there are problems. To begin with, there are objections in principle to the method. The continued study of people may, it is argued, lead them to modify their behaviour. The act of observation contaminates the data. There are objections to the procedures typically used to implement the longitudinal approach. The choice of sample may be influenced by considerations of accessibility, co-operativeness and ease of retaining contact. Together with initial non-response, there is a risk that the base population may be unrepresentative. During the course of the study, attrition is likely and this may have a differential impact on different groups: for example, it may be less easy to maintain contact with low-income families. These considerations mean that the conduct of an effective longitudinal study is bound to be highly labour-intensive and expensive. Finally, the work is long-term in nature and, if commenced *ab initio*, will not produce results for a very considerable period.

Retrospective surveys
The simplest form of retrospective survey would take a sample of

adults, and obtain information from them about their current income and about the income of their parents at the same age. Thus we would interview Mr Ash, aged 35, question him about his current earnings (and other income), and ask him whether he can remember what his father earned when he was aged 35, which would typically be some 20–40 years ago, so that in 1980 we would be asking about earnings in 1940–60. A more complex procedure would be to approach the parents themselves, where they are still alive, and again seek retrospective information. Alternatively, the survey could start from a sample of parents, obtaining retrospective data, and then seeking to contact the children.

The appeal of the retrospective approach is that it avoids the long lag with the longitudinal method, and that, although careful interviewing is required, it does not involve the same complex research organisation. The central problems, however, are whether people would in fact be able to answer such retrospective questions and, if they did provide an answer, whether it would be as reliable as contemporaneous reports.

There are three main methods by which the validity of retrospective reporting has been assessed: (1) reliability studies in which respondents are re-interviewed at a later date; (2) studies in which the retrospective interview reports can be checked against independent records; and (3) studies in which the consistency of answers by the same individual to different questions, or of different individuals (for example, brothers) to the same question (father's job), can be estimated. These methods of checking have been employed in a variety of fields. The first type was used in the Douglas longitudinal study, where responses at different stages were compared: for example, mothers were asked on more than one occasion if, and when, the child had had measles. The finding of 'a generally high rate of contradictory reporting and retrospective distortion of events' (Cherry and Rodgers, 1979, p. 40) is not encouraging. The second method is illustrated in a quite different field by an inquiry into the purchase of cars, where comparison could be made with the official vehicle registration records, and 'substantial inconsistencies' were found (Kemsley, 1979, p. 122).

The retrospective method has, in fact, been extensively used in studies of intergenerational occupational mobility, and this experience is especially relevant to our own inquiry. In the United States, considerable success has been claimed for the retrospective approach. Dealing first with the reliability of the reporting of *own* occupation, Featherman and Hauser argue that 'there appears to be marked ability of persons to report their occupation held five years in the past, with nearly the same reliability as they report current statuses' (1977, p. 55). They go on to reject the view that reporting of occupational information is subject to distortion and decay as time passes. They recognise that the use of *proxy* reporting, for example, where children report their father's occupation, introduces a further range of problems. But in an analysis of response error based on the first and third of the methods outlined above, they 'find no evidence that social background variables are measured substantially less reliably than are contemporaneous achievement variables' (Bielby, Hauser and Featherman, 1977, p. 734).

It is important, however, to stress that the experience with occupation does not necessarily carry over to earnings or income. There are indeed good reasons to expect recall to be less accurate and the problems of proxy reporting to be more serious. Occupation is a more stable characteristic over time than money income. It is a reasonable bet that people who could say without hesitation what job they were doing five years ago would have, in many cases, considerable difficulty in recalling their average take-home pay. Occupation is certainly a more 'visible' characteristic. A person may know quite well that thirty years ago his father was a bus driver, but have no idea what he was earning. (Do you know what your father earned thirty years ago?) Although results in the United States suggest that people do provide answers (for example, to the question 'when you were about 16 years old, what was your family's annual income?' – Featherman and Hauser, 1975), the interpretation of the response is open to question: 'it is not clear what the item measures, that is, whether it should be regarded as a report of annual income, as a global perception of relative economic standing, or as a distorted and perhaps ideologically colored reconstruction of the past' (Treiman and Hauser, 1977, p. 274). In this connection, it may be noted that the comparison of American proxy reports with census records – the second method of checking described above – showed a correlation between son's report and father's recorded status of 0.78 for occupation and 0.76 for age, but 0.28 for family income (Featherman, 1980, p. 166). This last correlation may understate the accuracy of the report, and adjustments by the author raised it to 0.57, but it remains substantially below that for occupation. Finally, it is not obvious that results for the United States apply to the United Kingdom. Incomes are much less discussed in Britain both publicly and within the family, and are subject to taboos which do not apply in the case of occupation.

Record linkage

A record-linkage study would ideally work forward from records on a past population a generation ago, tracing the children and obtaining current information from them. In this case, one needs a representative initial sample, with reasonably accurate income or earnings data, and with the information required to trace the next generation. Alternatively, one could start from a sample of the present generation and work backwards by tracing the records of the previous generation. This is illustrated in the occupational mobility field by Benjamin's (1957) use of the 1951 census record of occupation, which he compared with birth certificates to obtain the father's occupation. This method depends on there being a body of earlier records with comprehensive coverage and also that the relevant member of the earlier generation can be identified.

The most important difficulty with the record-linkage approach concerns the availability of past records from either official or private sources. Availability, it should be emphasised, means not just the existence of records, but also the possibility of access and the provision of records in a form which allows tracing. The difficulties may be illustrated by reference to the income-tax records in Britain, and the possibility that they might be used to obtain evidence about incomes in, say, 1950. First, as far as we have been able to ascertain from informal inquiries, the records do not exist in a usable form, but even if they did, they would be far from comprehensive, since many people's incomes are below the tax-exemption level. Second, in contrast to a number of other countries, the government has not to date released individual ('micro') income-tax data for academic analysis. Third, even if income-tax data were made available in the same form as those from the household surveys (the Family Expenditure Survey and the General Household Survey), this would not be sufficient to allow us to link the data across generations, since they are anonymous.

The limitations on the use of official data stem from a very understandable concern with the protection of confidentiality. In the United States, attempts have been made to devise arrangements which permit the information to be released without breaching confidentiality: for example (Sewell and Hauser, 1975, p. 203):

We send a tape to the Social Security Administration that includes all of the information we have on the men in our sample. By matching Social Security numbers, they are able to add earnings information to the tape; they then eradicate all identification information . . . scramble the order of the cases, and return the tape to a senior member of the staff of the Madison Academic Computer Center. This person . . . is under instructions to insure the security of the tape.

The authors go on to comment that this scheme 'meets all legal and ethical requirements for the security of individual records'. At the same time, it is clear that it is a highly expensive operation, and one that necessitates close liaison between the government statisticians and the researchers.

For reasons of resources alone, it seems unlikely that official records will be available in the required form in the foreseeable future. The use of record linkage to examine intergenerational income mobility depends therefore on the existence of suitable sources from academic or private investigations. This is, in fact, the route we pursued, and the possible sources are discussed later in this chapter.

The State of Knowledge: Occupational Mobility

The most active area of socio-economic research on intergenerational continuities is that on occupational mobility. It was of considerable assistance in planning our own investigation. We begin therefore with a brief summary of the methods employed and findings of two major studies of occupational mobility in the UK. These were carried out by Glass and colleagues at the London School of Economics (Glass, 1954) in 1949, and by the Oxford Social Mobility Group (Goldthorpe, 1980; Heath, 1981) in 1972.

National studies of mobility in Britain

Both studies were based on representative national samples of a substantial size. The central results for the Glass study relate to 3497 men resident in England and Wales (the Scottish data were analysed separately). The original sample was 10 000; from this there were 7751 completed interviews (a response rate of 77.5 per cent), of which 6914 were in England and Wales. A further 1357 'substitute' interviews were carried out to replace the non-respondents, giving an overall total of 8271, of which 3703 were men. The Oxford inquiry of 1972 was based on a sample of the male population aged between 20 and 64 years in England and Wales. Successful interviews were carried out with 10 309 men, representing a response rate of 81.8 per cent.

In both studies the information was obtained retrospectively. In the Glass study, respondents were questioned about their own occupation and the last main occupation of their father (Glass, 1954, p. 179). The occupations of the two generations (in the case of the respondent it related to 1949) were classified according to the (Hall–Jones) scale of occupational prestige and the results were presented in terms of seven categories ranging from 'professional and high administrative' to 'unskilled manual'. The respondents in the Oxford mobility inquiry were asked to provide details of the occupation of the head of household, normally the father, when the respondent was aged 14, and of his own occupation: on first entry into full-time employment; ten years after entry; and in 1972. Considerable time was devoted to the construction of a new classification of occupations (the Hope–Goldthorpe scale), giving a quantitative index of the 'social standing' of occupations.

As is often the case with pioneering research, the Glass investigation has been the subject of considerable criticism (see, for example, Payne, Ford and Robertson, 1977); in any event the findings do not necessarily apply to the social conditions of the latter part of the twentieth century. For these reasons, we concentrate on the findings of the more recent

Table 2.1   Intergenerational occupational mobility: evidence from the Oxford survey

| Percentage in father's class | Percentage in respondent's class | | | | | | | Total (% of sample) |
	I	II	III	IV	V	VI	VII	
I	45.2	18.9	11.5	7.7	4.8	5.4	6.5	100.0 (7.3)
II	29.1	23.1	11.9	7.0	9.6	10.6	8.7	100.0 (5.9)
III	18.4	15.7	12.8	7.8	12.8	15.6	16.9	100.0 (7.3)
IV	12.6	11.4	8.0	24.4	8.7	14.4	20.5	100.0 (14.1)
V	14.2	13.6	10.1	7.7	15.7	21.2	17.6	100.0 (11.5)
VI	7.8	8.8	8.3	6.6	12.3	30.4	25.9	100.0 (27.5)
VII	6.5	7.8	8.2	6.6	12.5	23.5	34.9	100.0 (24.6)
Total	13.6	11.5	9.2	9.4	11.6	21.2	23.5	

Note: The results include farmers, small-holders and farm workers, and relate to 9434 men aged between 20 and 64 years.

Source: Goldthorpe (1980), Table 2.2.

Oxford study. In Table 2.1, we show one set of results, relating the current occupation of the respondent to that of his father when the respondent was aged 14. In both cases occupation is classified according to a sevenfold class schema, obtained by aggregating categories from the Hope–Goldthorpe scale. The seven categories are:

Class I   higher-grade professionals, administrators, managers and large proprietors;

Class II   lower-grade professionals, administrators, and managers; higher-grade technicians, and the supervisors of non-manual workers;

Class III   routine clerical workers, sales personnel and other non-manual workers;

Class IV   farmers, small proprietors and self-employed;

Class V   supervisors of manual workers and lower-grade technicians;

Class VI   skilled manual workers;

Class VII   semi-skilled and unskilled manual workers, including agricultural workers.

For each class of fathers, we show the percentage of sons who entered different categories: that is 45.2 per cent of sons with fathers in class I remained in that class, 18.9 per cent were in class II, etc.

The results of the Oxford survey are summarised by Heath (1981, p. 75) as follows:

Britain is not a society in which individual position in the class structure is fixed at birth. The sons of foremen and technicians (Class V), for example, are spread out across the class structure in an apparently random manner . . . Occupational inheritance, however, is more in evidence when we look at the extremes.

The last point may be illustrated by calculating the differential chances of being in class I. From Table 2.1, we can see that 45.2 per cent of sons with fathers in class I were themselves in that class, whereas the corresponding percentage for sons with fathers in class VII was 6.5 per cent. The differential odds, or disparity ratio, are in favour of the sons from class I by a ratio of 7 : 1. Similarly, if we compare the chance of being in class I with that of being in class VII, then it is 7 : 1 for sons from class I, but 1 : 0.19 for sons from class VII. These considerations led Goldthorpe to conclude that 'British society today is still very far removed from the goal of openness' (1980, p. 251), and to draw attention to the 'enormous discrepancy [which] emerges if one compares the chances of men whose fathers held higher-level service-class positions being themselves found in such positions rather than in working-class ones with the same relative chances of men who are of working-class origins' (p. 252).

The presentation of the data in Table 2.1 is in the form of transition proportions, as with the quintile ranges of height. If it were legitimate to use the Hope–Goldthorpe scale as a quantitative index of occupational status – which, as we shall see shortly, is highly debatable – then we could calculate the correlation between the status of fathers and sons. According to the results given by Heath (1981, p. 253), the correlation between father's occupation and son's present occupation is 0.363, and that with son's first occupation is 0.303. Both are below the figure of 0.50 taken for heights. Interestingly, the correlation with the present occupation is higher, indicating the need to examine the career pattern.

Occupation and earnings

The reasons why occupation has featured so prominently in research on mobility are well summarised by Kelsall and Kelsall (1974, p. 105):

First, people are not on the whole averse to furnishing information of this particular kind in sufficient detail for classificatory purposes. Secondly, such data are thought, rightly or wrongly, to be relatively objective . . . Thirdly, knowledge of a person's precise occupation and his position within it gives some indication also, however rough, of such matters as income, style of life, social status and level of formal education reached. Fourthly, there is really no practical alternative.

The last of these reasons has undoubtedly been important, and the practical difficulties in constructing alternative indicators will receive a great deal of prominence in what follows. We should explain, however, the reasons why we feel that alternative indicators are necessary, and why studies of occupational mobility need to be complemented by research on income mobility.

The first problem is one which has given rise to a lot of discussion in the social-mobility literature: the translation of occupational categories into a continuous indicator of occupational status. In the case of the seven occupational classes shown in Table 2.1, Goldthorpe takes pains to emphasise that they should not be regarded as a hierarchy, and in particular that the intermediate classes III–V should be seen as occupying a broadly similar position. He states (1980, p. 42) that:

Our class schema should not then be regarded as having . . . a consistently hierarchical form . . . In general, we shall in fact speak of upward mobility only in the case of movement into Classes I and II, whether from the intermediate classes or from Classes VI and VII, and conversely of downward mobility only in the case of movement out of Classes I and II.

Given the uncertain relation between the occupational groupings and economic function (for example, the inclusion of shop assistants in III and of foremen in V), this caution is quite understandable. However, it limits the usefulness of the evidence for our purposes.

What about the Hope-Goldthorpe scale, which lies behind the class categories in Table 2.1, or similar occupational gradings? After all, the scale, which in its 'collapsed' version ranges from 18 for unskilled manual workers and street vendors to 75 for self-employed professionals such as doctors and lawyers, is intended to provide a quantitative index of the 'social standing' of occupations. Moreover, it could be argued that such an index provides a better measure of the long-term desirability of occupations than does current earnings. As we have seen, earnings are subject to temporary fluctuations and there is a marked pattern of life-cycle variation. Use of occupational status may avoid these difficulties. To know that a person is a houseman in a London hospital may convey a more accurate picture of his lifetime income than the fact that he currently earns £x.

The use of the occupational scale in this way would, however, rest on a number of strong assumptions. The cardinal scale is clearly debatable. For example, according to the collapsed version, the scale implies:

service workers: lower grade (e.g. caretakers)   27
semi-skilled manual workers in construction
   and extractive industries (e.g. roofers)   30
skilled manual workers in manufacturing:
   lower grade (e.g. locksmiths)   33

Use of the scale implies therefore that the difference between caretakers and locksmiths is twice that between caretakers and roofers. Goldthorpe himself has counselled caution in the use of occupational status as an independent variable in analysis of mobility (as would be necessary, if we used occupation as an indicator of family background). The ordinal properties too are open to question. As with the broad classes I–VII, it is not necessarily appropriate to regard occupation in hierarchical terms. People may relate to occupations in different ways and it may not be possible to reduce the different considerations to a single-dimensional index.

The dimension in which we are interested is that of economic reward. The scale, which was based on the 'general desirability' of occupations, as assessed by a sample of the population, must have been heavily influenced by the level of earnings. However, other features of the occupations must also have been included. Phelps Brown has drawn attention to the 'looseness of the relation between the status of a particular occupation and its relative pay' (1977, p. 110). In Figure 2.1 we reproduce his analysis of the median earnings of 107 occupational groups, as observed in the New Earnings Survey of April 1973, and their relation to the Hope–Goldthorpe scale. Taking occupations with the same, or closely similar, scale values, the dots indicate the average of the median earnings and show a fairly systematic relationship. The fitted straight line indicates that a rise of one unit in the scale is associated with an increase of 1.031 per cent in earnings. What is more striking, however, is the spread around the averages, the vertical lines indicating the range of median values for a given Hope–Goldthorpe number. Thus the occupations with a scale value of 32.6 include butchers (median £28.1), footwear workers (£34.9), fork-lift truck-drivers (£37.3) and furnacemen (£41.8).

The variation shown in Figure 2.1 is that between the median values for different occupations; it does not include the variation *within* occupational groups. Yet the evidence suggests that the within-occupation dispersion is very considerable, and this is a final reason why occupational status gives only a partial picture. In his classic study of earnings, Lydall concluded, on the basis of data from the United States, that 'not more than about 25 per cent of the total variance of earnings is attributable to the variance between occupations . . . The important conclusion which emerges is that . . . the proportion of total variance of

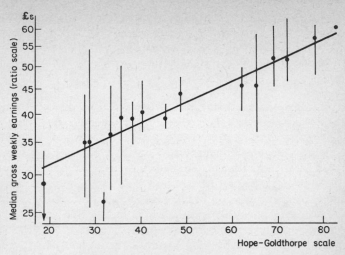

Figure 2.1 *Range of median earnings of various occupational groups*
Source: Phelps Brown, 1977, p. 108.

. . . earnings which is attributable to the between occupation variance
is remarkably small' (1968, p. 104). More recently, the Royal Commission on the Distribution of Income and Wealth (1979b) concluded
that in Britain there is a definite association between occupation and
earnings, but there is a great deal of dispersion within groups. The
median earnings of doctors in 1978 were more than double those of
bricklayers, but the top decile for bricklayers was *higher* than the
bottom decile for doctors.

This evidence must, of course, be treated with caution. The transitory and life-cycle factors may account for a sizeable part of the
within-occupation variability; the extent to which the variation in
earnings can be attributed to occupational differences depends on the
fineness of the classification. On the other hand, it seems likely that
within-occupation variability will remain, even when allowance is made
for it. For example, on the basis of an analysis of 441 occupations, the
Royal Commission formed the view that 'the amount of dispersion
explained is not very great, even using this fine classification' (1979b, p.
61).

We are in no way seeking to devalue the investigations which have
been made of occupational mobility. Our argument has been that these
studies are concerned with rather different features of society and that
the results cannot be applied directly to earnings mobility. There is no
doubt that, as Kelsall and Kelsall claim, occupation gives an indication
of life-style and social status, but it is open to question whether the
evidence on occupational mobility can be used to reach conclusions

about mobility of incomes. We share the view of Rutter and Madge that 'it would be misleading to view occupation as the sole basis for a social class hierarchy . . . Economic inequality and social inequality are not synonymous' (1976, pp. 140–1).

State of Knowledge: Income Mobility

We are seeking evidence relating earnings or income in one generation to earnings or income in the next generation. By earnings, we mean all cash receipts from employment (wages, salaries, bonuses, commission, etc.) together with all other economic benefits (that is, including fringe benefits), although any actual measure is likely to fall short of being comprehensive. Income is defined to include, in addition to earnings, capital income (interest, dividends, rents, etc.), state transfers (pensions, child benefit, unemployment benefit, etc.), and private transfers (occupational pensions, friendly society benefits, etc.). The unit of analysis is typically taken in what follows to be the individual in the case of earnings and the family in the case of incomes, the family being defined to include husband, wife and dependent children (but not non-dependent members of the same household).

Studies of family background

At first sight, it appears that there are a number of studies on which we can draw. The 1970s, particularly in the United States, saw the publication of several investigations of the role of family background in the determination of earnings. Closer inspection, however, reveals that in nearly all cases they used proxies for income in one generation. Thus the article of Bowles (1972), with its promising title 'Schooling and inequality from generation to generation', reports a correlation between the income of non-Negro males in the USA aged 25–34 and their parents' income of 0.3004. This is, however, an assumed value, based on the assumption that the correlation is equal to that between income and father's occupation. Similarly, Morgenstern's study (1973) of socio-economic background uses father's and mother's education (and the Duncan measure of occupational status). Treiman and Hauser (1977) make a series of ingenious calculations to estimate the correlation of incomes across generations as 0.25–0.5, but they have no direct evidence on parental income and warn that 'all of our calculations might better be regarded as quantitative speculations than as "estimates" in the usual sense' (p. 271).

The position in the United States was reviewed in 1976 by Corcoran, Jencks and Olneck (1976), and in Table 2.2 we summarise the background information available in the eight major studies which they considered. In only one case – the Wisconsin inquiry – were data

Table 2.2 *Information on family background in major United States studies*

	Father's education	Occupation	Mother's education	Income
Occupational changes in a generation	√	√		
Productive Americans	√			
Panel study of income dynamics	√	√		
NORC Brothers	√	√		
National longitudinal	√	√		
Talent twins and siblings	√	√		
Kalamazoo Brothers	√	√	√	
Wisconsin	√	√	√	√

Source: Taken from Corcoran, Jencks and Olneck, 1976.

collected on parents' income. This important investigation is discussed in more detail below.

In the United Kingdom, the literature has been even more sparse. There have been studies of the influence of family background and earnings by Psacharopoulos (1977) and Papanicolaou and Psacharopoulos (1979), but these again employ occupation as the background variable. The averaged correlation between earnings and father's 'usual occupation', the latter measured by the Hope–Goldthorpe scale, is 0.20 for men aged 25–64 (Psacharopoulos, 1977, Table A). To our knowledge, there are no studies which contain data for a sizeable, representative sample on incomes in two generations. There have, of course, been studies of elite groups, such as the very interesting research of Harbury and Hitchens (1979) on inheritance, but these by definition are concerned with an exceptional group.

Two Scandinavian studies
It is to Scandinavia that we have to look to find the pioneering work in this field. First, there is the investigation by Soltow (1965) of the incomes of fathers and sons in the city of Sarpsborg in Norway. This adopted the record-linkage approach, exploiting the fact that income-tax records are open to the public in Norway (Chancellor of the Exchequer, please note!). He began with a sample of 771 fathers aged 55–64 in 1960 and resident in Sarpsborg, but the sample was progressively reduced by the requirements for record-linking. First, to ensure full family records, all those not living in the city in 1930 were eliminated. This reduced the number to 476, of whom 211 were known

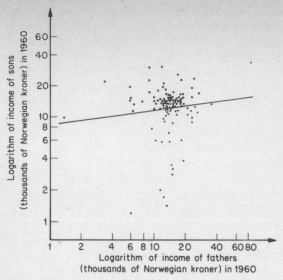

Figure 2.2   Incomes of fathers and sons in Sarpsborg, Norway

to have sons aged 25 or over in 1960. However, since the records were kept on a city basis, it was then necessary to exclude those sons not living in Sarpsborg in 1960, so that the final sample was 115. The results are illustrated in Figure 2.2, where the logarithm of the father's income in 1960 is plotted along the horizontal axis and the logarithm of the son's (or the average of sons') income in 1960 is plotted along the vertical.

As is clear from Figure 2.2, the Soltow data for Norway do not indicate anything more than a weak association across generations. (The fitted regression line does not yield a statistically significant coefficient.) But there are clearly a number of respects in which the data are unsatisfactory. Two points in particular should be stressed. The first concerns the unrepresentativeness of the sample as a result of the procedures adopted in linking records. As Soltow recognises, the sub-sample of fathers resident in Sarpsborg in both 1930 and 1960 may represent the less dynamic group of fathers, and the exclusion of sons who have left the city seems likely to be a serious source of bias. The second point is that Soltow is comparing the incomes of fathers and sons at the same calendar date, and hence at quite different stages in the life cycle. For these reasons, only limited weight can be attached to the findings; however, Soltow's study remains of value as a demonstration of what can be achieved (with the aid of publicly available income-tax data).

The second Scandinavian study illustrates the longitudinal approach, based on a prospective investigation started in 1938. In that year, Hallgren collected data on children in the third grade of school (aged 9–11) in Malmö, Sweden, together with records on their parents; further information was obtained in 1942, 1948 and 1964 (see Husén, 1969). In the last year, data on taxable income in 1963 were obtained for 545 male respondents (65 per cent of the original sample) from the Swedish tax authorities. These respondents were aged 35–37, and the observations were twenty-five years apart, so that the data are closer to overcoming the life-cycle difficulties.

The Hallgren–Husén study shows how a longitudinal cohort started a generation earlier could be used to analyse the relation with family background, and this has been done by Hause (1972) and Wolff and van Slijpe (1973). It also brings out the problems with the design of the study. Given that the original intention was to monitor school performance, the family-income data appear to have been collected in a rather limited form. The analyses of earnings have for this reason used a categorical social-class variable, based in part on income, but also on occupation and on whether the family was in receipt of social welfare. The source is therefore less rich than if the parental-income data had been assembled expressly for the purpose of examining the degree of mobility.

The Wisconsin study

The Wisconsin study is parallel in several respects to that by Hallgren and Husén for Malmö. It builds on an earlier survey of schoolchildren, in this case high-school graduates in 1957. It is limited to one geographical area, the state of Wisconsin; the participants have been followed-up over a number of years (1965–75); and use has been made of data from income-tax records. The original sample was not a random drawing from the age cohort, since a number did not graduate from high school, but it represented in the case of boys about 75–80 per cent of Wisconsin youth (Sewell and Hauser, 1975 App. D). In 1962 a follow-up study was initiated by Sewell. It started with the parents, from whom information was obtained in 1964 on the post-high-school educational and occupational attainments of the children, together with details of marital status, military service and present residence. The response rate for males was 87.9 per cent (91.5 per cent contacted, of whom 96 per cent responded), yielding a sample of 4571. Following this, information was obtained on a confidential basis from the Wisconsin Department of Taxation on parents' occupation and reported income from the 1957–60 state income-tax returns, and the same information for the children for the period 1957–65. Finally, the Social Security Administration, Washington provided data on the earnings of male students and their parents for 1957–67, and later this was extended to 1971 (Hauser and Daymont, 1977). A further telephone follow-up of the respondents was carried out in 1975, with a response rate of 88 per cent (Clarridge, Sheehy and Hauser, 1978).

The analysis of this survey contained in Sewell and Hauser (1975) is confined to those with a non-farm background (primarily because of the difficulty of measuring the income of farmers) and excludes those who had died since 1964, who were enrolled in college or in the military, who were unemployed or not in the labour force. This reduced the effective sample to 2069. Taking the parents' average *income* for the three years 1957–60, the correlations with the son's *earnings* for the three years 1965, 1966 and 1967 were 0.128, 0.175 and 0.177. In a structural equation incorporating an index of ability, educational attainment and occupational status, three parental background variables had no independent significance (father's education, mother's education, and father's occupational status), but parental income was significant. In terms of the model described in Chapter 1, there appears to be a *direct* association with parental income: 'after all intervening achievements are taken into account, $1000 in parents' income is still worth $112 in son's earnings' (Sewell and Hauser, 1975, p. 108). The subsequent analysis by Hauser and Daymont (1977) of a larger sample of more than 3000 showed that the direct impact of parental income remained broadly stable as one took earnings for successive years 1965–71, but that the indirect effect via education tended to increase.

The Wisconsin study is the fullest available to date and provides a valuable point of reference. It has very considerable merits, including:

(1)   the existence of reliable sources of data on incomes in the two generations;
(2)   the relatively large sample size;
(3)   the high success rate in tracing the children, including the fact that data were obtained for those who had left Wisconsin;
(4)   the extensive additional information available about the children (for example, on education or IQ).

At the same time, attention should be drawn to a number of potential difficulties, which need to be borne in mind in using the data and assessing the findings, including:

(1)   the local nature of the original sample (Wisconsin) and the fact that it did not cover the entire population (particularly those from low-income families less likely to graduate from high school);
(2)   the sample involves working back from sons to fathers, with the resulting problems of interpretation;

(3) the income data relate to rather different stages in the life cycle, the gap being some fifteen years or shorter, and early career earnings may be unrepresentative (the sons were aged 26–33 in 1965–71).

Implications

From this survey of the existing state of knowledge, it transpires that, although research on occupational mobility is well developed, there is to date no corresponding evidence on intergenerational income mobility in Britain. This led us (in 1974) to consider how such evidence might be secured.

Of the three methods outlined at the start of this chapter, the longitudinal is in many respects the most attractive. However, the existing longitudinal cohorts do not provide a basis on which to build an income follow-up survey, there being no parental income information comparable with that in the Wisconsin, or indeed the Hallgren–Husén study. The prospect of mounting a new longitudinal project was ruled out by considerations of cost and of the time-scale involved. If a new longitudinal investigation had been launched in 1975, satisfactory intergenerational results would not have been available before the twenty-first century.

The retrospective approach has been used in the study of occupational mobility, but we have earlier argued that it is much less likely to yield reliable results with earnings or income. For the reasons explained there, we rejected this line of attack, although we recognise that further exploration of the technique may succeed in overcoming the difficulties of inadequate recall and of the need to use proxy information.

This left us with the third approach – via record linkage – although even here we have seen that considerations of confidentiality rule out the use of official data. Progress in this direction depends on the existence of academic or private surveys which collected data suitable for our purposes and which could be used as the foundation for a follow-up survey. The list of desiderata rapidly narrows the field. We are looking, in effect, for a reasonably large sample survey (larger than Soltow's 115 cases), with fairly accurate income or earnings data (better than the parental income data in the Hallgren–Husén study), carried out some 20–30 years previously (so as to provide income data at a broadly comparable stage of the life cycle).

It appeared to us that there were two main possibilities. One was the series of savings surveys carried out by the Oxford University Institute of Economics and Statistics from 1952–5, containing data on income, occupation, household composition, etc. Since we started work, the original computer cards have been discovered, and are being made available via the SSRC Survey Archive (*Survey Archive Bulletin*,

September 1978). This could well provide the basis for a follow-up study, but at the time we were planning our investigation we were not aware that the original material was still extant. We decided therefore to explore the second main prospect as a base survey: the survey of York carried out in 1950 by Seebohm Rowntree in conjunction with G. R. Lavers.

3 The Rowntree Survey and Tracing the Children

Introduction: the Rowntree Surveys of York

The 1950 social survey of York was the third and last carried out by Seebohm Rowntree. He had begun in 1899 with the inquiry which is one of the landmarks of social science research. The 1899 survey covered 'working-class' families in York and consisted of questionnaire returns for 46 754 people, or about 61 per cent of the population of the city. The identification of the 'working-class' sample was based on local knowledge, and the bulk of the interviews were carried out by one investigator during the period March–September 1899. Details of occupation and, where possible, earnings were obtained by the interviewer. Where the earnings data could not be collected, Rowntree made estimates, drawing on information provided by employers.

In 1936, Rowntree carried out a second social survey, covering 55 206 people in 16 362 'working-class' families, located by sending interviewers into 'all the streets where such people were likely to live' (Rowntree, 1941, p. 11). Within the identified population, Rowntree sought to interview all families, but in a famous supplementary chapter he examined the reliability of taking samples of one in ten, one in twenty . . . one in fifty. Rowntree concluded that the difference between the results using the sample and the population method were 'immaterial' (Rowntree 1941, p. 479). (It is interesting to learn from material in the archives of the Joseph Rowntree Memorial Trust that Rowntree was a reluctant convert to sampling techniques. Chapman, one of Rowntree's assistants in the 1936 survey, states that Rowntree refused to use sampling techniques at the outset and that he believed the objective of the supplementary chapter was to discredit such techniques.) In the 1936 survey no attempt was made to get information about earnings from the interviews, and Rowntree relied heavily on information supplied about individual wages by the employers. In about 60 per cent of cases the employer furnished such information; in the remaining cases Rowntree made estimates of normal earnings in the occupation concerned.

By the time Rowntree came to prepare the third social survey of York in 1950, he had evolved a procedure by which he sought to interview only the 'working-class' section of the community (variously defined), obtaining occupation, family composition and other information at the interview, but relying on employers to provide much of the earnings data from their payroll records. It is important to see the 1950 survey in this historical context, since otherwise some of its features may seem rather strange – at least judged by current standards. This applies to the sample design, which certainly appears amateur, and to the willingness of employers to provide earnings information, which may appal those concerned with issues of privacy. It has also to be remembered that by the time of the 1950 survey Rowntree was aged 80 and resident in Hertfordshire (170 miles south of York). Commander G. R. Lavers was recruited to assist Rowntree with the survey, but he made only weekly visits to York and the general supervision of the survey seems to have been much less than in the preceding surveys. This lack of supervision in the execution of the survey is paralleled by a lack of clarity in the presentation and analysis of the results in the reports of the survey (Rowntree and Lavers, 1951). The implications of these aspects of the survey are discussed further in the next section, where we consider the feasibility of using it as the basis for a follow-up study.

The 1950 survey

The 1950 survey concentrated as before on the 'working-class population', defined as those households with total earnings (husband and wife) of £550 or less per year. The method by which it was selected is described by Rowntree and Lavers (1951, p. 2):

> We took a list of all the streets of York, and a man who has lived in the city for more than half a century, who knows the city intimately, and has also a wide knowledge of, and sympathy with, our work, marked on our list every street where working class families live.

From the streets defined in this way, a sample of one in nine households was drawn. In this respect, Rowntree modified his earlier procedure. Unfortunately, the execution of the sampling does not appear to have been closely supervised; and there is evidence of departure from the sample originally selected. Moreover, the response appears to have been considerably less than 100 per cent. These aspects are not described in the published account of the survey, but we have been able to piece together information from the Rowntree papers (deposited at the University of York) and from discussion with those involved. The conclusions drawn involve an element of judgement, but the available evidence seems to tell a consistent story.

The drawing of the sample appears to have been based on the York City Year Book for 1949, taking in general every ninth address in the order listed. This we assume to be the case on the basis of the typed street list, containing some 2000 names and addresses, found among the Rowntree papers. When the interviewing came to be carried out in the summer of 1950, the sample was extended to include two new estates, as described in the report to Rowntree by T. J. Brooke (who was the local director of the survey):

Of the 2182 interviews contained in the original street-list, 1893 were carried out. These, together with 102 interviews carried out on the new Gale Lane estate, and 59 on the new portion of the Carr Lane estate, bring the total number of interviews completed in the four weeks to 2054.

He goes on to say that the reasons for the shortfall from the original list include: streets not occupied (for example, because of slum clearances); streets above the £550 cut-off; streets where it was 'impossible for the interviewer to find the requisite number of households in at the time'; and organisational faults. The 289 non-responses from the original list implies a non-response rate of some 13 per cent. This is quite low by the standards of surveys such as the Family Expenditure Survey, where the non-response rate has been of the order of 30 per cent (although this survey does involve a much more detailed questionnaire). None the less, this non-response should have received more attention from Rowntree and Lavers in their report of the results; and it would also have been helpful if they had discussed the implications of adding a further 161 interviews (some 8 per cent of the final total).

More importantly, there appears to have been considerable departure from the original street list. The comment by Brooke about interviewers failing to find the requisite number of households in a street gives the impression that they viewed their task more as finding a specified quota from the street than as being to interview specified households. This impression is supported by discussions we have had with those involved in the interviewing. Further evidence is provided by the typed street list: there are broadly the 'right' number in each street. But the proportion which correspond to the actual house numbers on the list is considerably lower. Although in some streets there is a 100 per cent correspondence, in others there is none. For example, for Crombie Avenue, all eight schedules are given on the list, whereas for Rowntree Avenue, not one of the ten schedules agrees with the list. This may well reflect the differential success/conscientiousness of different interviewers. To the extent that those interviewed were those who could be readily contacted, the resulting interviews may be unrepresentative. Households where both husband and wife worked may, for instance, have been under-represented.

On the basis of the available evidence, it seems reasonable to conclude therefore that the 1950 survey suffered from problems of non-response and of departure from the survey design. The reasons for these shortcomings are easy to understand, but they mean that the results are not necessarily fully representative. Brooke, for example, reported the general conclusions reached by the interviewing team:

Name of Householder Mr. XYZ

Street and Number 22 Lake Success Terrace

Rent   £1.2s.9d.   Total number of occupants 8 (including lodger)

Rates   Number of rooms 6

Bathroom (Yes or No) Yes

Members of Household and status.	Age.	Sex.	Occupation and where employed.	Wage.
Mr.XYZ	57	M	Railway Worker	£5.19s.6d.
Mrs.XYZ	50	F	Housewife	
Daughter	18	F	Packing Dept. of -- & Co	
Daughter	17	F	Packing Dept. of -- & Co	£2. 5s.0d.
Daughter	15	F	Open-Air School. Value of School milk	2s.3d.
Son	9	M	School Family allowances	10s.0d.
Son	8	M	School Value of vegetables grown	2s.6d.
Mr.ABC. (Lodger)	31	M	Bus Driver Paid by lodger	£1.10s.0d.

(Say if children are at school, and if 15 or over and unemployed, if they are attending any classes).

Do the children receive free School meals?   No; pay 2s.6d. each per week

Do the children receive free milk (*a*) at School ?   Yes

                                (*b*) in holidays ?   No

Amount paid by each child in employment for board and lodging   Eldest 25s. a week; Second 20s.

Amount paid by lodgers   30s. a week

Amount received from sub-tenants not boarded   None

Sums received for:—

Unemployment Insurance   None

National Assistance (*i.e.* "Public" Assistance)   None

Health Insurance   None

Sick Clubs   None   War Pension   None   Widow's Pension   None

Old Age Pension (including supplementary)   None

Are all/most/some of vegetables consumed home grown?   Yes - some

GENERAL OBSERVATIONS ON HOUSEHOLD:– A modern council house. The family have not really recovered from four years' continuous unemployment 1934-37. Buying furniture on instalment system (15s.9d.) per week. Complained of high cost of children's clothes and poor quality of shoe leather.

Figure 3.1   A specimen hypothetical schedule from the 1950 survey

'streets in the centre of the city tended to be too highly represented as against the suburbs and that old-age pensioners and young couples were the most cooperative in answering questions'.

The full number of respondents is nowhere stated explicitly by Rowntree and Lavers (1951). The report by Brooke refers to 2054 interviews being carried out. On the other hand, it is clear from the Rowntree papers that the published results are based on a multiplier of 9, and working back from the 18 099 working-class families referred to in the report, we arrive at a figure of 2011. This is corroborated by working documents among the Rowntree papers. We therefore assume that, although 2054 interviews were carried out, 43 were not used for some reason.

The number of respondents would be easily determined, if we had access to all the original schedules; unfortunately the Rowntree papers at the University of York only contain schedules relating to 1363 households, or 67.8 per cent of the assumed total of 2011. We have not been able to provide a satisfactory explanation of why the schedules are missing; however, a comparison of the surviving two-thirds of the schedules with the results for the full sample reported by Rowntree and Lavers (1951) does not suggest that they are grossly unrepresentative (see below).

The interviewers collected information on the age, sex and occupation of each member of the household, the rent and condition of the house (this description was sometimes highly unflattering). A hypothetical schedule, taken from Rowntree and Lavers (1951, pp. 4–5) is shown in Figure 3.1. As in 1936, Rowntree went directly to the employers and requested them to supply details of the net earnings of their employees who were in the survey. Where respondents received income from sources such as pensions, unemployment or sickness benefit and public assistance, Rowntree approached the institutions concerned, and acquired and checked the relevant data.

Is the 1950 Survey Adequate as a Base for a Follow-up Survey?

The Rowntree 1950 survey is far from ideal as a source of information and we have argued elsewhere (Atkinson, Corlyon *et al.*, 1981; Atkinson, Maynard and Trinder, 1981) that it led people to draw misleading conclusions about the extent of poverty in post-war Britain. The question we have to ask here, however, is whether its shortcomings are such as to render it inadequate as the base for a follow-up study. Or can it, with due qualifications, be used to throw light in an area where no other source seems available?

The nature of the sample

If we consider the 1363 families for whom the 1950 Rowntree survey

National Population

City of York — Population 105,000

Exclusion of upper/middle income ranges by selection of streets — Population about 60% 18,099 families

1 in 9 sample, not necessarily random — 2,011 families

Loss of schedules — 1,363 families

Figure 3.2   Stages in the selection of the 1950 sample available as base for the 1975–8 follow-up survey

schedules survive, then they are obviously far from a random sample of the national population. As in the case of the Soltow study, we have to examine the possible bias introduced by the method by which the sample was obtained. The main stages, summarised in Figure 3.2, are discussed in turn.

The first problem is that the survey relates to a single city. In this respect it is no different from the base surveys described in Chapter 2, but we have to ask how representative or unrepresentative York is of the national population. Rowntree himself, in embarking on his 1899 survey, expressed the hope that the conditions of life in York 'might be taken as fairly representative of the conditions existing in many, if not most, of our provincial towns' (1901, pp. xvii–xviii). In the 1936 survey, he elaborated on this theme, arguing (1941, p. 10):

On the whole, I think, we may safely assume that from the standpoint of the earnings of the workers, York holds a position not far from the median, among the towns of Great Britain. If on the one hand there is no important industry employing a large number of highly skilled and highly paid workers, on the other hand there are no large industries (although unfortunately there are isolated small businesses) where wages are exceptionally low.

This claim was repeated in 1950 (Rowntree and Lavers, 1951, p. 6).

In certain respects, York does indeed seem reasonably typical of the national population. If one takes the information on demographic structure contained in the 1951 Census of Population, then the sex and age composition is relatively close: for example, 21.9 per cent in York are aged under 15, compared with 22.2 per cent in England and Wales. In other respects, the position in York appears rather different from the national picture. The proportion of married women working, for example, was rather higher. The level of unemployment in York has tended to be below the national average: for example, in 1950 it was below 1 per cent when the average for England and Wales was 1.5 per cent.

Perhaps most important are the differences in industrial structure. In 1951, according to the census, some 9500 men and women were employed in cocoa, chocolate and sugar confectionery. British Railways employed over 5500 people, and a further 3000 were engaged on the manufacture and repair of wagons. The categories 'food, drink and tobacco' and 'transport and communication' together accounted for 35.4 per cent of total employment in York in 1951, compared with 10.8 per cent for England and Wales. In contrast, employment in textiles, clothing and agriculture was considerably below the average for England and Wales. The Rowntree survey is likely, therefore, to reflect the characteristics of the dominant industries, and may well not be representative of the country as a whole. Even if it is close to the median, it is quite possible that 'the city would not reflect the "spread" of incomes typical for the country as a whole' (Townsend, 1952, p. 37). The claim made by Rowntree appears therefore to have been overstated, and we do not share his view that York can be taken as a microcosm of Great Britain. We cannot simply extrapolate the findings to national conclusions. This does not, however, mean that the sample is useless for our purpose; what we must do is to take account in the analysis of the particular features of York, notably the predominance of the confectionery industry and of British Railways.

The second element in the selection of the sample is the restriction to 'working-class' households and the method by which this was put into effect. The exclusion of households where total earnings exceeded £550 a year would, in theory, have eliminated the top 20 per cent or so of the income distribution. According to our estimates of the national distribution of earnings in 1950 (see Chapter 6), 20 per cent of men earned £540 or more; according to our estimates based on the Blue Book figures for the national distribution of income for 1949–50, 14 per cent of tax units had incomes in excess of £525 a year. The reduction in the population shown by the Rowntree figures of 40 per cent is substantially larger. This includes domestic servants and those living in institutions, which may account for part of the discrepancy, but it is also possible that the method of selection, based on the identification of streets, may have caused a sizeable number of those below the earnings limit to be wrongly excluded. The investigators' local knowledge was no doubt considerable, but the method itself was a crude instrument for the purpose.

The shortcomings of the procedure by which the sample of one in nine was drawn have been described in the previous section. To this must be added the failure to distinguish adequately between households and families as units of analysis. The investigation in effect focused on the position of the family belonging to the household head, with only limited information for non-dependent members of the household. In 1950, when lodgers were common and there were more multiple-generation households, this was an important factor.

Contemporary commentators on the Rowntree 1950 survey drew attention to the possibly unrepresentative nature of the sample. Kaim-Caudle (1953), for example, noted that the proportion of the sample who were children eligible for family allowances (that is aged 14 or under) appeared to be only 10.7 per cent (Rowntree and Lavers, 1951, p. 42), whereas from the census figures for York in 1951 one would expect a figure of 22 per cent. This figure does not, however, include the children of lodgers and other family units, illustrating the point made in the previous paragraph. Our calculations from the surviving schedules, in fact, give a total proportion of 25 per cent so that on this basis families with children do not appear to be under-represented. On the other hand, Kaim-Caudle was clearly correct in drawing attention to a number of questionable features of the Rowntree sample. For example, our own reanalysis (Atkinson, Maynard and Trinder, 1981) shows that the number of recipients of National Assistance was only around a half that which could be expected on the basis of the national figures. This may reflect a difference between York and the country as a whole, but more likely to be important is the fact that the information relates primarily to heads of households.

Finally, the loss of a third of the original schedules is undoubtedly a major handicap, and there is no reason to expect those that remain to be representative in all respects. From our comparison with the reported results for the full sample, there seems, for instance, to be some under-representation of working wives. On the other hand, for a number of other characteristics the surviving schedules appear reasonably typical. For example, the proportion of owner-occupiers is 29 per cent compared with 28 per cent in the full sample, and the average family size is 3.6 compared with 3.5. Of especial interest is the comparison of the numbers classified in relation to Rowntree's poverty line. (see Table 3.1). It appears that there is a slight over-representation of classes A and B. The proportions are, however, in general in fairly close agreement.

A partisan supporter of the Rowntree survey could describe the surviving 1363 schedules as a resonably representative sample of the 'working-class' population of a not atypical provincial city. A severe critic, on the other hand, could describe them as the unexplained remnant of a survey conducted without due care, relating to an ill-defined sub-population of a city dominated by two industries scarcely characteristic of the country as a whole. In our view, the position lies between these two extremes. The method of sample selection does not

Table 3.1   Percentage of households covered by survey (that is, working-class population)

Class	Description of household	Original	Surviving schedules
A & B	Below minimum	4.6	5.1
C	At minimum or less than 23% above	19.4	18.7
D	At least 23%, but less than 46% above	17.4	17.5
E	At least 46% above	58.6	58.7

match up to modern standards, but Rowntree and his colleagues did possess considerable local knowledge. The results are not representative, certainly not of the national population, but examination of the characteristics of the 1363 schedules does not reveal any gross bias. There are aspects of the sample which must lead us to qualify any conclusions, but these can be taken into account in the analysis.

Quality of the data

In the course of our research, we have obtained information from a number of those involved in the conduct of the 1950 survey, and this certainly raised doubts in our minds about the quality of the data. The survey was mostly carried out by students, with little previous experience of this kind of work, and there was limited supervision. Rowntree and Lavers themselves felt that the data were adequate, and reported how Lavers revisited some households to verify the data, finding 'no cases in which they furnished inadequate or incorrect information' (1951, p. 2). However, examination of the schedules and interviewing of the children in our 1975–8 follow-up survey suggest that this conclusion was over-optimistic. The schedules contain errors in such details as the Christian names of the respondents, in addresses and in respondents' ages. From the correspondence between Rowntree and employers it is clear that the occupation information was in some cases incorrect. One Whitehall department, when asked for earnings data on one respondent, supplied the information, but commented: 'I do not know how Mr X's occupation came to be described as Secret Service Work. He has been identified as a packer in the Department's local store.' This may, of course, be a 'cover up', but corrections were made by a number of employers; and our discussions with those involved suggest that Lavers did not, in fact, make any substantial checks.

It may appear from this catalogue of deficiencies that the 1950 data were not worth using. This conclusion is, however, too hasty for three reasons. First quite a lot of the information can be checked and corrected. Rowntree and Lavers did this themselves, as is evident from the notes on the schedules, and we have been able to make further corrections: for example, where earnings were wrongly transcribed as £15 rather than £5. Secondly, errors on the original schedules may cause difficulties with the tracing of the children, but if we can locate the children, then it may be possible to correct the information from interviews with the children. This use of retrospective data did indeed prove of value for characteristics such as age.

The third – and most important – reason why errors in the interview stage may not prove fatal is that Rowntree drew a significant part of his information from other sources. In particular, he obtained a major part of the data on earnings and other income from employers and government bodies. Only a brief account of this aspect is given in the published report, but from the Rowntree papers it is possible to form some idea of the reliability of the information. In December 1950, one of the interviewers described how the large firms (for example, the railways and the confectionery companies) had been most helpful, but that the small firms had been less co-operative. The correspondence indicates how refusals of information were not unusual. For instance, the local authority refused to divulge details of their employees' earnings and, as a result, the authors had to estimate the earnings of 61 of their respondents. Of the 102 respondents in the building industry, 89 had their earnings estimated from basic rates. A further 104 had given incorrect replies about their place of work. However, from the correspondence it appears that there were over 1000 employees for whom data were collected direct from the employers. Moreover, many employers seem to have taken a great deal of care in answering the questions, and in correcting and supplementing the interview information: for example, 'I have taken the liberty of supplying the details on a new form, as on your original list some of the titles, initials, ages and occupations, etc. were incorrect.' The earnings data supplied by *employers* in this way may well be more reliable than those obtained from *employees* in modern surveys.

The quality of the earnings data collected from employers is a major strength of the 1950 survey. Moreover, for other items of income, too, Rowntree was able to obtain reliable information from the source of payment. In particular, the National Assistance Board supplied details for 127 families, indicating whether or not they received assistance and, if so, how it was calculated. Thus he knew that Mr Arnold (fictional name) received National Assistance of 12 shillings a week, in addition to 42 shillings retirement pension and 10 shillings occupational pension. With this degree of co-operation from government departments, a high standard of accuracy could indeed be achieved.

Can the 1950 survey be used?

The answer to this question is a matter of judgement. The Rowntree 1950 survey has evident weaknesses and strengths. Overall, as a source about living standards at that time, the former probably outweigh the latter. But for our purposes, the merits of the Rowntree survey, notably the quality of the earnings data and the fact that the survey was carried out approximately a generation ago, were felt to be sufficient to warrant exploring whether we could locate the children of the 1363 families as the basis for a follow-up study.

Tracing the Rowntree Children

The problem of tracing the second generation may be simply described. We were trying to find, in a typical case, Smith (male) and Smith (female, probably now married with different surname), children of Mr and Mrs J. Smith, resident at 1 Rowntree Drive, York in 1950, as well as establishing whether or not there were other children not yet born in 1950 or who had already left home at that time. The problem is simply stated, but at the outset we had no idea whether or not it was soluble.

The tracing of respondents has played a major role in a number of studies. In the follow-up by Husén in 1964 of the original sample of children (aged 9–11) in Malmö in 1938, 'practically every individual' was eventually traced, apart from those who had emigrated. The problems of tracing were, however, less severe than with the Rowntree sample, for two main reasons. First, the initial data cover all children, whereas we have first to establish the potential population and then locate the children. Second, the Malmö study had carried out follow-up surveys of part at least of the group in 1942 and 1948. When the later follow-up survey started in 1962, therefore, the gap was 14 rather than 26 years. Repeated contact has been an important factor for the longitudinal investigations in Britain of Douglas and the National Children's Bureau. They have succeeded in retaining a high proportion of the original sample by collecting information at frequent intervals: for example, nine contacts in fifteen years. Nearer to the problem we face, in terms of the time interval, is the study by Olneck (1977) of brothers in the Kalamazoo, Michigan school system. He sought to trace in 1973 a sample who had records drawn from the period 1928–50 and achieved the remarkable success rate of 57.9 per cent.

A pilot study

Since there was little to guide us as to the likelihood of success, we began in 1974 with a pilot study. For this we first drew a random sample of 201 from the 1363 schedules in our possession. The figure of 201 was chosen as representing 10 per cent of the original Rowntree sample (at that time we entertained hopes that the missing schedules would still be found). This subsample included 126 families headed by a man in full-time work (in 1950) and 50 headed by retired persons. The remaining 25 included those where the head of household was unemployed, sick or widowed. After considering the evidence available, we decided to concentrate in the pilot study on the 126 families headed by a man in work. The probability of being able to trace the children appeared greater in these cases, since the children were more likely to have been living at home in 1950.

For the 126 we adopted the simplest possible tracing procedure, based on readily available public sources. These were the Kelly's Street Directory for York and the voting lists. (The York edition of the former – an invaluable tool for this kind of research – unfortunately ceased publication in 1975.) The easiest cases to locate are, of course, those where the family are still living at the same address. This depends on the rate of mortality and on the degree of mobility. A very approximate guide to the numbers which one could expect to trace this way is provided by the following calculation, based on the national figures on length of residence (General Household Survey, 1971) and the national life tables (Annual Abstract of Statistics, 1967). Suppose that in two-thirds of the cases one member at least of the family survived and that, of these, one-third remained at the same address. This suggests that we should expect to find at the same address some two-ninths of those interviewed in 1950. The lower-income groups covered by the survey may have had a higher degree of mobility, and have been more likely to have been affected by council redevelopment schemes, but against that we would expect York to have a more stable population than nationally. The experience with the pilot study showed, in fact, that the percentage at the same address was close to 40 per cent: in 51 out of the 126 cases, at least one of the Rowntree parents was alive and at the same address, and in a further two cases, one of the children was living at the address, having taken over the house.

The next, relatively straightforward step was to check whether the parents, or children, had moved elsewhere in York. In such cases, at least with names less common than Smith, the present address could be deduced from the 1975 directory alphabetical listing. (That the identification was in fact correct was of course checked at a later stage.) The result of this procedure was that we thought we might have located the present address of at least one member of 94 families of the 126 families in question. Of the remainder, some had died without children. Others could doubtless have been traced with a more exhaustive procedure, but we went on to see how many of the 94 would provide the addresses of the children necessary to establish the sample.

In order to obtain the names and addresses of the children, we wrote to the 94 people, enclosing a simple form. A reminder was sent after two weeks. This elicited a total response from 45 families – slightly under half. This was less satisfactory than we had hoped, and in some cases reflected the fact that our original 'identification' of the family member had been incorrect. Of the 45:

> 33 provided details of children (54 sons, 31 daughters);
> 8 had no children;
> 4 refused to help.

The 'success' of tracing may be measured by the ratio of those for whom addresses were obtained plus those with no children, giving a combined total of 41, to the original total of 126 families. This success rate of 32.5 per cent was clearly unsatisfactory. On the other hand, it was based on only the very simplest tracing procedures, and no attempt had been made to follow up the 49 households for whom 'leads' had been obtained, but who had not responded to the postal inquiry. The response to the pilot study should therefore be regarded as a base on which we could build.

The experience with the pilot study encouraged us to embark on the main investigation and provided a number of lessons about the techniques of tracing. Although the overall success, in terms of the final sample of children, was not adequate as it stood, we had made considerably more progress in the limited time available than we had originally expected, and there were a number of pointers in the pilot study that more intensive methods could be highly effective in raising the success rate.

(The pilot study went on to interview the 54 sons located, achieving a response rate of 87 per cent. The results are not discussed separately here, being combined with those from the main investigation.)

Main tracing exercise

The main tracing operation drew on the findings of the pilot study, and began in the same way with the public sources, notably Kelly's Street Directory. As in the pilot study, a substantial number could be identified from the 1950 address: 356 of 1363 (in all cases we include the pilot families in numbers reported). Of these, 285 were the Rowntree parents. A further 297 Rowntree parents could be traced from the alphabetical listing in the directory, or, more accurately, we could obtain 'leads' on these families. This brings the total (653) to just under half the schedules.

We then supplemented the street directory by more extensive use of the voting lists than had been the case in the pilot study. The latter have the advantage that they give the full names of all members of the household entitled to vote. This enabled us to add to the information contained on the 1950 schedules: for example, to know that the male Smith child aged 10 in 1950 was actually Alexander Bernard Smith (a fact that would be recorded, if he was registered as a voter from 1961). Tracing through the different registers allowed us to obtain leads on a further 263 families.

At the end of this first stage (in May 1976) we had therefore addresses which gave 'leads' on 916 families (67 per cent). To each of these addresses, we sent a letter explaining the research and asking for the addresses of the Rowntree children. Enclosed was a short form on which to provide the information and a stamped addressed envelope. (In some cases the recipient was the Rowntree parent, in others it was one of the Rowntree children.) At the same time, the *Yorkshire Evening Press* (based in York) carried an article (14 May 1976) describing the purposes of the research, which we hoped would improve the response. A repeat mailing was made in June 1976 to those who had not replied, and there was a further article in the *Yorkshire Evening Press* (9 July 1976). A copy of the press article was enclosed with the reminder. The response to this mailing was:

Supplied addresses of children	500
Mailing revealed that they had no surviving children	65
Not willing to help	37
Reply incomplete, wrong family, letter returned by GPO	128
No reply	186
Total	916

Measuring 'success' by those who supplied addresses or had no surviving children, the rate was 565/1363 (41 per cent) at this stage. This was higher than the 32.5 per cent in the pilot study and may reflect the fact that the research now had a base in York and the press coverage. The substantial numbers where the 'leads' failed to yield addresses were in part accounted for by cases where the identification was uncertain and by the fact that the street directory for 1975 (the last one published) was rather out of date.

At the end of the second mailing, there were therefore 565 cases accounted for, and 37 refusals. In addition, in 46 cases there were firm grounds for believing that there were no children, for example, spinsters over 50 years old. This left 715 'difficult to trace' cases. From a preliminary investigation of these, and the possible lines of inquiry, it became clear that the next stage would be highly labour-intensive. Personal visits would have to replace postal and telephone inquiries, and these visits would have to include neighbours, distant relatives, present occupiers of the house, etc. We therefore decided that, with the resources available, we could only sample these 'more difficult to trace' cases. We therefore took a random 10 per cent sample. The choice of a sample of 10 per cent was dictated by the available resources. With the benefit of hindsight, it might have been preferable to transfer resources from interviewing those located at the first stage (taking a random sample) to tracing the 'more difficult' cases, allowing a higher fraction than 10 per cent to be taken. In our defence, we would note that we had, at the outset, little basis to judge the likely costs of tracing these cases. Subsequent investigators may find our experience helpful in this respect.

In view of the fact that we drew a sample of these cases, the analysis which follows typically *grosses up* the observations from the 10 per cent sample, so as to arrive at a representative set of results. The procedure is described in more detail below. The main exception to this is that we do not employ grossed figures in the regression analysis (see Porter, 1973) or in Chapters 8 and 9, where extensive use is made of individual case studies.

The 'difficult to trace'

The 10 per cent sample of 'difficult to trace' families, 73 in all, fell into three broad categories. The most straightforward case was that where we had obtained an address, but had received no reply to the mailings. When these families were visited, it became clear that the majority were in fact willing to help. In several cases they felt guilty about not having returned the form, and excused themselves by saying that 'they were no good at filling in forms'. In other cases, the information given was incomplete and required further investigation. Thus, one respondent was only willing to give surnames and streets for her six brothers and sisters. Four of these could be traced from the voting lists, but this was not easy where two families with the same surname lived in the same street. (They had to be traced back through the electoral registers until it was discovered that in 1959 one of them, together with her husband, had lived with the 1950 respondent.) In one case, contacting the family produced the information that the 1950 schedule gave the wrong surname. This necessitated a second visit. The respondents showed remarkable patience as the interviewer sorted out what had happened.

The second category consisted of cases where the information collected from the mailing had been incomplete. In some cases it was simply a matter of returning to the 'lead' address and collecting the information. This was so where the respondent had not himself believed that he was the correct person, but we were able to establish that the correct identification had in fact been made. The range of methods used with less straightforward cases may be illustrated by the following three families.

The Green Family   The reply to the mailing contained incomplete information on two of the children and seemed likely to yield further details on a personal visit. In particular, we hoped to trace a son living in a particular district. Closer examination revealed that the person identified from the voting list was not a son, but a cousin of the 1950 family (a confusion caused by the fact that he had lived with the Rowntree respondents in the 1950s). He confirmed the existence of a son, but was unable to give an address.

The Cooper family   The problem arose because they had moved from the address we had located. Visits to the house revealed, at the fifth attempt, that the occupant did not know the address of the 1950 respondent, but could describe the involved route to his house ('the one with the purple front door'!). Eventually, the right house was found and the address of both daughters obtained.

The Hurst family   We had been unable to get a reply because they too had moved, and the house had been demolished. A neighbour gave the information that the respondent worked as a plumber and, she thought, lived out of York. From the electoral registers, the Christian names of the sons were obtained and the Yellow Pages revealed a person of that name working as a plumber some miles away. A visit produced the information that he did not know the addresses of his brother or sister, but could tell us the current address of the parents. A visit there gave the daughter's surname, and she was traced through the electoral register. No address could be given for the other son, but he was a student and could be traced through the university.

The third category of 'difficult to trace' families was that where we had no 'lead'. Tracing here was much more time-consuming and the success rate considerably lower. The general approach adopted was to check through the electoral registers to identify the neighbours at the date when the family left the 1950 address. Where the neighbours had not themselves moved, contact could easily be established. Where the neighbours had moved, we attempted to trace them through the directories. If no neighbour could be traced in this way, then there was usually no other line of approach.

Where neighbours were traced, they were typically helpful and appeared to have no compunction about giving away information, even if they did not know why it was being requested. In many cases, precise information was not available, but either helpful facts were given (for example, that the parents definitely had children) or useful 'leads' were offered. Two examples may illustrate the help provided and the way in which intensive effort devoted to tracing can pay dividends.

The Brett family   The street in which the parents were living in 1950 had been demolished and there were no clues as to the present address. Through the street directory, a then neighbour was discovered to be living in Heworth and he recalled that the 1950 respondent had moved to a particular street in Acomb. No person with the correct name was identified in that street, but with the aid of a street map and the electoral register a search was made of all streets leading off that given to us by the neighbour. This yielded a person with the correct name, who turned out to be the Rowntree father and supplied addresses of three children.

The Dore family   We succeeded in finding one of the neighbours from 1950. She confirmed that the parents interviewed in 1950 were no longer alive, but knew of the existence of a married daughter whose surname she remembered (the husband's brother had been a footballer of local fame!). She did not know the address, but suggested an area of York where they might be living. A lengthy search through the electoral register located someone with the right surname. A visit to the house produced the information that this person had moved. A systematic check with neighbours was made until one of them recalled the new address of the required person. She was indeed the daughter and gave the addresses of two other children, one living in another part of Yorkshire and the other in Australia.

Success of the tracing

The combined success rate for the two stages is shown in Table 3.2. In drawing the sample for the 'difficult to trace' cases, the sampling fraction differed slightly for the three categories described in the previous section. As a result, the average grossing factor is 9.8, so that 73 cases in the sample gross to 715. However, for the convenience of the reader, and to avoid discussing fractions of families, we have taken throughout a grossing factor of 10. This slightly overweights the difficult to trace cases, and leads to a total of 1378 rather than 1363.

We have treated as 'success' cases where we have either obtained the addresses of the children or established that there are no surviving children. On this basis, the 'success rate' is 76.3 per cent. This falls quite a long way short of being ideal, but – given the limited information from which we had to work and the fact that more than a quarter of a century had elapsed – it seemed to us a highly satisfactory outcome.

There are, of course, good reasons for supposing that those not traced are different in significant respects (for example, they are more likely to have left York). The representativeness of the traced sample is discussed in the next chapter, but it is interesting to note the results of a comparison of those located at the second stage with those traced in the first round. This shows that the 1950 families where the children were traced at the second stage had, on average, a smaller number of children, a much larger proportion receiving retirement and widows' pensions, a smaller proportion with a man in employment, and a lower mean income in relation to the National Assistance scale. This brings out the importance of the intensive stage of the tracing procedure.

The 500 families traced at the first stage and the 33 from the second stage had, according to the information supplied in the tracing exercise, 1262 and 98 children, respectively. Grossing the difficult to trace by a factor of 10, this gave a total of 2242 children, who formed the basis for the follow-up survey. More than half of them still lived in York, but we succeeded in tracing a substantial number who had moved away. The addresses for the children included Aberdeen, Dundee, Whitehaven, Brecon, Minehead and Plymouth. Indeed 4 per cent of children located lived overseas.

Table 3.2   Tracing of the children from the 1950 survey

	First stage	*Grossed figures for second stage*	*Total*	
	Number of original Rowntree parents where children traced			
Supplied addresses of children	500	330	830	76.3%
No surviving children	111	110	221	
Not willing to help	37	20	57	23.7%
Not traced	—	270	270	
Total	648	730	1378	

Note: By 'grossed' figures we mean those obtained by multiplying all observations from the 10 per cent sample by a factor of 10.

4 The Follow-up Survey in 1975–8

Introduction: the Questionnaire and Response to the Survey

Our success in tracing the children of the 1950 families was greater than we had anticipated; as a result, we were not able to hold personal interviews with all 2242 second-generation families. (In what follows, we refer to the second generation as 'Rowntree children', although it should be borne in mind that by the time of our follow-up survey they were mostly adults – and some indeed were grandparents.) What we did was to interview 1097 of the Rowntree children traced at the first stage and to send postal questionnaires to 165, including 50 of the 54 overseas (the remaining four were interviewed while visiting the UK). In the case of those traced at the second stage, we were constrained by limitations on resources to interviewing those in or around York, 67 in all. The remaining 31, including three overseas, were sent postal questionnaires, so that the proportion was higher for this group. The figures, including the totals grossed for the 10 per cent subsample, are shown in the first column of Table 4.1.

The basic interview questionnaire consisted of three types of schedule. The first (Schedule A) was for the household as a whole. It checked that the parents did in fact take part in the 1950 survey and requested details of household composition, housing, etc. This was followed by a set of individual schedules for all those aged 16 and over, dealing with employment, income, education and job history. There were different schedules for those in employment (Schedule B) and those retired (Schedule C). The UK postal questionnaire was in the same format, with a household schedule and individual schedules (Type I for those not retired and Type II for those retired). Less information was requested, however, so as to make the document less daunting. The same applied to the overseas schedule, where we also modified certain questions (for example, those relating to social-security benefits).

The interviews, apart from those in the pilot study, were carried out over the period June 1976–July 1978. The procedure was to send a letter prior to the interview. This explained the purpose of the research, enclosing a copy of the *Yorkshire Evening Press* cutting, and said that an interviewer would be calling. (For interviews outside York, appointments were made in many cases.) The interviews were commonly in the evenings, which typically allowed both husband and wife to be present – and in some cases brothers, sisters, aunts and uncles as well. They were often lengthy, sometimes involving sessions of four hours or more or requiring two or three visits. The interviews frequently yielded a great deal of detailed and relevant information in addition to that requested. The interviewers were encouraged to write up their general impressions, and these provide valuable qualitative evidence.

The income and earnings questions were naturally rather sensitive and some people responded with what were obviously rounded figures. In general, however, people were willing to provide considerable detail of their income and its composition, often consulting pay-slips and other records. The interviewers also took care to collect additional information where earnings appeared to vary significantly from week to week, an aspect not covered as fully in the questionnaire as would, in retrospect, have been desirable.

The postal questionnaires were sent out in 1978. In each case the same materials were sent as with the letter to families to be interviewed, in addition to the questionnaires and a stamped addressed envelope. Where no reply was received, a reminder was sent.

Response to the questionnaire

Experience with questionnaires containing detailed questions on income suggests that non-response is likely to be a significant problem. The Family Expenditure Survey, which is a more extensive but well-established interview survey, has in recent years had a response rate of around 70 per cent: in 1979, for example, it was 68 per cent. The response rate in its first year of operation (1959), which is perhaps the best comparison with what we were attempting, was only 59 per cent. In the case of postal questionnaires dealing with income, the response has been very considerably lower. The Census Income Follow-up Survey in 1971 achieved a response rate below 40 per cent (OPCS, 1978).

The response to our Rowntree follow-up survey is summarised in Table 4.1. To begin with the least satisfactory aspect, the response to the postal questionnaire was low. Measured in terms of fully completed replies, the (grossed) response rate was only 29 per cent; even if we include partially completed replies, the response rate only reaches 40 per cent. In contrast, the response to the interviews was in excess of that which might have been expected. In 81 per cent of cases (grossed) we obtained a complete response, and when partial replies are included the rate is nearly 90 per cent. This no doubt reflects the skill of our interviewers and the way in which they briefed themselves thoroughly for each interview. We also have the impression that people liked to take part in a survey in which their parents had been involved.

From Table 4.1, it can be seen that 177 provided incomplete replies and that 487 did not respond (both grossed figures). In the case of

Table 4.1   Response to the Rowntree follow-up survey

	Total	Complete response	(Percentage)	Complete or partial response	(Percentage)
Interview (UK and abroad):					
traced first stage	1097	899	(82)	963	(88)
10% sample	67	54	(81)	60	(90)
Postal (UK and abroad):					
traced first stage	165	59	(36)	72	(44)
10% sample	31	8	(26)	12	(39)
Total	1360	1020	(75)	1107	(81)
Grossed up total					
interview	1767	1439	(81)	1563	(88)
postal	475	139	(29)	192	(40)
Overall total	2242	1578	(70)	1755	(78)

non-respondents, there is little that can be done, although we comment below on the characteristics of their parents in 1950. The main cause of incomplete replies (94 out of 177) was the refusal to answer the income questions. This does not mean that the interview was necessarily useless for our purposes. For example, in some cases the missing information concerned investment income, and the earnings data could be utilised. In other cases, we have complete information for the Rowntree child, but lack data on the spouse. In such situations, we could use the results to analyse, say, mobility from father to son.

Included in the 1755 complete or partial responses are 39 from abroad. These include four cases where we were able to interview them in person, when they were temporarily visiting Britain (brothers and sisters still living here were most helpful in arranging this). The countries in which the overseas respondents were living included Australia, Canada, New Zealand, South Africa and the United States. Since the earnings and income data cannot be readily compared with those for UK respondents, we have not included those from overseas in the main analysis. It may be interesting none the less to note two features. The first is that none came from families classified by Rowntree as being in poverty in 1950. The second is that the occupations suggest that they were in relatively well-paying jobs. The occupations of the Rowntree sons who had gone overseas included: one schoolteacher, two accountants, three managers (including one with Rowntree Mackintosh), a welfare officer with local government, and a technician in a university. The possible links between family background and geographical mobility, and between geographical mobility and economic success, are discussed in a UK context in later chapters.

Representativeness of the sample

In assessing the representativeness of our respondents as a follow-up of the children of the original 1950 survey, we have to bear in mind that there are two major sources of possible bias: that arising from the failure to trace all the children, and that from non-response to our survey. Moreover, in considering these, we need to use different units of analysis. In terms of tracing, the unit is the 1950 family; the left-hand part of Table 4.2 is drawn up in these terms (the total is 1378 rather than 1363 because of the grossing up). In terms of response to our survey, this is measured in terms of the number of children, so that each traced 1950 family appears in the potential sample as many times as it has children.

Table 4.2 shows a number of the characteristics of the families in 1950 which were traced and of those who responded (in whole or in part). It should be noted that it is in the nature of the method that we know considerably more about non-respondents than is typically the case, although whether there was more non-response amongst mobile children cannot, of course, be tested. If we consider, first, these 1950 families 'accounted for' (that is, where we traced the children or established that there were no surviving children), then there do not appear to be any marked differences: for example, the percentage with retirement or widows' pensions is identical, and the percentage with a man earning is virtually the same. The income of the family, expressed relative to the National Assistance scale (details given in the next chapter), is 196 for those accounted for, compared with 197 overall. The most noticeable difference is that the mean number of adults is higher for those families accounted for, and we would expect families with at least two adults in 1950 to have been easier to trace.

The difference between the second and third column in Table 4.2 reflects the exclusion of those with no surviving children. This is, of course, an aspect which is concealed by studies, such as the Wisconsin one, which work back from children to parents. Examination of the characteristics of the group with no surviving children (not shown separately in Table 4.2) indicates, as is to be expected, that the number of children in these households was small and these were typically either grown up in 1950 or not the child of the Rowntree parent. In many cases (34 per cent) the household was headed by a single woman, and the proportion receiving National Insurance retirement/widows' pension was nearly twice that for the rest of those traced. The proportion with a man in employment is low – some 46 per cent compared with 65 per cent in the sample as a whole. For those men with earnings,

Table 4.2   Representativeness of the sample

| | Unit: 1950 family | | | Unit: Children in 1975–8 survey | | |
	Whole sample (1)	Those accounted for (2)	With surviving children (3)	Potential sample (4)	Response (complete or partial) (5)	Non-response (6)
Total number (grossed up)	1378	1051	830	2242	1755	487
Mean number adults	2.17	2.26	2.26	2.26	2.26	2.28
children in household	1.34	1.30	1.59	2.08	2.02	2.29
Percentage with man earning	65	64	69	65	69	52
Mean earnings[a] (£ per year)	361	359	359	351	353	342
Percentage with National Insurance, retirement or widows' pension	28	28	24	27	26	30
Mean income in relation to National Assistance scale[b] (£ per year)	197	196	193	180	185	160

Note: [a] For a small number of cases, information was not available on earnings. The mean relates to all cases with earnings for which the information was known.

   [b] For a small number of cases, information was not available. The mean relates to cases for which information was known.

the mean is fairly similar to that for the population as a whole.

The 2242 total shown in the fourth column of Table 4.2 corresponds to the 830 families with surviving children, weighted by the number of children. As a result, the characteristics are rather different; and in particular the mean number of children rises from 1.6 to 2.1. The comparison of the respondents (column 5) and the non-respondents (column 6) indicates that there are significant differences. The non-respondents were less likely to have had a man at work in 1950, and where they did the earnings were significantly lower. The percentage with a pension was higher among non-respondents, and the mean income in relation to the National Assistance scale is substantially lower for the non-respondents. These differences arise particularly on account of the low response to the postal questionnaire. The mean earnings of non-respondents to the interviews were only £3 a year less than those of respondents, whereas the earnings for postal non-respondents were nearly £20 a year lower.

This analysis of non-response suggests that the results of our survey need to be qualified. At the same time, it indicates that the findings are likely to be more reliable for some groups than for others. One distinction of especial importance is that between families where the father was at work in 1950 and those where he was not, or where there was no father. The former constitute 1457 of the potential sample and the number of respondents was 1209. This gives a response rate of 83.0 per cent, which is considerably higher than that for the remaining families, where it was 69.6 per cent. The results for families where the father was in work, which receive particular attention in our analysis, may therefore be more representative than those for other groups.

Characteristics of Our Respondents

The design of our study is such that there is no reason to expect the respondents to be representative of the national population in any respect. Only if their characteristics were totally unrelated to those of their parents would we expect them to constitute a representative sample. It may nevertheless help to put our findings in perspective if we present a brief description of some of the major characteristics and compare these where possible with the national statistics. In the final section of this chapter, we begin to compare the position of parents and children.

Geographical location

The most obvious respect in which our respondents are unrepresentative is the concentration on York or, more broadly, Yorkshire and Humberside. If one drew a random sample of 2000 families in England and Wales, one would expect to find about four in the city of York. Of the 1716 respondents in the UK to our survey, no fewer than 1113 were resident in York. (Unless otherwise stated, all figures are grossed up for the random 10 per cent.) A further 374 were resident in Yorkshire and Humberside.

The distribution of the 1113 respondents in York between the thirteen different wards of the city is shown in Figure 4.1. Given the concentration of the original 1950 survey on 'working-class' streets, there is no reason to expect a uniform distribution. Comparison with the Census of Population Small Area Statistics for 1971 suggests that the respondents are fairly evenly spread as a percentage of the population, with some over-representation of Bootham and Beckfield and under-representation of Walmgate.

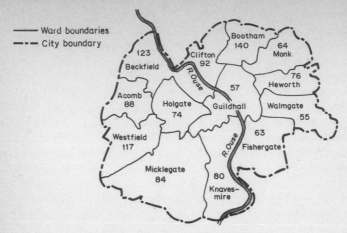

Figure 4.1   Distribution of York respondents to 1975–8 survey by wards

The use of the city boundary to identify those families which have stayed in York is to a considerable extent arbitrary. There are, for example, a significant number of respondents who live just outside the city boundary, and some of these commute daily into York to work. We may similarly expect there to be differences between those families who have moved, say, 30 miles away and those who have gone to the south-east of England. In order to allow for this, we have divided the respondents into three groups, on the basis of whether they live in York, elsewhere in Yorkshire and Humberside, or in the rest of the United Kingdom.

The respondents from the rest of the UK correspond to 148 un-grossed observations, and their location by county is shown in Table 4.3. From these figures it can be seen that the largest single concentration is in London (12), but that Surrey (10) is not far behind. The respondents are by no means evenly distributed between counties, and twenty out of the forty-five counties have 2 or fewer respondents whereas, in addition to London and Surrey, Bedfordshire and Nottinghamshire each have 7 and Cleveland has 8. It is also the case that in only two families does more than one sibling live in the same county (in Cleveland and in Nottinghamshire). Although seven brother/sister pairs live in the same region, in general there is no clear tendency to concentrate. For example, the Morris children live in Greater London, Hertfordshire and Norfolk, and the Austin children in Dorset, Cumbria and Scotland.

Age and household composition
The Rowntree children in the UK are somewhat weighted towards

daughters (922) and against sons (794). Although there is a slight tendency for the response rate to be higher for daughters, the main source of the difference is the, perhaps surprising, finding that more daughters were traced; thus any bias has been introduced at that stage rather than via non-response.

The ages of the sons and daughters are shown in Table 4.4. The respondents, whom we have been referring to as 'Rowntree children', do in fact range from teenagers to octogenarians. A substantial proportion are, however, concentrated in the range 25–54: 62 per cent of sons and 60 per cent of daughters. The percentage over 65 is 15 per cent for sons and 12 per cent for daughters.

Table 4.3   Respondents outside Yorkshire by county

County	Number (ungrossed)	County	Number (ungrossed)
London	12	Hereford	0
Bedfordshire	7	Worcester	0
Berkshire	2	Salop	0
Buckinghamshire	0	Staffordshire	4
Essex	3	Warwickshire	2
Hampshire	6	Derbyshire	3
Hertfordshire	4	Leicestershire	3
Isle of Wight	0	Lincolnshire	4
Kent	6	Northamptonshire	2
Oxfordshire	2	Nottinghamshire	7
Surrey	10	Greater Manchester	3
Sussex	4	Merseyside	0
Cambridge	1	Cheshire	4
Norfolk	2	Lancashire	3
Suffolk	5	Tyne and Wear	5
Avon	3	Cleveland	8
Cornwall	0	Cumbria	5
Devon	1	Durham	5
Dorset	2	Northumberland	0
Gloucestershire	2	Wales	6
Somerset	1	Scotland	6
Wiltshire	3	Northern Ireland	0
West Midlands	2		
Total		148	

The classification of households by composition is shown in Table 4.5. In looking at these results, two points should be borne in mind. First, our survey was concerned only with *surviving* Rowntree children. We did not interview the widows of Rowntree sons or the widowers of Rowntree daughters. This accounts for the — entries in Table 4.5.

Table 4.4   Ages of respondents to 1975–8 survey

Age-range	Number of sons	Number of daughters
<25	36	45
25–34	193	172
35–44	142	204
45–54	155	181
55–64	133	179
65+	123	114
Not known	12	27
Total	794	922

Secondly, it is quite possible that the Rowntree son or daughter was living with another family unit. For example, a child of 25 may still be living at home. The composition shown in Table 4.5 relates to the *household*, and the multiple family-unit households appear in the 'other' category.

From Table 4.5, it can be seen that 33 per cent of sons were married and had children aged under 16 years and that a further 31 per cent were married, without children under 16 and were below retirement age. For daughters, the percentages were virtually identical: 34 per cent with children and 30 per cent without children under 16 and the household head below retirement age. It is interesting to compare these figures with those for the national population sampled in the Family Expenditure Survey for 1977. The classifications cannot be matched exactly, but the 1977 survey shows 28 per cent of households as consisting of a man, a woman and between one and three children (Department of Employment, 1978, Table 39), and that 19 per cent were married couples where the head was below retirement age. The latter is less extensive than our category (which may include cases where a child over 16 years of age is still at home), but our sample certainly includes fewer pensioner households than the national population. The Family Expenditure Survey shows 11 per cent of households consisting of a couple with the head aged over retirement age and 13 per cent as consisting of a single person over retirement age.

Housing and consumer durables
Since there are noticeable regional differences in tenure patterns, we distinguish in Table 4.6 by location as well as tenure. The proportion of owner–occupiers is lower in York (45 per cent) than in the full sample (55 per cent), but a larger fraction of these have paid off their mortgages. The lower proportion of owner-occupation in York could be due to the fact that much of the postwar building has taken place outside the

Table 4.5 Household composition of respondents to 1975–8 survey

Household	Sons		Daughters	
	Number	Percentage	Number	Percentage
MC + 1 child under 16 years	47	5.9	57	6.2
MC + 2 children all under 16 years	108	13.6	137	14.9
MC + 3 children all under 16 years	39	4.9	40	4.3
MC + 4 children all under 16 years	7	0.9	8	0.9
MC + children both under and over 16 years	58	7.3	70	7.6
MC head under retirement age without children under 16	249	31.4	278	30.2
MC head over retirement age without children under 16	108	13.6	78	8.5
One parent family (children under 16)	2	0.3	50	5.4
One woman under retirement age	—	—	33	3.6
One woman over retirement age	—	—	84	9.1
One man under retirement age	27	3.4	—	—
One man over retirement age	5	0.6	—	—
Other	144	18.1	87	9.4
Total	794	100.0	922	100.0

Note: MC denotes married couple

city boundary (for example, in Huntington).

As may be seen from Table 4.6, there are a sizeable number in the 'other' category. This consists mainly of children still living with their parents, but also includes those in rent-free accommodation. It may therefore be simpler to think in terms of the ratio of owner–occupiers to council tenants, which is 1.29 in York and 2.02 for the sample as a whole. A comparison with national figures may be of interest, although again there is no reason to expect our respondents to show the same pattern. From the Department of Environment data (Central Statistical

Table 4.6   Respondents to 1975–8 survey by housing tenure and location

	York No.	York %	Yorkshire and Humberside No.	Yorkshire and Humberside %	Rest of UK No.	Rest of UK %	Total No.	Total %
Own outright	220	19.8	72	19.3	64	27.9	356	20.7
Own on mortgage	284	25.5	206	55.1	106	46.3	596	34.7
Rent from council	390	35.0	44	11.8	38	16.6	472	27.5
Rent privately	75	6.7	9	2.4	10	4.4	94	5.5
Other	141	12.7	43	11.5	11	4.8	195	11.4
Not known	3	0.3	—	—	—	—	3	0.2
Total	1113	100.0	374	100.0	229	100.0	1716	100.0

Office 1979, Table 9.4), we can derive the corresponding ratios for different regions:

Yorkshire and Humberside	1.64
England	1.83
Great Britain	1.69

This suggests that our sample as a whole contains rather more owner-occupiers than would be found in a national sample, even when comparison is made with England (that is, excluding Scotland where owner-occupation is lower).

In the survey we asked about consumer durables, and the results are summarised in Table 4.7. Usually those with only one of the four durables (car, central heating, telephone and refrigerator) have a

Table 4.7   Respondents in 1975–8 survey with consumer durables (car, central heating, telephone and refrigerator)

	Number of sons	Number of daughters	All children
None of the above	29	55	84
Any one of the above durables	187	194	381
Any two of the above durables	171	211	382
Any three of the above durables	192	202	394
All four of the above durables	196	257	453
Don't know	19	3	22
Total	794	922	1716

refrigerator. The next most common are a telephone (931 out of 1716 respondents) and a car (936 respondents). The figures may be compared with those from the national Family Expenditure Survey (FES) (Department of Employment, 1978, Table 57). In 1977, 57.2 per cent of households in the FES had cars, compared with 54.5 per cent of our respondents, and 56.8 per cent had telephones, compared with 54.3 per cent of our respondents. The proportion in the FES with central heating was not so close (50.8 per cent compared with 41.5 per cent), although there may be differences in definition. Finally, the proportions with refrigerators were virtually identical: 89.9 per cent in the FES, 90.9 per cent in our sample. In their access to consumer durables, our respondents do not seem very different from the national population.

Parents and Children
In the previous section, we have seen that our respondents differ from a random sample of the national population in ways to be expected. They tend to be concentrated in York or its vicinity. There is a lower proportion of pensioners. In other respects, they do not appear to be particularly unusual. What our principal concern is here, however, is whether or not they resemble their parents.

Age and the life cycle
The intention of the follow-up survey was to interview the children at broadly the same stage of the life cycle as their parents in 1950. The gap between 1950 and our survey was approximately a generation, but clearly there can be considerable variation around this value. Mr and Mrs Gooch were aged 30 when interviewed by Rowntree in 1950; their children were born in 1946, 1952 and 1958. When we interviewed the children in 1976, the eldest was the same age as his parents had been in 1950, but the youngest was only 18. In contrast, Mrs Boycott's first child was born when she was 17, so that when we came to carry out the follow-up interview in 1978, the child was eleven years older than his mother had been in 1950.

In Table 4.8, we show the pattern of age differences for the parent/child pairs in our sample. It should be noted that here, as with other observations on parent/child pairs, parents with x responding children appear x times in the table. Thus the Gooch family contribute three entries to the second row, two in the first column and one in the second diagonal column. In 108 cases, the age of one generation is not known. If we take the remaining 1608 parent/child pairs, then 751 are in the same age-range in both generations (these figures are printed in italic). If we include the neighbouring age-bands, the number rises to 1450, or 90 per cent of the total.

Table 4.8   Age of respondents and parents of respondents

Parents	Age of Rowntree child respondents							
	<25	25–34	35–44	45–54	55–64	65 or over	Don't know age	Total
<25	—	1	—	2	—	—	—	3
25–34	61	168	29	—	—	—	3	261
35–44	13	165	160	13	—	—	—	351
45–54	6	26	124	180	71	55	20	482
55–64	—	5	23	109	110	16	2	265
65 or over	—	—	10	18	110	133	15	286
Don't know age	—	—	—	14	21	33	—	68
Total	80	365	346	336	312	237	40	1716

Note: The age of the parents is defined as that of the household head (that is, the father, unless there is no father, in which case, the mother).

The grouping by age-ranges may give a misleading impression. After all, if all the Gooch family had been one year older, then two rather than one would have been on the diagonal. An alternative presentation of the data is in terms of the age difference between parents and children:

Age difference	Number of cases
less than 10 years	1172
10–15 years	274
more than 15 years	162
don't know	108
Total	1716

This too suggests that the timing of the follow-up survey has been fairly successful in securing data at an interval of a generation. None the less, we cannot ignore the age differences that exist, and particular attention will be paid to the question of adjusting for the age factor.

The stage in the life cycle is obviously related to age, but there are likely to be differences in the age at which parents have children. The cross-tabulation of household composition provides, therefore, a valuable additional check. This is shown in Table 4.9. If we exclude the 108 for whom the age information is not available, then 755 of the 1608 (or 47 per cent) had children aged under 15 (the school-leaving age) in 1950. Of these 755, 455 had children under the age of 16 in the 1975–8 survey. In the same way, of the 285 households without children under 15, where the head was over retirement age in 1950, 180 had children in this category in 1975–8. Combining the entries for couples with

Table 4.9 Household Composition of Respondents and Parents of Respondents

Parents in 1950	Respondents to 1975–8 survey					
	Couple + child(ren) under 16	1 parent + child(ren) under 16	Others – head of household under retirement	Others – head of household over retirement	Age or composition not known	Total
Couple + child(ren) under 15	406	38	293	3	3	743
1 parent + child(ren) under 15	11	0	4	0	0	15
Others – head of household under retirement age	146	12	335	75	22	590
Others – head of household over retirement age	7	1	97	180	15	300
Age or composition not known	1	1	33	33	0	68
Total	571	52	762	291	40	1716

children and for one-parent families, the number on the diagonal (indicated by the numbers printed in italic) in Table 4.9, comes to 60 per cent. Again this is reassuring, but indicates that the stage of the life cycle must continue to be an important element in the analysis. We cannot simply compare the incomes of the two generations without allowing for the fact that in nearly 300 cases the parents had dependants when they took part in the original inquiry, but their children did not when they responded to our 1975–8 follow-up survey.

Comparison of income and earnings
Our main aim is to compare the income and earnings across the two generations. However, this cannot be done for the full sample of 1716 respondents in the UK. The first reason is that data are not complete in all cases. The figure of 1716 relates to complete or partial responses (see Table 4.1, from which has to be subtracted 39 overseas responses). As we have noted, a major reason for replies being classified as incomplete is that income information is missing.

The basis for the analysis of income continuities in the next chapter is therefore the complete replies, which come to 1545 when we subtract those from overseas. Even for these it is not possible to calculate in all cases the Supplementary Benefit assessment (described in more detail in Chapter 5). Those which had to be excluded consist broadly of two groups; first, 79 cases where the questions, although all answered, yielded estimated figures for earnings or pensions, and hence were not as accurate as those giving precise amounts. Secondly, those where the Rowntree child was in fact still at school (20), or long-term sick in hospital (5), or in transition (7) (for example, being between work and retirement, having just set up in business or having been made redundant on the day of the interview). In these cases too, despite full replies, we did not feel that an accurate Supplementary Benefit assessment could be made. Finally, there were cases where the complexity (for example, of maintenance payments) defeated us. As a result, the sample was reduced by 115 to 1430. It is this sample which forms the basis for Chapter 5.

The second reason why the sample is smaller applies to the analysis of earnings in Chapter 6 and subsequent chapters. Continuities in earnings can only be assessed where both generations are in employment at the relevant dates. Mr Cook was 55 when interviewed by Rowntree in 1950; his son, aged 35 in 1950, had already taken early retirement when we interviewed him in 1977. This father/son pair could not therefore be included in the investigation of earnings mobility.

5 Income Continuities across Generations

Our main purpose in carrying out the follow-up survey is to collect evidence about income mobility. In this chapter, we take a first look at the evidence about intergenerational continuities. It is a *first* look in the sense that many of the difficulties of interpretation are left for the present on one side. In particular, we largely ignore in this chapter the problems which arise from the method by which our sample was obtained: the exclusion by Rowntree of upper income-groups, our failure to trace all the second generation, and non-response to our survey. We begin by discussing the measurement of living standards and the National Assistance/Supplementary Benefit scale. The analysis then considers the transition between different income-ranges and the differential 'odds' of entering different income-positions. Particular attention is paid to movements in and out of the low-income group and to the characteristics of 'movers' and 'stayers'. The alternative regression approach is then presented, and used to introduce consideration of the implications of measurement error. Finally, we explore the role of the life-cycle factor and the effect of taking different indicators of living standards.

Measuring Living Standards
In considering the comparison of incomes across two generations, it may be helpful to begin with a case-study. For this we take Mr and Mrs Parks and their son Robin. When Mr and Mrs Parks were interviewed by Rowntree in York in 1950, they were both aged 35 and had a daughter aged 8 and two sons of 7 and 4. Mr Parks worked as a welder earning £8.50 a week (all amounts are expressed in decimal currency, even though at the time it would have been £8 10s 0d). Mrs Parks did not work, but they received family allowances of £0.50. When we interviewed Robin Parks, the younger son, in 1978, he was earning £9700 a year as an accountant. He was married, with two children aged 5 and 7. His wife did not work, and they had no other income apart from child benefit of £2.50 a week.

From consideration of their occupations, Robin appears to have risen relative to his father, but a comparison of their incomes cannot be made as directly as this – even in this relatively uncomplicated example. First, we cannot compare money amounts without allowing for the general rise in prices and incomes. Between 1950 and 1978, national income per head rose by a factor of slightly over 10. This factor of 10 is a fairly useful one to bear in mind when converting money amounts from 1950 to the 1975–8 survey, but it is of course only a crude adjustment. After all, between 1975 and 1978 national income per head rose in money terms by some 50 per cent, so that the adjustment applied to interviews in 1978 would not be appropriate to those carried out as part of the pilot study in 1975.

The second factor for which allowance has to be made is that the deductions from pay for income tax and National Insurance contributions have increased in relative importance. In 1950 Mr Parks had to pay the National Insurance stamp, but, even though his earnings were well above the median, he paid virtually no income tax. Since that time, the income-tax threshold has fallen, and Robin Parks pays more than a quarter of his income in tax.

Thirdly, we have to allow for the differing requirements of the two families, reflecting differences in the life cycle and other circumstances. Mr and Mrs Parks had three children to feed rather than two, but they were more favourably placed in terms of housing. Mrs Parks had inherited the house from an aunt, whereas their son Robin in 1978 had substantial outgoings on a recently acquired mortgage.

There are several ways in which these factors could be accommodated, but in this chapter we concentrate on just one. The 'resources' of each family are calculated, by subtracting tax, other deductions and housing outlay, and are then compared with the ruling National Assistance (in 1950) or Supplementary Benefit (in 1975–8) scale. The method is described in more detail below. The wisdom of adopting this approach may be questioned, and we draw attention later to some of its shortcomings, but it has a number of merits.

With a line of descent from the Poor Law, National Assistance and Supplementary Benefit (its 1966 replacement) have been the basic form of means-tested income maintenance in Britain. The National Assistance/Supplementary Benefit (referred to below as NA/SB) scale represents therefore 'in a sense the "official" operational definition of the minimum level of living at any particular time' (Abel-Smith and Townsend, 1965, p. 17). For this reason, the NA/SB scale has frequently been taken as the basis for studies of poverty, if only to judge the effectiveness of government policy by its own standards. *The Poor and the Poorest*, the study closest in time to that of Rowntree, employed a criterion of the basic NA scale plus 40 per cent. More recently, Layard, Piachaud and Stewart have taken the long-term SB scale, describing it as a 'familiar benchmark' (1978, p. 10).

In addition to being widely used, the NA/SB scale seems appropriate in view of our particular concern with the experience of low-income families. How many families who had low incomes in 1950 (this does not include the Parks) have children who are at or close to the poverty line in 1975–8? In this context, we should note that our assessment for 1950, using the NA scale, may well differ from Rowntree's poverty classification (A–E). Although Rowntree's earlier investigations played a significant role in the development of the NA standard, his calculations differed in several respects. They were based on a different unit of assessment, giving special treatment to the amounts paid by lodgers and adult children; they included income in kind; the level of the scale was different. The implications of these differences are explored in Atkinson, Corlyon *et al.* (1981). From our reanalysis of the surviving schedules, we estimate that 14 per cent of these involved families who were below the NA scale, compared with 5 per cent in poverty according to Rowntree's classification. Although his approach may well be the right one for the purpose of making comparisons with his earlier inquiries in 1936 and 1899, our use of the NA scale seems more appropriate if one is looking forward rather than backwards.

National Assistance/Supplementary Benefit classification
The resources of the family are expressed relative to the NA/SB scale. This may be defined more fully as follows:

Husband's (normal) earnings
    plus wife's (normal) earnings   } **Gross**
    plus state income   **income**
    plus other income (e.g, interest, lodger's contributions)

    minus tax payments
    minus National Insurance payments
    minus other deductions (e.g. superannuation payments)
    minus housing costs
Equals **Net resources**

NA/SB ratio equals Net resources divided by NA/BA scale and multiplied by 100

In applying these calculations, the income unit is assumed to be the 'family' rather than the 'household': that is, we follow NA/SB practice. This is important where more than one family live in the same household, as where grandparents live with their children, or where there are lodgers. In 1950 this was relatively common. Under the NA/SB assessment, a limited allowance is made for the contribution of other household members to the income of the family in question.

In the definition of income, we have departed from the NA/SB practice in two respects. First, we have not followed their special treatment of capital income, which imputes a 'tariff' income typically in excess of the actual income. We have taken the actual interest or other investment income. Secondly, we have not applied 'disregards' to income, as embodied in the NA/SB regulations. In 1950, for example, the first 10s 6d of private pensions or friendly society benefits was disregarded, and there was a further disregard for earnings. In 1975–8 the provisions for disregards took a different form, but had the effect of again exempting certain amounts of particular types of income. In our assessment we have, in both generations, included all income. To this extent, our assessment is a more severe one than would be applied by the NA/SB practice.

The method may be illustrated by reference to the Parks family. Mr and Mrs Parks in 1950 had a gross income of £9.00 a week. From this we have to subtract National Insurance contributions and the housing outlay, which total £1.23, leaving a disposable income of £7.77. The National Assistance scale at that time was £2.18 for a married couple plus £1.40 for the three children. The percentage ratio of resources to the NA scale, referred to as the NA ratio, is therefore 217 per cent. Mr and Mrs Parks were comfortably above the National Assistance level. In 1978, Robin Parks's earnings were £186.54 a week, to which has to be added child benefit of £2.50. When we subtract income tax, National Insurance contributions and his mortgage payments, then his net resources are £115.13. The Supplementary Benefit long-term scale for a couple was £28.35, to which £9.90 was added for the children, so that his percentage SB ratio (ratio of resources to the SB scale) was 301 per cent. Viewed in this way, he was significantly better off than his parents in 1950, even without taking account of the fact that the SB scale itself was higher in purchasing power than the NA scale in 1950.

Incomes in relation to the NA/SB scale

Before considering the degree of mobility across generations, it may be helpful to describe the overall distribution in our sample at the two dates which will be presented in the next section.

The figures in Table 5.1 relate to the 1430 parent/child pairs which are the subject of analysis in this chapter. (All figures, unless otherwise indicated, are grossed up to allow for the random 10 per cent.) The unit is the 1975–8 survey respondent, so that a 1950 family with three children responding to our follow-up survey will appear three times in Table 5.1. For this, and other, reasons, the results should *not* be interpreted as throwing light on the extent of poverty in 1950.

Of the 1430 pairs, 295 (that is, slightly over 20 per cent) are below the NA scale in 1950. A further 170 cases are within 40 per cent of the NA scale. If therefore we were to adopt the Abel-Smith and Townsend criterion of NA plus 40 per cent about a third of the sample would be in the 'low-income' category in 1950. The upper third of our sample begins approximately with Mr and Mrs Parks. We can see that 374 cases had

Table 5.1   Incomes in relation to the NA scale in 1950 and the SB scale in 1975–8

Percentage of NA/SB scale	Parents		Children	
	No	%	No	%
⁻79	149	(10.4)	7	(0.5)
80–99	146	(10.2)	95	(6.6)
100–119	72	(5.0)	183	(12.8)
120–139	98	(6.9)	192	(13.4)
140–159	117	(8.2)	156	(10.9)
160–179	160	(11.2)	142	(9.9)
180–199	91	(6.4)	160	(11.2)
200–239	223	(15.6)	196	(13.7)
240–299	263	(18.4)	173	(12.1)
300⁻	111	(7.8)	126	(8.8)
Total	1430	(100.0)	1430	(100.0)

NA ratios in excess of 240 per cent, and 111 were above 300 per cent.

If we look at the families at the extremes of the distribution, there were six families who in 1950 appeared in the lowest category with a NA ratio below 50 per cent. None of them had a head of household in full-time employment at the time of the interview. Two were widows aged 61 years and 58 years, one was a (probably) divorced or separated woman aged 64 years, two were retired men aged 65 years and the last was a younger man (age not stated) not in employment because of illness. All except one family were in rented accommodation. At the upper tail, there were eight families with a NA ratio of 400 per cent or more. All contained a male aged between 41 and 65 years in employment. Their occupations included self-employed builder, Gas Company employee, optical glass worker, cashier, projectionist, clerk and employee of a firm of wholesale chemists. Earnings ranged between £10 a week for the self-employed builder and £5.62 for the clerk, but their domestic positions varied greatly. Two were widowers, four were married, one was single and one was not married but had a house-keeper. All except the single men had children living at home, but none of the children was less than 14 years of age (the majority of the children were in their twenties and in employment).

The distribution of the 1430 respondents in the 1975–8 survey is shown in the right-hand part of Table 5.1. A considerably smaller proportion, 7 per cent, is below the SB scale than was the case for the parents in 1950, but the number within 40 per cent of the scale is correspondingly higher. As a result, the number with a low income (less than the SB scale plus 40 per cent) is almost exactly a third: 33.3 per cent, compared with 32.5 per cent for the parents. We should repeat that nothing can be deduced from this about the trend in the extent of poverty in Britain over the period. At the upper end, the top third begins at about 200, and Robin Parks finds himself comfortably in the top 10 per cent of the sample.

Some of the characteristics of the 1975–8 respondents by income ranges are shown in Table 5.2. From this certain distinct features appear. The elderly and one-parent families seem most likely to have low incomes. The cases consisting of one or two persons under 65 years with no children, have the highest proportions with incomes over 240 per cent of SB (43.8 per cent). Families with dependent children are spread fairly evenly over the middle categories, with relatively few at either extreme and the majority above the 140 per cent line. The lower

Table 5.2 Characteristics of 1975–8 families by SB ratio

	SB ratio percentage					
	−99	100–139	140–179	180–239	240+	*Total percentage*
Family type						
Married couple and children under 16	11	108	190	139	46	494 (39.1)
One-parent families	16	26	6	1	0	49 (3.9)
One or two people, under 65 years [a]	15	50	60	119	190	434 (34.4)
One or two people, 65 years or over [b]	40	172	18	47	7	284 (22.5)
Other	20	19	24	50	56	169 (11.8)
Total	102	375	298	356	299	1430
Percentage	(7.1)	(26.2)	(20.8)	(24.9)	(20.9)	(100)
Employment status of male head						
At work [b]	19	138	249	300	284	989 (79.3)
Sick	6	20	16	6	4	52 (4.2)
Unemployed	6	7	0	0	0	13 (1.0)
Retired	17	134	20	19	3	193 (15.5)
Total	48	299	284	325	291	1247
Percentage	(3.8)	(24.0)	(22.8)	(26.0)	(23.3)	(100)

Notes: [a] By age of head of family.
  [b] Includes those on holiday at date of interview.

part of the table shows the employment status of the Rowntree son or son-in-law (that is, excluding cases where the head of household is a Rowntree daughter). A clear pattern emerges. The majority of those below SB are not at work, although it should be noted that in nineteen cases the family was below SB despite having a male head in work. There are relatively few unemployed (if our interviews had been carried out five years later the number would undoubtedly have been much higher), but they all fall into the low-income category below SB plus 40 per cent.

If we look at the extremes of the distribution in 1975–8, we find that seven cases have SB ratios less than 80. None was married when interviewed: two were separated, one was divorced and four were single. Their ages ranged from 19 to 51 years. Unemployment and/or sickness were the principal characteristics of the group. At the other extreme, there were thirteen 1975–8 families with a SB ratio equal to 450 or above: eight containing Rowntree daughters and five containing sons. The ten who were not self-employed were evenly distributed inside and outside York. There was one unmarried Rowntree daughter of 55 years and one unmarried son aged 31; the remaining eight were married. In seven of these eight cases the wives worked outside the home (in all instances full-time). The wife who did not go out to work had a 12-year-old child. None of the other families had dependent children; in fact only one other family had a child living at home and she was in employment, as was the older child of the first-mentioned family. With the exception of two cases, all the husbands' occupations were non-manual. Home-ownership was a feature common to them all. Of the three self-employed families with an SB ratio of 450 or more, one contained a married Rowntree son. He was a partner in a shop. One of the Rowntree daughters was married to a managing director and the other to a doctor. Two of the three had low housing costs; the other owned their house outright. Also, two of the three had second incomes.

Income Mobility: the Evidence
In this section, we bring together the circumstances of the Rowntree children with those of their parents. We begin in Table 5.3 with a detailed 10 × 10 transition matrix. Each cell in the matrix corresponds to a specific combination of origin and destination. We take a particular range of NA ratios, corresponding to one of those shown in Table 5.1, and see how many of the children whose parents were in that range ended up in a particular range of SB ratios: for example, the Parks are found in the cell printed in italic in Table 5.3.

The transition matrix shows an interesting pattern with some tendency for concentration on the diagonal, but also quite a lot of cases of movement from low incomes to high and vice versa. For example, there are four families where the parents were below 80 per cent of the NA scale in 1950, but the children are at more than 300 per cent of the SB scale. Conversely, there are four families where the parents were above 300 per cent of the NA scale, but the children were below the SB level in 1975–8.

The matrix in Table 5.3 also brings out the small numbers in many cells. Even with the grossed data, there are 40 out of 100 cells with fewer than ten entries. In view of this, we concentrate on the less detailed 5 × 5 matrices shown in Table 5.4 for all Rowntree families and sons/daughters separately (all grossed).

Indicators of the extent of mobility

The evidence from the simplified transition matrices of Table 5.4 suggests that the off-diagonal entries are numerous and that predictions of the children's living standards based on the parental NA ratios would not be particularly accurate. At the same time, the transition matrix does not appear to be consistent with a situation of 'perfect' mobility, defined such that the 1975–8 income category of the children is independent of their parental income in 1950. In order to reach more concrete results, we need to standardise the data to allow for the differing numbers in different groups.

The first set of calculations are of the transition proportions. For each row, we compute the percentage of cases entering different income-ranges. Thus, for the first row, of children whose parents were below the NA scale in 1950, the destinations were:

10.5 per cent below SB (31 ÷ 295)
37.6 per cent in the range of 100–39 per cent SB (111 ÷ 295)
18.0 per cent in the range of 140–79 per cent SB (53 ÷ 295)
24.1 per cent in the range of 180–239 per cent SB (71 ÷ 295)
9.8 per cent in the range of 240 per cent or more SB (29 ÷ 295)

So about one child in ten remained below SB, and – at the other end – about one child in ten was comfortably above SB (240 per cent plus). Nearly half were within 40 per cent of the SB level. The corresponding transition proportions for the children of parents at 240 per cent or more of the NA scale in 1950 are: 4.0 per cent, 22.5 per cent, 16.0 per cent, 27.5 per cent and 29.9 per cent. So three children in ten remained in the same category, and over half had resources of at least 180 per cent of the SB scale.

If there were perfect mobility, then the transition proportions would be the same for all rows. The chance of entering a particular income-range would be the same from whatever income class one came. That this is not the case is shown in Table 5.5. For the first row, of children

Table 5.3 Transition matrix for incomes

NA ratio (percentage) for parents	SB ratio (percentage) for children										Total
	1 <79	2 80–99	3 100–119	4 120–139	5 140–159	6 160–179	7 180–199	8 200–239	9 240–299	10 ≥300	(percentage)
1 <79	1	13	36	35	3	15	32	7	3	4	149 (10.4)
2 80–99	0	17	17	23	33	2	14	18	19	3	146 (10.2)
3 100–119	0	3	29	8	6	5	3	11	4	3	72 (5.0)
4 120–139	0	15	22	5	20	6	16	9	3	2	98 (6.9)
5 140–159	0	15	13	8	16	11	12	21	7	14	117 (8.2)
6 160–179	1	6	9	20	15	25	17	25	25	17	160 (11.2)
7 180–199	0	2	3	18	7	13	13	14	13	8	91 (6.4)
8 200–239	0	14	29	16	40	21	16	25	27	35	223 (15.6)
9 240–299	5	6	20	40	12	31	26	45	50	28	263 (18.4)
10 ≥300	0	4	5	19	4	13	11	21	22	12	111 (7.8)
Total	7	95	183	192	156	142	160	196	173	126	1430 (100)
(Percentage)	(0.5)	(6.6)	(12.8)	(13.4)	(10.9)	(9.9)	(11.2)	(13.7)	(12.1)	(8.8)	

Table 5.4   Simplified (5 × 5) transition matrices for incomes
(a)   All families

NA ratio (percentage) for parents	SB ratio (percentage) for children					Total (Percentage)
	1 <99	2 100–139	3 140–179	4 180–239	5 ≥240+	
1 <99	31	111	53	71	29	295 (20.6)
2 100–139	18	64	37	39	12	170 (11.9)
5 140–179	22	50	67	75	63	277 (19.4)
4 180–239	16	66	81	68	83	314 (22.0)
5 >240	15	84	60	103	112	374 (26.2)
Total (Percentage)	102 (7.1)	375 (26.2)	298 (20.8)	356 (24.9)	299 (20.9)	1430 (100)

(b)   Rowntree sons

NA ratio (percentage) for parents	SB ratio (percentage) for sons					Total (Percentage)
	1 <99	2 100–139	3 140–179	4 180–239	5 ≥240	
1 <99	13	62	28	28	22	153 (22.3)
2 100–139	2	29	13	12	6	62 (9.0)
3 140–179	14	15	38	44	52	163 (23.8)
4 180–239	2	28	31	38	51	150 (21.9)
5 >240	6	36	25	47	44	158 (23.0)
Total (Percentage)	37 (5.4)	170 (24.8)	135 (19.7)	169 (24.6)	175 (25.5)	686 (100)

(c)   Rowntree daughters

NA ratio (percentage) for parents	SB ratio (percentage) for daughters					Total (Percentage)
	1 <99	2 100–139	3 140–179	4 180–239	5 ≥240	
1 <99	18	49	25	43	7	142 (19.1)
2 100–139	16	35	24	27	6	108 (14.5)
3 140–179	8	35	29	31	11	114 (15.3)
4 180–239	14	38	50	30	32	164 (22.0)
5 >240	9	48	35	56	68	216 (29.0)
Total (Percentage)	65 (8.7)	205 (27.6)	163 (21.9)	187 (25.1)	124 (16.7)	744 (100)

Table 5.5 Transition proportions derived from Table 5.4 (for all families)

| Class of parents | Class entered by children | | | | |
	I	2	3	4	5
I	10.5	37.6	18.0	24.1	9.8
2	10.6	37.6	21.8	22.9	7.1
3	7.9	18.1	24.2	27.1	22.7
4	5.1	21.0	25.8	21.7	26.4
5	4.0	22.5	16.0	27.5	29.9
Total	7.1	26.2	20.8	24.9	20.9

Note: For definition of classes, see Table 5.4.

whose parents were below the NA scale, the chance of being below SB is 50 per cent higher than if there were perfect mobility ($10.5 \div 7.1 = 1.5$), and the chance of being at or over 240 per cent of the SB scale is half that expected with perfect mobility. In Figure 5.1, we show the position for sons and daughters separately, giving for each of the parental income-ranges the transition proportions expressed relative to those expected with perfect mobility. If there were perfect mobility, then all the lines (continuous for sons, broken for daughters) would be horizontal. In fact they tend to slope down for children from low-income families, indicating lower chances of entering upper income-ranges, and tend to slope up for those whose parents were at least 80 per cent above the NA scale. Interestingly, there appears to be no marked difference between the patterns for sons and daughters.

The comparison with the case of perfect mobility brings out certain aspects of the data, but it may also be helpful to consider the differential chances of being in different classes. Take the case of Robin Parks, whose parents were in class 4 in our 5×5 matrix. The proportion of children from that class entering class 1 was 5.1 per cent; the proportion entering class 5, like Robin himself, was 26.4 per cent. One could therefore say that the odds favouring entry to class 5 relative to class 1 is $26.4/5.1 = 5.2$. In contrast, Arthur Hazall, whose parents were below the NA scale, had a more or less equal chance of staying below the SB scale or of entering class 5. The odds favour those coming from better-off backgrounds.

At the same time, inspection of Table 5.5 shows that the calculation of differential odds is sensitive to the choice of categories, and that the picture in the middle of the table is blurred. (The same phenomenon is illustrated by the ups and downs of the lines for the middle ranges in Figure 5.1.) In part at least this must reflect the relatively small numbers with which we are working; after all, Table 2.1, taken from the study of occupational mobility by Goldthorpe (1980), is based on

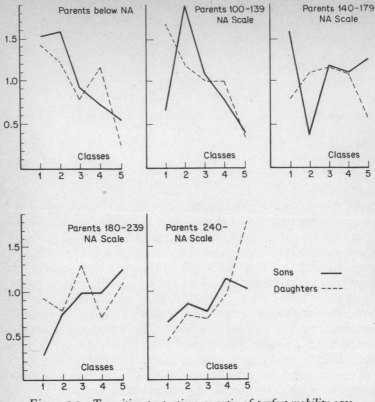

Figure 5.1   Transition proportions as ratio of perfect mobility case

over 9000 observations. We consider below an even more aggregated version of the mobility table.

Movement in and out of low-income group
We are particularly interested in movements in and out of the low-income group, which we take to be those below 140 per cent of the NA/SB scale. For this purpose, we consider only the three classes:

'low income' below 140 per cent of NA/SB scale
'intermediate' 140–199 per cent of NA/SB scale
'comfortably off' 200 per cent or more above the NA/SB scale

As we have seen earlier, these categories divide the sample in both generations approximately into thirds.

The 3 × 3 transition matrix is shown in Table 5.6, together with the transition proportions. This again brings out the differential odds.

Table 5.6   Aggregated 3 × 3 transition matrix

Parents		Children			
	Low income		Intermediate		Comfortably off
Low income	224	(48.2)	155	(33.3)	86	(18.5)
		'Stayers'		'Movers out'	
Intermediate	95	(25.8)	129	(35.1)	144	(39.1)
		'Movers in'			
Comfortably off	158	(26.5)	174	(29.1)	265	(44.4)

Note: The figures in parentheses are transition proportions.

Those from the low-income group stand a 2.6 higher chance of remaining than of entering the comfortably-off group; whereas those from the latter group are 1.7 times as likely to stay there as to enter the low-income group. Nevertheless, some of those from the low-income group do escape: 86 out of 465 ended up in the comfortably-off class. Conversely, of the 477 in the low-income group in 1975–8, 158 were recruited from those whose parents had been classified as comfortably off in 1950.

Particular interest attaches to those 'staying' in the low-income group, those 'moving out' and those 'moving in' – see the classification drawn in Table 5.6. In Table 5.7 we summarise some of the main characteristics of the different income-groups. Given our concern with the differential features of movers and stayers, we have calculated the relative percentages: that is 120 out of 241 (or 49.8 per cent), moving out of the low-income group, came from families with five or more children, whereas this was true of 79 out of 224 'stayers' (or 35.3 per cent), giving a relative percentage of 49.8/35.3, that is, 1.41.

The first aspect considered is family size. For upward mobility, the pattern seems rather mixed, but for downward mobility there is evidence that movers are more concentrated in large families. Of those moving down, 45 per cent came from families with four or more children, compared with 34 per cent of stayers. Secondly, there is geographical location. It appears that a smaller fraction of those Rowntree children who were upwardly mobile were living in York, and that a larger fraction of those downwardly mobile had remained in the city. There appears to be some association between income mobility and geographical mobility – an issue which is taken up in later chapters. (With the factors considered in this paragraph, the direction of causation may, of course, run either way.)

The lower part of Table 5.7 shows the pattern by age. (Unfortunately the age information is missing in some cases.) It appears that upward mobility is particularly associated with young Rowntree children (aged

Table 5.7   Characteristics of 'movers' and 'stayers'

Characteristics	Stayers	Movers out		Movers in	
		Number	Relative percentage	Number	Relative percentage
Size of 1950 family			-		
1	3	19	—	16	0.41
2	43	16	0.35	62	0.82
3	48	61	1.18	62	1.19
4	51	25	0.46	65	1.33
5 or more	79	120	1.41	48	1.27
All	224	241		253	
Geographical location (1975–8)					
York	177	170	0.89	199	1.37
Yorkshire and Humberside	41	57	1.29	39	0.64
Rest of UK	6	14	—	15	0.32
All	224	241		253	
Age of father in 1950 (information missing in some cases)					
Under 25	0	0	—	1	—
25–44	10	34	2.96	109	0.88
45–54	34	12	0.31	86	1.36
55 and over	71	86	1.06	36	0.81
All	115	132		232	
Age of son/son-in-law in 1975–8 (information missing in some cases)					
Under 25	0	0	—	4	—
25–44	11	64	4.53	100	1.01
45–54	27	41	1.18	13	0.29
55 and over	130	111	0.66	61	2.37
All	168	216		178	

under 45 years old in 1975–8) and young Rowntree parents. In the case of downward mobility, the differences are less marked for the age of the father – there appears, however, to be much more concentration among sons aged 55 plus and many fewer downwardly mobile in the age-group 45–54. This suggests that life-cycle differences may be important – a subject which is taken up below.

A regression analysis
The results so far have been presented in terms of transitions between

income-ranges. However, the alternative method of presentation – an estimate of a regression model – has a number of attractions, among them that it does not depend on the choice of categories. As has been stressed by Hart (1976), where there is a specified bottom (top) group such that no downward (upward) movement is possible, then these diagonal entries tend to give an exaggerated impression of the degree of immobility. This is illustrated by the large entries in the top left-hand and the bottom right-hand corners of Table 1.1.

In applying the regression model, we have to recognise that we do not have the classic 'Galtonian' situation, illustrated for the heights of fathers and sons in Figure 1.1. The first reason for this is that Rowntree's sample was, as we have seen, effectively truncated at the top. This causes the variance of NA ratios to be less than in the population as a whole. The second reason, which may also apply to heights, is that the dispersion of incomes may have changed from one generation to the next. As a result the correlation coefficient may not coincide with the estimated regression coefficient in the linear model. In our discussion, we focus on the estimated regression coefficient; the ordinary least squares estimates are unbiased even when the distribution of fathers' incomes is truncated.

Our regression analysis is equivalent to fitting a straight line, as in Figure 1.1, except that we have measured the logarithm (to base e) of the NA and SB ratios along the axes. The choice of the *logarithm* is based on the view that this is more likely to capture the way in which the association with family income is likely to work. Consider, for example, a rise in the NA ratio from 50 to 100. With a logarithmic formulation, this is equivalent in effect to a rise from 100 to 200; whereas with a simple, non-logarithmic formulation, it would be equivalent to a rise from 100 to 150. It also makes is more likely that the assumptions of the linear regression model are satisfied (see the section entitled 'Statistical Terms: an Explanatory Note' at the end of the book).

The fitted regression line has a slope of 0.143, with an estimated standard error of 0.027. This is based on 917 ungrossed observations (as noted earlier, we use ungrossed data for the regression analysis), corresponding to the 1430 grossed observations shown in the transition matrices. This estimated regression coefficient is much smaller than the value of 0.5 discussed in the case of heights.

In order to see what the estimated coefficient means, let us compare the position of the Parks family with an NA ratio of 217, with that of the hypothetical Smith family, where the parents were on the margin of our low-income category in 1950, the NA ratio being 140. The difference in the expected SB ratio of their children with the estimated coefficient of 0.148 can be calculated as:

$$\left(\frac{217}{140}\right)^{0.148} = 1.067$$

In other words, the Parks children had an expected advantage of some 6.7 per cent.

Using the regression approach, it is possible to carry out a number of experiments with the data. These show, for example, that there are no apparent significant differences between the 10 per cent subsample and the rest of the survey, and that there is no significant difference between the estimated regression coefficients for sons and daughters. The latter bears out the conclusion drawn by eye from Figure 5.1.

Measuring Income Mobility: some difficulties

The reader may well feel that we have been cavalierly ignoring some of the difficulties in interpreting the material we have collected, especially if he recalls the warnings given in Chapter 1 about the misleading nature of the analogy with heights. What about the transitory variations in income? After all, the apparent success of a Rowntree son in moving out of the low-income group may simply reflect the fact that in the week we interviewed him he received an exceptional bonus. By ignoring this, we may be overstating the degree of mobility. What about the life-cycle factors? Our sample design is intended to reduce the life-cycle differences, but they still remain, and in any case the similarity of status across the generations may simply mirror our success in this respect. The fact that both parents and children are 'stayers' may arise merely because they were both retired, rather than recording any genuine similarity of life experiences. Finally, what about the different dimensions of income? Income expressed relative to the NA/SB scale is only one of a number of possible indicators.

Temporary variations in income and errors in recording

We begin with temporary variations in incomes, which we consider together with errors in recording, since – despite the care which we have taken – the latter are certain to have crept in. What are the implications of the fact that we do not observe the 'true' permanent value of each of the variables, but only the true value plus an error term, which we assume to be uncorrelated with the true values and across the variables?

The impact is perhaps most easily seen in the regression analysis. First, measurement error in the dependent variable, that is, the income of the children, does not lead to bias in the estimated regression coefficient. What it does do is to introduce additional variation in the sample, so that part of the unexplained variance in the regression equation may be attributable to transitory fluctuations, or to recording

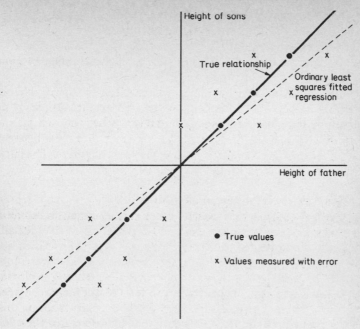

Figure 5.2   Illustration of measurement error problem

error, in the incomes of the children. Error in the measurement of parental income, on the other hand, does introduce the possibility of biased estimates of the regression coefficient. This is the classical measurement error problem of econometrics, and it can be shown that in the simple model considered here the coefficient tends to be biased downwards.

To see how this arises, let us take a highly simplified example. Suppose that the true height of each son is b times the true height of his father (where b is not equal to 1, this implies that the distribution of heights is changing across generations). But the height of the fathers is measured with error, in such a way that, of the fathers with a specified true height, half are recorded h inches shorter than they really are and half are recorded h inches too high. This does not affect the average height of the fathers, since on average the errors cancel out. However, it does affect the ordinary least squares estimates of the relation between heights in the two generations. This is illustrated in Figure 5.2, where the dots show the values and the crosses those observed. The sons' heights are assumed to be measured without error (although this makes no difference to the argument), so that the points move horizontally. The 'true' regression line fits the dots exactly. The ordinary least squares fit to the crosses is shown by the broken line, where the slope is less. Intuitively, this may be explained by the fact that if we take low values of the observed heights for fathers, then there is a predominance of those with negative errors: people recorded as (5 feet 4 inches) are more likely to have been under- rather than over-measured. Conversely, those with large values are more likely to have errors in the opposite direction.

Calculation of the least squares estimate of the regression coefficient in our simplified example shows that it is given by:

$$b \times \frac{1}{(1 + (h/\sigma)^2}$$

where σ is the standard deviation of the true height. So that an error, h, equal to half the standard deviation causes the estimated coefficient to be only four-fifths of the true value. The expression can also be interpreted in the following terms:

$$b \times \frac{\text{variance of true value of parents' variable}}{\text{variance of measured value of parents' variable}}$$

With the example given, and $h = \frac{1}{2}\sigma$, the observed variance is 25 per cent higher than the true value. This reinterpretation is of interest, since it may be shown that it characterises in the general case the probability limit of the least squares estimator when the explanatory variable is measured with error (see, for example, Johnston, 1972, p. 282).

The analysis just given provides a basis for assessing the likely impact of measurement error on the estimated regression coefficient. For example, the variance of the measured variable is likely to be at least 10 per cent higher than that of the true variable, in which case an estimated coefficient of 0.148 would correspond to a 'true' value of 0.163. Alternatively, we may consider the case where the combined effect of recording error and transitory variations increases the variance by 50 per cent. In the latter case, the estimated coefficient would correspond to a 'true' value of 0.222.

Measurement error could therefore have a sizeable impact on the regression analysis. What about the implications for the transition matrices? (This is a subject which does not seem to have received a great deal of attention in studies of occupational mobility.) Again, a highly simplified example like the one just used may help to illustrate the consequences. Suppose that both parents and children are spread uniformly over the range from 80 per cent to 260 per cent of the NA/SB scale, with a total of 240 in each of the three categories of low income (below 140 per cent), intermediate (140–200 per cent), and comfortably off (200 per cent and above). The true relation is such that children have exactly the same position as their parents. However, there is a measurement error of the type assumed earlier, with half the values being recorded as 30 percentage points too low and half recorded as 30 points too high. As a result, half of those in the range 110–140 per cent are wrongly reported as being in the intermediate range, and so on. It is immediately clear that, in the case of the transition matrices, errors in the status of the children now affect the conclusions drawn. In Table 5.8a we show the transition matrix which results from our hypothetical example. The hypothetical error of 30 per cent may appear to be quite large, but it corresponds broadly to half the standard deviation and this fraction was taken earlier. The effect is, in fact, quite striking.

To sum up, our discussion of measurement errors suggests that they may be of considerable importance, and that further examination is necessary. In the next chapter, we explore the subject in more detail, when we consider the degree of earnings mobility.

Life-cycle factors
The notion of a family 'life cycle' was well captured by Rowntree in his original 1899 survey, when he produced the celebrated diagram of

Table 5.8   Hypothetical transition matrices

(a) Complete immobility but measurement errors

NA ratio (percentage) for parents	SB ratio (percentage) for children		
	Low income	Intermediate	Comfortably off
Low income	180	60	0
Intermediate	60	120	60
Comfortably off	0	60	180

(b) Perfect mobility but life-style effects

NA ratio (percentage) for parents	SB ratio (percentage) for children		
	Low income	Intermediate	Comfortably off
Low income	192	48	48
	(66.7)	(16.7)	(16.7)
Intermediate	48	64	80
	(25.0)	(33.3)	(41.7)
Comfortably off	48	80	112
	(20.0)	(33.3)	(46.7)

Note: Figures in parentheses denote transition proportions.

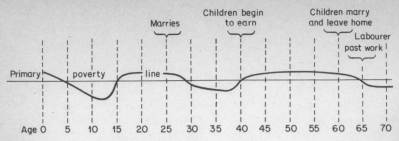

Figure 5.3   Rowntree's life-cycle profile
Source: Rowntree, 1901, p. 171

alternating periods of want and plenty, reproduced in Figure 5.3. The first question we address is whether the same pattern is revealed by our sample. Figure 5.4 shows the mean values of the NA ratio and SB ratio for different age-ranges in our sample.

It is interesting to compare the life-cycle pattern for the two generations and also with Rowntree's profile. Taking age-groups from 30 upwards, our two cycles have similar shapes, with turning-points at approximately the same ages: early forties and late fifties. There are some differences between them, however. For those aged between 50 and 60 years old, income is higher in relative terms for the 1950 sample than the 1975–8 one. For the elderly, income falls sharply in both samples, but by a greater amount in 1950, so that for the 'over-60s' income is lower in 1950 than in 1975–8. The difference might be due to earlier retirement in 1975–8, together with higher and more extensive pensions than in 1950.

Compared with the profile described by Rowntree, the pattern after half a century is strikingly similar, except that the trough in old age is more pronounced in 1950 and 1975–8 than in Rowntree's 1901 diagram. The reasons for the shape may, however, be somewhat different. In Rowntree's case, the rise after the age of 40 is associated with the children going out to work and contributing to the income of the household. In the present case, the assessment is based on the nuclear family, as embodied in the SB practice, so that children growing up contribute by reducing needs rather than in terms of income. In our case, the most important factor is that the wife is more likely to be able to work, particularly in 1975–8.

Substantial life-cycle differences of the kind revealed may have a sizeable impact on the findings. This may be illustrated by a simple hypothetical example of the kind already employed. Suppose that a third of parents and children are in each of our three categories, but that this time there is perfect mobility. Of the 240 children with parents in the bottom range, 80 enter each of the ranges, and the same applies to those originating from the other categories. However, incomes vary

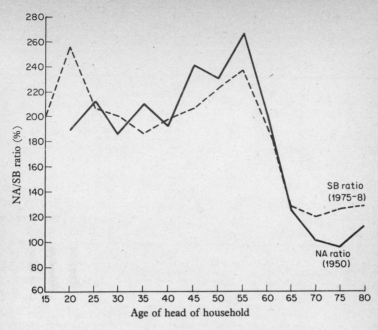

Figure 5.4   Mean NA ratio and SB ratio by age

with the stage of the life cycle, and parents and children are all at the same stage. Suppose that one-fifth are retired and, regardless of their income in work, they are all in the low-income group. Moreover, of those at work, a quarter are at their 'peak' incomes, which shifts both parents and children one cell upwards, where this is possible (upwards in terms of income; however this is downwards in terms of the table). The resulting hypothetical transition matrix is shown in Table 5.8b, and is remarkably different from the perfect mobility case. This – admittedly artificial – example brings out the importance of the life-cycle element.

In an attempt to see the effect of life-cycle factors on our results, we consider the subgroup where the Rowntree father and Rowntree son/son-in-law are in the same age-group, taking for this purpose the age-groups 25–34, 35–44, 45–54, 55–64, 65 or over (there were no cases below 25). The sample size is, of course, substantially reduced, both by the age requirement and because in a number of cases the age is not known. In view of the relatively small numbers, we combined the two older age-groups, 55–64 and 65 or over (although we did not relax the criteria for inclusion, so that a son of 55 with father of 70 would be excluded). The numbers in each case are shown in Table 5.9, which summarises the degree of mobility in the 5 × 5 transition matrices in

Table 5.9 A summary of income matrices for various subsamples at the same stage of their income life-cycle (Percentages on, above or below the leading diagonal as percentages of their respective sample sizes)

Age-group of Rowntree father and son/son-in-law	Number of cases	Below diagonal		On diagonal		Above diagonal	
		Actual	Expected under perfect mobility	Actual	Expected under perfect mobility	Actual	Expected under perfect mobility
25–34	131	32.8	33.1	22.1	23.2	45.0	43.7
35–44	131	41.2	35.0	17.6	27.3	41.2	37.7
45–54	127	43.3	49.9	39.4	23.9	17.3	26.4
55 plus[a]	132	22.7	38.4	52.3	20.3	25.0	41.1
Whole sample	1430	36.0	39.9	23.9	19.6	40.1	40.5

Note: [a] To qualify for this group, which is formed by combining 55–64 and 65+, the father and son-in-law must be both 55–64 or both 65+.

terms of the percentage below, on, or above the diagonal compared with that expected with perfect mobility.

The results for different age-groups are most interesting and indicate much less mobility for the older age-groups. For those aged 45 or over, the predicted proportion on the diagonal, combining the two older age-groups, is 46 per cent, which may be contrasted with a predicted proportion under perfect mobility of under half that (22 per cent). However, for the younger age-groups, the proportion on the diagonal is actually less than that expected with perfect mobility – a finding which is surprising, if not paradoxical. This overall pattern could have several explanations. It could reflect a cohort effect, with mobility having substantially increased. It could be that there is 'counter-mobility', with children reverting later in life to an income position closer to that of their parents. In the context of occupational mobility, Goldthorpe has drawn attention to 'work-life movement which has the effect of returning an individual back to his class of origin, following some initial shift away on his entry into employment, and which thus serves to promote intergenerational stability' (1980, p. 53).

Different dimensions

Income expressed relative to the NA/SB scale is only one of a number of indicators which could be used, and it is open to criticism. The NA/SB practice treats housing costs as an unavoidable outlay, but it may be felt that this is an inappropriate method of allowing for this aspect of 'requirements'. The differential scales for children applied under NA/SB have been attacked as insufficiently generous, and we might argue that other types of 'need' should be taken into account.

In order to give an impression of the sensitivity of the results to the indicator employed, we give below the estimated regression coefficients (and standard errors) for two variants:

	Coefficient in logarithmic regression (standard error)	
NA/SB ratio	0.148	(0.027)
Net resources	0.227	(0.025)
Gross income	0.383	(0.033)

(The reader can find the definitions of the variables on p. 71.) To understand the meaning of these results, we may go back to the Parks and Smith families. Mr and Mrs Parks had a gross income of £9.00 a week and net resources of £7.77. Mr and Mrs Smith, also with three children, are assumed to have a gross income of £6.50 a week and net resources, after subtracting National Insurance contributions and their rent and rates, of £5.29. The predicted advantage to the Parks children, using the results for the NA/SB ratio, was some 7 per cent. Using net resources, the differential (£7.77 ÷ £5.29) implies an advantage of 9 per cent; using gross income, the predicted advantage is 13 per cent.

The different indicators measure different things, and the results cannot be directly compared. None the less, the results hint that the degree of mobility may appear rather different, if we consider gross income, and in the next chapter we explore the continuities in gross earnings.

Conclusions

Our results suggest a number of interesting conclusions. The observed chances of entering different income classes differ considerably across income-ranges. A child whose parents were below the NA level in 1950 is $1\frac{1}{2}$ times as likely to be below the SB level in 1975–8, than if there were perfect mobility. Those from the low-income category, below 140 per cent of the NA scale, stand some $2\frac{1}{2}$ times the chance of remaining there than of entering the comfortably-off category of 200 per cent more of the SB scale. Those from the comfortably-off group are 1.5 times as likely to stay there than to fall to the low-income class.

The regression coefficient, relating the status of the children to that of the parents, is estimated to be substantially less than that for heights, when status is measured in terms of the NA/SB scales, but is closer to that for heights when measured in terms of gross incomes. There appear to be no marked differences between the mobility of sons and daughters. Upward mobility out of the low-income group appeared more likely for those who had left York; downward mobility into the group was more common among those who stayed in York and those from larger families.

At this stage, however, we should emphasise the qualifications rather than the conclusions. At the start of the chapter, we made it clear that we were leaving on one side the problems arising from the special nature of our sample, which certainly preclude any straightforward extrapolation of the findings to the national population. In the course of the chapter, we have seen that measurement error and life-cycle variations are not minor considerations, meriting attention only in footnotes.

There are reasons to believe that the objective of trying to measure the extent of income mobility for the population as a whole is over-ambitious. After all, the studies of occupational mobility concentrate on the working lifetime and do not venture into the fields which determine income arising from sources other than earnings. The life-cycle element is certainly more easily handled, if the sample is limited to those in work; and this restriction would also recognise that our sample is too small to allow us to say anything meaningful about groups such as the unemployed or long-term sick. By concentrating on earnings, more information can be brought to bear about the likely incidence of transitory variations, and it is easier to relate our sample to the national population. We saw, in fact, in Chapter 4 that there are indications that our sample is more likely to be representative of those in work.

These considerations lead us to conclude that we should go on to focus on the degree of earnings mobility among those in work, and this is the subject of Chapter 6.

6 Earnings in Two Generations

This chapter is concerned with the extent of continuity in earnings across the two generations. For this purpose, we concentrate on those families where the father was at work, either employed or self-employed, in 1950 and where the Rowntree son or son-in-law was an employee in full-time work in 1975–8. This reduces the size of the sample. Of the 1716 (grossed) pairs of parents and children in 1975–8, 1494 were families headed by a man, of whom 988 were employees in full-time work. The potential sample is therefore reduced to under a thousand. When we restrict attention to those cases where the father was at work in 1950, it is still smaller. Finally, we have to deduct those cases where the information on earnings is incomplete (although this is a less serious problem than with Supplementary Benefit assessments), leaving 406 father/son pairs and 374 father/son-in-law pairs with whom we are concerned here.

Earnings in 1950 and 1975–8

It is hard for the reader today to conceive of the levels of earnings recorded by Rowntree in his 1950 survey. There were a handful of fathers with earnings of more than £10 a week, and they were the best paid in the sample. They included a 36-year-old draughtsman, a 50-year-old optician, a 38-year-old manager of a garage, two fitters at British Railways and the manager of a tailoring company. Just below them, on some £9–10 a week were a policeman, a scientific-instrument maker and a chemist. Between £7 and £10 were a nurse, a civil servant, a welder, a labourer, a clerk, just to take a few examples. The same occupations are found in the £5–7 range, together with a British Railways shunter and platelayer, a milkman, a hairdresser and an ambulanceman. Then, at the bottom, were ten people earning less than £5 a week. Their jobs included builders' labourer, porter, labourer, car-park attendant and milkman.

These amounts are difficult to grasp – just as the fact that beer was 1s 2d a pint, tea 3s 4d a pound, shoes cost £1 10s and you could get (if you were lucky) a new Morris Minor for some £300. Prices have gone up and so have money earnings. In the previous chapter, we made allowance for this by taking the National Assistance/Supplementary Benefit scale. Here we take a different approach, seeking to compare observed earnings with those ruling nationally at the time. The aim is to relate our sample to the national population and hence to allow more general conclusions to be drawn about mobility. The earnings of fathers and sons will be viewed in relation to those of the whole labour force in the country and not just in relation to those of the small – and rather special – sample of Rowntree families. We want to translate knowledge that Mr Briggs earned £7 as a platelayer in 1950 into his position in the national earnings scale. Was he in the bottom 20 per cent, in the next 20 per cent up, or where?

Unfortunately, very little is known about the national distribution of earnings in 1950. The New Earnings Surveys, on which much current analysis is based, only began in 1968. Before that, information was only collected in special inquiries at irregular intervals (for example, 1938 and 1960) covering mainly manual workers. We had therefore to proceed by using the *average* earnings figure for 1950, and the assumption that the distribution of earnings was the same as in 1968. This assumption may appear a heroic one, but it is in line with the prevailing wisdom that the distribution of earnings has remained remarkably stable over time. Evidence from the special government inquiries for male manual workers in Britain suggests that from 1886 to the present day, when median earnings have risen in money terms by a factor of about 100, the *shape* of the distribution has changed little (Royal Commission on the Distribution of Income and Wealth, 1975, Table 22). These comparisons, particularly that with 1886 (see Williamson, 1980), need to be treated with considerable caution, since there are a number of respects in which they may well not be comparable. However, the results for the subperiod with which we are concerned do not, on the face of it, suggest that we should be far out in assuming that the distribution in 1950 had the same shape as in 1968 (see Table 6.1).

Table 6.1   *Comparison of earnings of male manual workers between 1938 and 1968*

| Year | | Male manual workers | |
| | Median earnings (£ per week) | Lower quartile | Upper quartile |
		(as percentage of median)	
1938	3.40	82.1	118.5
1960	14.20	82.6	121.7
1968	22.40	81.0	122.3

Source: Royal Commission on the Distribution of Income and Wealth, 1975, Table 22.

We have chosen the post-war figure, rather than 1938, on the grounds that the distribution is more likely to have shifted, if it has, during the Second World War. We have used 1968 since the New Earnings Survey in that year covered both manual and non-manual workers, whereas the 1960 inquiry was limited to manual workers.

   In attaching cash amounts to the points on the distribution in 1950, we worked from the average weekly earnings for adult male manual workers in October 1950, as reported by the Ministry of Labour (Department of Employment, 1971, p. 101), which was £7.52. The base figure we are seeking is the median earnings for all male workers. This differs in that the median can be expected to be below the average. (The median is the halfway point in the distribution; the average is typically higher because earnings stretch further upwards than they do downwards.) It also differs in the coverage. The inclusion of non-manual workers may be expected to raise the figure; the inclusion of workers below the age of 21 may lead to a reduction. Balancing these considerations, and making use of evidence from the New Earnings Surveys for more recent years, we arrived at an estimate for the national median level of earnings for men in 1950 of £7.60 a week. This is undoubtedly subject to a sizeable margin of error, but we hope that it is sufficiently accurate for our purposes.

Earnings of our sample in 1950
From the percentile points expressed as a percentage of the median in 1968, and the median earnings of £7.60 for 1950, we calculated the quintile points shown in Table 6.2a. Thus, the 1968 New Earnings Survey showed that the bottom 20 per cent of all workers, manual and non-manual, earned less than 75.9 per cent of the median. Applying this percentage to £7.60 yields £5.77, which is the bottom quintile shown in Table 6.2a.

   In Table 6.2a, we have shown the distribution of the fathers in our sample, where we have included those cases where the hourly earnings of the son/son-in-law can be calculated (see Table 6.2b). There are 378 father/son pairs and 340 father/son-in-law pairs. The results are broadly in line with those expected, given the method by which the sample was constructed and the characteristics of York. Rowntree deliberately excluded the upper earnings ranges, and this is borne out by the small numbers in the top 20 per cent. As we have seen in earlier chapters, the industrial composition of employment in York is not representative of the country as a whole; and the under-representation of groups such as agricultural workers, and of low-paying industries such as textiles, may be expected to cause the number of low-paid workers to be smaller than found nationally. From Table 6.2a, the bottom 20 per cent does indeed appear to be under-represented, and there are only a small number in the bottom 10 per cent (under £5 a week, not shown).

   In interpreting these results, we need to bear in mind that each father

Table 6.2   Earnings distribution
   (a) 1950

National distribution percentile	Gross weekly earnings	Income-range	Our sample	
			Number	Percentage
		Top 20%	10	(1.4%)
20	£10.36			
		Second 20%	88	(12.3%)
40	£8.29			
		Middle 20%	163	(22.7%)
60	£7.00			
		Fourth 20%	330	(46.0%)
80	£5.77			
		Bottom 20%	127	(17.7%)
			718	(100.0%)

   (b) 1975–8

National distribution percentile	Gross hourly earnings	Income-range	Our sample	
			Number	Percentage
		Top 20%	91	(12.7%)
20	£2.24			
		Second 20%	118	(16.4%)
40	£1.81			
		Middle 20%	154	(21.4%)
60	£1.51			
		Fourth 20%	169	(23.5%)
80	£1.28			
		Bottom 20%	186	(25.9%)
			718	(100.0%)

appears with a weight equal to the number of sons or sons-in-law in the sample. Examination of the results for 'distinct' fathers (with each father only appearing once) shows, however, a rather similar pattern.

Earnings in 1975–8
The analysis of the 1975–8 earnings data is less complicated, in that we can relate the distribution to that in the New Earnings Survey (in this report we use the results of the April 1977 survey). At the same time, there is the problem that wages were rising rapidly and discontinuously

over the survey period. The main interviews took place between June 1976 and March 1978, but there were, in addition, a number of interviews carried out in 1975 as part of the pilot study. In this period there were substantial increases in wages, and the timing can make a great deal of difference. In order to make an approximate adjustment for this, we have used the monthly index of average earnings to express everything in April 1977 levels. The quintile points shown in Table 6.2b are taken from the April 1977 New Earnings Survey.

The data for our sample of sons and sons-in-law are taken from the answer to the question 'what were your gross earnings last week/month/year (in your main job)?' In most cases, they related to the last pay period. (The alternatives of 'basic' and 'normal' earnings are discussed below.) In collecting the data, every effort was made to ensure accuracy, and the lengthy interview, coupled with the good relationship the interviewers typically established, mean that the evidence is probably more satisfactory than in many surveys. One may, for example, compare the questions in our survey with the much more limited scope of the income questions asked in the General Household Survey at that time. Moreover, many respondents supplied additional information and either showed their pay-slips to the interviewer or supplied figures direct from the pay-slip. None the less, we must recognise that there are undoubtedly errors in the reporting of the 1975–8 earnings data, and the significance of such errors in measurement is discussed later.

In the case of the 1950 earnings data, we used *weekly* earnings, since no information on hours of work was available. There are, however, good reasons for taking *hourly* earnings where those are recorded, and in our survey we asked for details of both basic hours and hours last week. The answers brought out a number of cases where differences in earnings possibilities were masked by differences in hours and vice versa. For example, we interviewed two brothers, both employed in the same trade and with virtually identical basic rates for a 40-hour week. The elder worked 57 hours a week and was comfortably above the median for weekly earnings; the younger worked 48 hours a week and was in the bottom 20 per cent. In this chapter, we concentrate on hourly earnings as the indicator of the earnings status of the second generation, and the distribution shown in Table 6.2b is based on hourly earnings. (The results of using weekly earnings, which are broadly similar, are given in our report to the DHSS/SSRC.) In calculating hourly earnings, we have simply divided weekly earnings by weekly hours. Where there is overtime, this gives a measure of the 'average' return to the job, but calculations of the basic hourly rates on the basis of different assumptions about the overtime premium lead to similar results.

In Table 6.2b, the distribution for our sample is compared with the national picture. The upper ranges are again under-represented, although to a lesser extent than for the fathers. Similarly, the bottom 20 per cent is also more fully represented. The spread of earnings is wider for the second generation than for the Rowntree fathers. This is also brought out by looking at the occupations of the sons and sons-in-law. Those in the top 20 per cent included doctors, engineers, airline pilots and teachers. The professions, essentially excluded by Rowntree, are quite well represented.

Study of the occupational pattern illustrates two of the reasons why we feel that earnings mobility is of importance in its own right and is a necessary complement to investigations of occupational mobility. First, the work done by our respondents demonstrates the significance of occupational change. Rowntree would not have found any traffic wardens in York in 1950, and electronic engineers and air traffic controllers would have been thinly represented even in a national sample. Not only has the nature of jobs changed, but there has been a systematic shift towards higher-status occupations. In the Oxford mobility survey (Table 2.1 above), the percentage of fathers in classes I and II was 13.2 per cent, but the percentage of sons was 25.1 per cent. This poses the problem of assessing the degree of mobility against a shifting background. In this respect, the apparently greater stability of the earnings distribution makes our results easier to interpret. Secondly, our interviews show how a particular occupational category may span a number of earnings ranges: for example, bus drivers, postmen and accountants are found in a number of our earnings categories. Just knowing a respondent's occupation would not have allowed us to place him accurately in terms of earnings.

Earnings Mobility

From father to son

We begin with the evidence for fathers and sons, where we have 378 pairs (all figures are grossed). The basic transition matrix is shown in Table 6.3a, relating the weekly earnings of the fathers in 1950 to the hourly earnings of the sons in 1975–8. The ranges are as identified in Table 6.2, and divide the national distribution into fifths, which we label, in descending order: top 20 per cent, second 20 per cent, middle 20 per cent, fourth 20 per cent and bottom 20 per cent. The top 20 per cent for fathers is virtually empty, and certainly unrepresentative of those in the overall population, so that we delete the five cases, reducing the sample to 373.

In the table, we show the transition proportions; again, we may compare them with those expected under perfect mobility. In this case, however, the latter are taken from the national distribution, which means – given the way that the ranges are defined – that we should expect a figure of 20 per cent in every cell. If the earnings of the son are unrelated to those of his father, we would find a 20 per cent chance of his entering any of the earnings ranges shown in Table 6.3a. To begin with the diagonal elements, which would be 100 per cent with complete immobility: in two cases they are actually below 20 per cent and only in the bottom range does the transition proportion differ at all noticeably from 20 per cent. Those with fathers in the bottom 20 per cent are $2\frac{1}{4}$ times more likely to be in the bottom 20 per cent themselves than if there were perfect mobility. Similarly, their chance of being in the top 20 per cent is about 60 per cent of that expected with perfect mobility.

An alternative measure of the extent of mobility is provided by the band formed by taking one cell either side of the diagonal (shown by the figures printed in italic in Table 6.3a). If there were perfect mobility, we would expect:

$$60\% \times (37 + 74 + 184) + 40\% \times (78) = 208.2$$

to be in the diagonal band, whereas we find 251. In other words, there are 67.3 per cent in the diagonal band compared with 55.8 per cent expected with perfect mobility. In this difference, the unfavourable chances faced by the bottom 20 per cent make a substantial contribution, but it also reflects the low probabilities of going from the fourth 20 per cent and the middle 20 per cent to the top 20 per cent, and of descending from the second 20 per cent and the middle 20 per cent to the bottom 20 per cent.

As we have emphasised in earlier chapters, the variation in earnings over the life cycle is an important factor. In Table 6.3b, we show the effect of adjusting earnings for the average variation with age. The data used in making this adjustment are taken from the 1976 New Earnings Survey; no evidence on the age pattern of earnings is available for 1950, and we assume that the same age profile applies as in 1976. By making this correction, we are not, of course, allowing for the differing profiles in different occupations, but on average it should put the earnings observations on a more comparable basis and, at the very least, provide some indication of the likely sensitivity of the findings. That it can make a substantial difference in individual cases is illustrated by the Mercer family. Mr Mercer earned £9.53 a week in 1950 and was about 30 per cent from the top of the national distribution. His son, Alan Mercer, was in the bottom 10 per cent in 1975–8. However, Alan was only 19 years old, and the age adjustment raised him fairly close to the median.

In theory, the age adjustment could shift the transition proportions in either direction. Figure 6.1 shows two hypothetical possibilities. In

Table 6.3   Transition matrix: fathers and sons
   (a) Hourly earnings

| Income-range for fathers | Income-range for sons | | | | | Total |
	Top 20%	Second 20%	Middle 20%	Fourth 20%	Bottom 20%	
Top 20%						
Second 20%	9	6	8	8	6	37
	(24.3)	(16.2)	(21.6)	(21.6)	(16.2)	
Middle 20%	12	18	13	22	9	74
	(16.2)	(24.3)	(17.6)	(29.7)	(12.2)	
Fourth 20%	24	28	42	41	49	184
	(13.0)	(15.2)	(22.8)	(22.3)	(26.6)	
Bottom 20%	10	14	11	8	35	78
	(12.8)	(17.9)	(14.1)	(10.3)	(44.9)	
Total	55	66	74	79	99	373

   (b) Age-adjusted hourly earnings

| Income-range for fathers | Income-range for sons | | | | | Total |
	Top 20%	Second 20%	Middle 20%	Fourth 20%	Bottom 20%	
Top 20%						
Second 20%	2	2	3	5	2	14
	(14.3)	(14.3)	(21.4)	(35.7)	(14.3)	
Middle 20%	8	8	18	11	6	51
	(15.7)	(15.7)	(35.3)	(21.6)	(11.8)	
Fourth 20%	23	23	40	47	40	173
	(13.3)	(13.3)	(23.1)	(27.2)	(23.1)	
Bottom 20%	12	23	19	21	61	136
	(8.8)	(16.9)	(14.0)	(15.4)	(44.9)	
Total	46	56	82	84	109	374

Notes: The figures in parentheses are the percentages for the row.
   There are two reasons for the difference in the sample size between the top and the bottom tables. First, age information is missing for one case. Second, the age adjustment reduces the number in the top 20 per cent of fathers, so that omission of this group leaves out three rather than five cases. There is therefore a net increase of one case.

the first, there are two possible lifetime earnings profiles, shown by the continuous lines, and there is a substantial amount of mobility between them: all of the four families switch position between the two generations. Yet the hump-shape of earnings is sufficiently marked for the peak earnings on the lower profile to bring a person into the upper

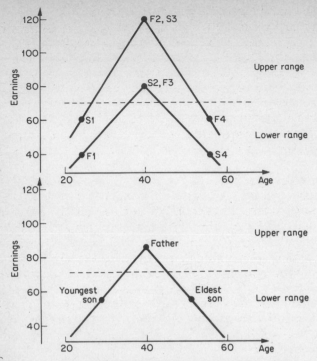

Figure 6.1 Two hypothetical examples of effect of age differences
Note: F1 and S1 denote the father and son from the first family, and so on.

range of observed earnings (above the broken line), and conversely, for those just embarking on their career, or nearing retirement, to be below the broken line on both profiles. Our observations of the four families will therefore record no mobility unless we make an age adjustment. As drawn, earnings at the peak are double those at the beginning and end points observed on the profiles. Suppose that the age adjustment involves increasing the latter by 50 per cent and reducing the peak by 25 per cent. This will take the son from family 1 above the cut-off (broken line), so that they will now be recorded as mobile.

In the second example, shown in the lower part of Figure 6.1, all the families are on the same age earnings profile, so that there is no lifetime mobility. But the families are not all observed at the same point in the life cycle. When the Brown family were interviewed in 1950, Mr Brown was 40 years old, and at the peak of the earnings profile. His eldest son was aged 22 and his youngest 2 at that time. When the sons came to be interviewed in 1978, they were therefore 50 and 30. As drawn in Figure 6.1, this means that they are below the broken line, so the unadjusted figures show apparent mobility where none exists.

Looking at the actual effect on the observed transition matrix in Table 6.3b, we can see that the diagonal elements are now more pronounced. The diagonal is greater than 20 per cent for three of the four rows. The sum of the diagonal elements is 128, compared with 74.8 expected under perfect mobility; the sum of the diagonal band is now 272 compared with 197.2 under perfect mobility. The transitions are clearly far from those that would be expected if there were no mobility, but the difference from perfect mobility is more marked with the age adjustment.

Movement in and out of 'low pay'

Of particular concern here is the experience of those in the lowest earnings ranges. The definition of 'low pay' is a matter which can be debated; however, for present purposes it seems reasonable to define as low paid those in the *bottom 20 per cent* of the hourly earnings distribution. The choice of this cut-off (in terms of hourly earnings, £1.28 in April 1977) is of course arbitrary, and by definition it implies that the extent of low pay can never change. It is not, however, intended as a normative measure nor to assess the success or otherwise of policies designed to help the low paid. Rather, it is simply a convenient dividing line when we wish to focus on the lower end of the distribution of incomes from employment.

From the transition matrix for age-adjusted hourly earnings, we can see that 136 of the fathers were in this category, or 36 per cent of the total. In view of the rather small numbers, which may be sensitive to grossing up, we discuss the results in terms of ungrossed figures. Of the 91 observations (86 + 5) on an ungrossed basis, 34 of the sons remained low paid. This group will be referred to as static (S); the remaining 57 will be called upwardly mobile out of low pay (U). The third group in which we are interested are the 39 sons of fathers not in the bottom 20 per cent who became low paid, referred to as downwardly mobile into low pay (D).

It may be interesting to look at some of the characteristics of these three groups, since this provides a bridge to some of the factors considered in the next chapter. The first characteristic is that of age. The definition of low pay is based on age-adjusted earnings, so that we should not be including those whose pay is low because they are just starting out or are approaching retirement. But differences in within-career movement will still appear. In the previous chapter, we noted that mobility appeared to be less for the older cohorts, and the same seems to be true here. Those in the static category (S) tend to be older – both fathers and sons. In the static group, 82 per cent of fathers were aged 40 years and over in 1950. In contrast, of the fathers of the mobile groups (both U and D) only 60 per cent and 69 per cent, respectively, were aged 40 and over. In the case of the 1975–8 generation, 76 per cent of the static sons were aged 40 or over, compared with 35 per cent of the mobile group. In other words, twice the proportion were aged 40 and over than in the mobile group. This is consistent either with a structural shift in the degree of mobility or with the hypothesis that continuities are more marked when comparing later stages in the life cycle.

The lower part of Table 6.4 gives information on family size. Rather surprisingly, this does not indicate any systematic relationship. In the case of sons, the proportions of families with three or more children are 65 per cent (S), 61 per cent (U) and 64 per cent (D). There is a certain amount of evidence that children from larger families are at a disadvantage with regard to physical development (Pringle, 1980) or educational performance (Douglas *et al.*, 1968). We might, then, have expected the downwardly mobile children to have been drawn disproportionately from larger families and the upwardly mobile families more than smaller families. On the other hand, in interpreting the evidence about the effect of family size, it is obviously necessary to control for differences in family incomes. Our results could be seen as suggesting that, when family income is held constant, the number of siblings is not a significant determinant.

Finally, there is geographical mobility, which we have already discussed in the context of incomes. Many of the 1975–8 sample are still living in York, but there appears to be a noticeable difference between those in group U and those in S and D. Of the latter groups, only 19 per cent had left York, whereas for the upwardly mobile the proportion was 39 per cent. This indicates again that geographical mobility may well be associated with economic mobility.

Fathers and sons-in-law

In considering the relationship between the earnings of fathers and their sons-in-law, it seems reasonable to posit a positive correlation between the earnings of husbands and wives (the latter being interpreted to include potential as well as actual earnings). To the extent that the earnings of daughters are positively correlated with those of their fathers, this will induce a positive correlation; we should, however, expect to find a weaker relationship than that between fathers and daughters. On the other hand, it is possible that the earnings of fathers and sons-in-law are positively correlated, even when the daughters' earnings are held constant: i.e. that there is an element of selection according to fathers-in-law' as well as daughters' earnings. (It has been put to us that a father may have more choice with respect to his son-in-law than to his son!)

In Table 6.5, we show the transition matrices for fathers and sons-in-

Table 6.4   Characteristics of those moving in and out of low pay

Characteristics		Sons	
	Static (S)	Upwardly mobile (U) from low pay	Downwardly mobile (D) from low pay
Age of father in 1950			
under 25	—	—	1
25–39	6	23	11
40–54	23	33	18
55 and over	5	1	9
All	34	57	39
Age of son in 1975–8			
under 25	1	5	3
25–39	7	36	18
40–54	24	15	14
55 and over	2	1	4
Family size (1950 family)			
1	2	9	3
2	10	13	11
3	7	6	10
4	7	12	4
5 or more	8	17	11
Geographical location of sons			
York	28	35	31
elsewhere in Yorkshire and Humberside	4	14	4
rest of UK	2	8	4

Note: All numbers in this table are ungrossed.

law comparable with those for sons in Table 6.3. The pattern is rather different, with the transition proportions being higher in the top right-hand corner and lower in the bottom left. Relatively few of the 1975–8 respondents in the top earnings ranges had fathers-in-law who were in the bottom 40 per cent in 1950. The concentration on the diagonal, however, is very similar for sons and sons-in-law, as indicated by the following summary statistics for age-adjusted hourly earnings:

Numbers relative to those expected with perfect mobility		
	On diagonal	*In diagonal band*
Sons	1.71	1.38
Sons-in-law	1.68	1.38

Table 6.5   Transition matrix: fathers and sons-in-law

(a) Hourly earnings

Income-range for fathers	Income-range for sons-in-law					Total
	Top 20%	Second 20%	Middle 20%	Fourth 20%	Bottom 20%	
Top 20%						
Second 20%	16 (31.4)	5 (9.8)	4 (7.8)	15 (29.4)	11 (21.6)	51
Middle 20%	10 (11.2)	15 (16.9)	29 (32.6)	20 (22.5)	15 (16.9)	89
Fourth 20%	6 (4.1)	25 (17.1)	39 (26.7)	31 (21.2)	45 (30.8)	146
Bottom 20%	2 (4.1)	5 (10.2)	5 (10.2)	21 (42.9)	16 (32.7)	49
Total	34	50	77	87	87	335

(b) Age-adjusted hourly earnings

Income range for fathers	Income-range for sons-in-law					Total
	Top 20%	Second 20%	Middle 20%	Fourth 20%	Bottom 20%	
Top 20%						
Second 20%	15 (46.9)	2 (6.3)	1 (3.1)	3 (9.4)	11 (34.4)	32
Middle 20%	3 (5.3)	14 (24.6)	9 (15.8)	9 (15.8)	22 (38.6)	57
Fourth 20%	4 (3.0)	13 (9.8)	38 (28.6)	37 (27.8)	41 (30.8)	133
Bottom 20%	5 (4.3)	9 (7.8)	19 (16.5)	17 (14.8)	65 (56.5)	115
Total	27	38	67	66	139	337

Notes: (1) There are two cases with age information missing.
(2) The figures in parentheses are the percentages for the row.

Earnings: A Regression Analysis

In this section, we examine the extent of mobility as measured by the regression coefficient in a simple regression equation relating earnings in one generation to earnings in the preceding one. As a summary measure, the regression coefficient has advantages and disadvantages. In trying to capture all features of the data in a single number, we are of course making strong assumptions. The simple regression model assumes an essentially symmetric process, not allowing, for example, for any differential tendency for movement up or down; it does not allow for the possibility that the extent of mobility may vary across the range of earnings. At the same time, it does not depend in any way on the choice of categories, as may be the case with the transition matrices discussed above. We have already noted the potential problem with open-ended top and bottom categories (although in our case the top is not likely to cause any difficulty in view of the truncation of the sample). Moreover, a small change in earnings can switch a person from one category to another, and in the case of earnings, unlike occupation, the use of a continuous variable seems appropriate. Finally, where the results are summarised in a single indicator, it is easier to examine their sensitivity to the choice of definitions and to aspects such as measurement error.

Regression towards the mean?

The regression model is similar to that employed in Chapter 5, where we assumed that the logarithm of income of the second generation was linearly related to the logarithm of income of the parents, with economic status being in part inherited and in part determined by a random factor which, on average, brought people towards the mean. In the case of earnings, the use of the *logarithm* of earnings, rather than earnings itself, is in line with the econometric literature on earnings determination, and this provides a bridge to the next chapter. It also means that there is no need to adjust for the general rise in money earnings over the previous quarter of a century. If all earnings are higher in money terms by a factor of 10 in 1975–8 than they were in 1950, then this simply adds a constant to the logarithm of earnings. The analysis which follows does not therefore depend on our assumptions about the position of the median or that the distribution of earnings has remained stable over time. Although we are reasonably confident that our findings are not unduly sensitive to these assumptions, it is clearly a merit of the regression analysis that it does not depend on assumed properties of the national distribution.

In considering the results, we begin with the case where the dependent variable is the logarithm of the hourly earnings of the sons and the independent variable is the logarithm of the weekly earnings of the father in 1950 (hourly earnings not being available). The sample is that used in Table 6.3a, except that we have used ungrossed data and have included all cases, so that the sample size is 288. The ordinary least squares estimates are:

$$-0.359 + 0.436 \log_e F \qquad R = 0.227$$

(where the estimated standard error of the coefficient of $\log_e F$ is 0.111).

These numbers need to be interpreted. First of all, F refers to the earnings of the father in 1950. The average value of the logarithm of earnings was 1.914 (corresponding to £6.78 a week), so that for the sons of a person at this level the predicted earnings are:

$$0.436 \times 1.914 - 0.359 = 0.475$$

which corresponds to hourly earnings of £1.61. One would expect the constant to be positive, not least because of the allowance for inflation, but it has to be remembered that we are going from *weekly* earnings to *hourly* earnings. Although the second generation can earn in a day what their fathers earned in a week in 1950, they cannot yet (even in 1982!) typically do it in an hour.

The regression coefficient, 0.436, is of particular interest as a measure of the extent of continuities across generations, with the estimated value lying between the cases of 0 (no continuities, or perfect mobility) and 1 (complete immobility). If the dispersion of the logarithm of earnings were the same in both generations, then the estimates of the regression coefficient and of the correlation coefficient (R) would be equal. However, the truncation of the 1950 sample at the top means that the variance of the father's earnings is substantially less, around a half, and this explains why the value of R is about half that of the regression coefficient. The truncation of the sample of fathers' earnings does not in itself necessarily lead to bias in the estimate of the regression coefficient, and it is on this that we focus. It may be noted that the estimated standard error of the regression coefficient (see the section on statistical terms at the end of the book) of 0.111 implies a 95 per cent confidence interval of ± 0.218, or from 0.218 to 0.654, which is fairly wide but which excludes zero and one.

The meaning of the estimated regression coefficient may be interpreted as follows. Let us take the example of the Parks family, introduced in Chapter 5, where Mr Parks earned £8.50 a week as a welder, and compare the prospects of Robin Parks, the son, with those of George Banks, whose father earned £5 a week in 1950 as a builders' labourer. Mr Parks was comfortably above the median; in fact, he was about a third down from the top of the national earnings distribution (according to our estimates). Mr Banks, on the other hand, was at the bottom decile. Taking the estimated regression coefficient, we can see that the predicted advantage for Robin Parks over George Banks is:

$$\left\{ \frac{8.50}{5.00} \right\}^{0.436} = 1.26$$

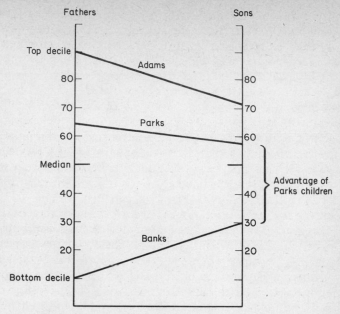

Figure 6.2   Regression towards the mean: earnings

That is, the predicted earnings of Robin are some 26 per cent higher.

The extent of regression towards the mean is illustrated in Figure 6.2, where we show the movement of the Parks family and the Banks family. The straight lines show the predicted earnings; the actual earnings, of course, are also influenced by the random factor (if it were not for this, then the distribution in the second generation would be more compressed than that in the first). In fact Robin Parks did considerably better than predicted and is in the top 10 per cent of earners in the second generation, but on average people in his position would be expected to have the advantage indicated in Figure 6.2. In the diagram we also show the position of the Adams family, where the father earned £12.25 a week in 1950 as a scientific-instrument maker. He was at the top decile, and his sons cannot expect, on average, to maintain this position, although their predicted earnings are none the less around the upper quartile.

Some variations on the theme

In the case of the Parks family, both father and son were in their thirties when interviewed, so that they were at a similar stage of the life cycle. This may, however, cause the degree of continuity to be overstated. The reader may like to consider, for example, what would have happened if we had fitted a regression model to data like those shown for the four hypothetical families in the upper part of Figure 6.1. One could generate a significant positive relationship, as a result of the common age factor, whereas the 'true' relationship is negative. In this case, the bias would be revealed, if we adjusted earnings for the age profile (in Figure 6.1, the peak earnings of 120 should then be compared with 60 in the lower range, and peak earnings of 80 should be compared with 40).

The effect of adjusting for age differences, using the profile derived from the New Earnings Survey for 1976, is shown in the second line of Table 6.6 (the first line reproduces the equation we have already discussed). For individual families, the age adjustment may make a considerable difference, but overall it appears that the regression coefficient is little affected. In terms of our comparison of the Parks and Banks families, the predicted advantage of Robin Parks is now 25 per cent, rather than 26 per cent. It may be noted that the correlation coefficient, R, is a little higher, corresponding to the greater concentration along the diagonal observed in the transition matrix (the equation is based on essentially the same data as Table 6.3b).

To this point, we have assumed that the earnings information has been measured without error and that it is free of 'transitory' variation.

Table 6.6   Estimated regression equations for earnings of sons and sons-in-law

	Constant term	Regression coefficient (standard error in parenthesis)	R
Sons			
1. Basic equation (as in text) (288 cases)	−0.359	0.436 (0.111)	0.227
2. Age-adjusted earnings (287 cases)	−0.333	0.418 (0.097)	0.247
3. Subsample where data derived from employer (198 cases)	−0.402	0.446 (0.126)	0.245
Sons-in-law			
4. Basic equation (232 cases)	−0.443	0.472 (0.129)	0.235
5. Age-adjusted earnings (230 cases)	−0.429	0.448 (0.123)	0.234
6. Subsample where data derived from employer (163 cases)	−0.380	0.434 (0.157)	0.212

As we have seen in the previous chapter, such 'measurement error' in the earnings of the sons does not lead to bias in the estimate of the regression coefficient (although it would tend to reduce R). Measurement error for the fathers' earnings data, however, may lead to a downward bias. In those cases where Rowntree obtained details of earnings from the employer, the records are likely to be relatively accurate; moreover, Rowntree and Lavers reported that 'in most cases the figures given were the average earnings for a period of three months' (1951, p. 6), so that the impact of transitory variations should have been reduced. Nevertheless, we should consider the implications of measurement error, if only on account of the minority of cases where earnings were estimated.

There are two ways in which we can seek to assess the importance of measurement error. The first is to consider theoretically the bias which may be induced by recording error, using the formula given earlier (p. 86), where it is assumed that the proportionate error in earnings is uncorrelated with the true value. By making different assumptions about the magnitude of the measurement error, we can calculate the value of the regression coefficient which would correspond to an observed value of 0.42:

Assumed increase in variance as result of measurement error	Implied regression coefficient
5%	0.441
10%	0.462
15%	0.483
20%	0.504
25%	0.525

If there is sizeable measurement error in fathers' earnings, it is therefore possible that the 'true' coefficient is closer to 0.5 than to 0.4.

The second approach is to confine attention to those cases where the father's earnings data were obtained from the employer's records and are therefore likely to be fairly accurately reported (see Chapter 3). The results for this subsample of 198 cases (out of 288) are shown in line 3 of Table 6.6. It should be noted that the subsample is not representative, as those who are excluded were concentrated in particular occupations; however, the subsample accounts for the majority (69 per cent) of the sample. The estimated coefficient is higher, as would be expected theoretically, but the effect is quite modest. At the same time, it has to be remembered that the data from employers may still be subject to some measurement error.

In case the reader is worried by the fact that we are using weekly earnings for fathers but hourly earnings for sons, it may be helpful to note that the estimated regression coefficients are broadly similar. Taking weekly current earnings, the estimate is slightly lower (0.370), as it is with normal weekly earnings (0.377); on the other hand, with basic weekly pay, the estimate is 0.481. In the country as a whole, some 20 per cent of operatives in manufacturing were working overtime in the early 1950s, with an average of some 8 hours per week (Department of Employment, 1971, Table 146).

Finally, we show in Table 6.6 the results for sons-in-law. The transition matrices suggested a rather similar degree of concentration along the diagonal, and this is borne out by the estimated regression coefficients. With age-adjusted earnings, for example, the value is 0.448 for sons-in-law, compared with 0.418 for sons. It appears as if the predicted earnings advantage for Christine Parks's husband is as large as for Robin Parks.

Earnings Mobility: a Summary

By concentrating on the mobility of *earnings*, we have been able to make further progress in this chapter. In particular, we have related the earnings of our respondents to the national distribution and have provided a more firmly based adjustment for differences in the lifetime profile.

In order to summarise the findings for fathers and sons, we draw on both the transition matrices and the regression analysis. Table 6.7 is an attempt to bring them together and to round out the analysis. For this purpose, we use the framework of the quintile transition matrix, and the transition proportions shown in the bottom four rows are derived directly from Table 6.3b (age-adjusted earnings). This latter table did not show the top 20 per cent. If, however, we are willing to treat the other figures as unbiased estimates of the transition proportions, then we can obtain the 'missing' entries in the top row as a residual. This procedure, which is based on strong assumptions, makes use of the fact that the underlying transition matrix must have column sums equal to one. Thus, we have:

	Columns				
	1	*2*	*3*	*4*	*5*
Sum of *percentages* in rows 2–5	52.1	60.2	93.8	99.9	94.1
Implied row 1	47.9	39.8	6.2	0.1	5.9

The regression analysis is brought in by the figures in parentheses in Table 6.7, which are the (rounded) proportions predicted where there is a bivariate normal distribution of the logarithm of earnings, with a

Table 6.7 *Earnings mobility: summary of evidence for fathers and sons*

Income-range for fathers	Income-range for sons				
	Top 20%	Second 20%	Middle 20%	Fourth 20%	Bottom 20%
Top 20%	47.9 (45)	39.8 (25)	6.2 (16)	0.1 (10)	5.9 (4)
Second 20%	14.3 (25)	14.3 (26)	21.4 (22)	35.7 (17)	14.3 (10)
Middle 20%	15.7 (16)	15.7 (22)	35.3 (24)	21.6 (22)	11.8 (16)
Fourth 20%	13.3 (10)	13.3 (17)	23.1 (22)	27.2 (26)	23.1 (25)
Bottom 20%	8.8 (4)	16.9 (10)	14.0 (16)	15.4 (25)	44.9 (45)

Note: The figures in parentheses represent the proportions predicted by a bivariate normal distribution with a regression coefficient of 0.5.

regression coefficient of 0.5. The value of 0.5 has been taken as broadly corresponding to the regression estimates, with an allowance for possible measurement error bias. It should be noted that by comparing the estimated transition proportions with those predicted by the bivariate normal distribution, we are in effect dealing with the problem of the overstatement of immobility at the top left- and bottom right-hand corners. The fact that the predicted transition proportions in these diagonal corners are 45 per cent, rather than 24–26 per cent as in the interior, takes account of the 'crowding' into these cells of the matrix.

The first set of conclusions concern the *extent* of mobility. From the evidence of our survey, there appears to be a definite tendency for the earnings of the son to be related to those of his father. Whether the degree of association is regarded as large or small is a matter of judgement. Jencks, for example, writing about the United States, suggests that a coefficient of 0.5 is 'surprisingly small' (1972, p. 179), but this view could well be disputed. As the figures in parentheses in Table 6.7 indicate, it implies that the odds of entering the top 20 per cent are ten times more favourable, if your father comes from the top 20 per cent than if he comes from the bottom 20 per cent. It implies that Robin Parks has a predicted earnings advantage relative to George Banks of some 30 per cent. This appears quite large, both absolutely and when compared with the kind of differences typically associated, for example, with the acquisition of educational qualifications. Interestingly, the degree of association is similar for fathers and sons-in-law.

The second, and more tentative, group of findings concerns the *pattern* of mobility. These findings are tentative since they depend on the transition proportions for the top row, derived as a residual, and since the small numbers in our survey (and other special features) limit the conclusions which can be drawn. None the less, comparing the transition proportions in Table 6.7 with those predicted by the regression model, one is struck by the difference between the bottom left-hand and the top right-hand corners. The proportion of upwardly mobile sons from the bottom 20 per cent appears to be considerably higher and the proportion of downwardly mobile sons from the top 20 per cent appears to be lower than the regression model would predict. The proportion entering the top 60 per cent from the bottom 20 per cent was around 40 per cent. This may be compared with the 30 per cent predicted with a regression coefficient of 0.5. Conversely, the proportion of the sons of the top 20 per cent who drop more than one range is 12.2 per cent, compared with a predicted 30 per cent. Put another way, the upper groups are more 'closed' in terms of distance moved when leaving than when entering. The process of mobility may be seen as involving upward jumps from a number of strata, including the bottom, but a more gradual 'trickling back'.

Finally, there have been a number of hints as to the possible *mechanisms* associated with mobility or immobility. The discussion of those leaving and entering the low-paid category suggested, for instance, an apparent association with geographical movement. This, and other mechanisms, is the subject of the chapters which follow.

7 Earnings: from Father to Son?

Introduction
In this chapter we concentrate on the observed association between the earnings of fathers and sons. That is, we leave until the next chapter any discussion of the relation between the earnings of fathers and sons-in-law (and of the position of daughters), and we take the earnings of the father as the sole indicator of family advantage (other measures, like the NA ratio, are considered in Chapters 8 and 9).

Factors determining earnings
What factors could lead to the observed association across generations? In Chapter 1 we identified some of the possible determinants. The correlation between the earnings of fathers and sons could result from the influence of 'ability', where this is causally related over generations. Suppose, for example, that the logarithm of earnings were determined solely by scores of intelligence tests and that the role of genetic factors was such that the IQ scores of fathers and sons have a correlation coefficient of around 0.5. We should then observe the kind of association recorded in our Rowntree survey. Not even the strongest advocates of the IQ explanation of earnings would be likely to accept this extreme version, but it serves to illustrate an important limitation of our analysis. With the information at our disposal, we cannot examine all the possible mechanisms, and there may well be major influences on earnings which are left out of our analysis. We have no data on measured intelligence or other indicators of ability. More generally, there are qualities of personality or character – for example, the 'D-factor' of Lydall (1976) which stands for 'drive, dynamism, doggedness or determination' – which may be associated across generations, and which we are not able to take into account.

Our discussion of the determinants of earnings concentrates therefore on only some of the links set out in Figure 1.2. We do not pretend that we can provide a full picture of what is a complex process. We begin with education, considering not just the length of schooling, but also the type of school attended and the qualifications acquired. We are especially interested in discovering whether or not there is a relation between these measures of educational performance and father's earnings. For example, on the basis of their cohort study, Douglas and his colleagues concluded (1968, pp. 40–1):

the social class inequalities in opportunity . . . have increased in the secondary [schools] and extend . . . even to the highest levels of ability. It seems that the able boys and girls from manual working class families . . . have been heavily handicapped in their later secondary school careers through relatively early leaving and poor examination results.

How far is this true of our sample, with our rather different measure of family advantage?

The second aspect on which we focus is labour-market experience, a term which we take to cover entry to apprenticeships, the local labour-market and geographical mobility, and macroeconomic conditions. Among other considerations are the special nature of our sample, including the industrial composition of employment in York, and the special features of the time-period spanned by our respondents, some of whom entered work in the 1930s whereas others left school in the 1970s. Again, family background may have a role to play. Bowles has argued (1972, p. S225) that the recruitment practices of employers may be such that:

children of parents occupying a given position in the occupational hierarchy grow up in homes where child-rearing methods and perhaps even the physical surroundings tend to develop personality characteristics appropriate to adequate job performance.

In more concrete terms, fathers may be able, for example, to secure for their sons preferential access into their own skilled trades.

The provision of superior education, or access to apprenticeships, are examples of *indirect* links between family background and earnings. Some writers argue indeed that all mechanisms must be indirect. Leibowitz, for example, writes (1977, p. 29):

it would be hard to argue that employers [are willing to] pay workers for having had richer families. The families' income must have been used to provide an attribute – such as higher quality schooling, or health – which increases productivity.

Similarly, Mincer states in Atkinson (1980a), pp. 124–5:

the preponderant evidence thus far [is] that employers pay for the characteristics and efforts of the workers, not of their parents. The economic analysis of human capital investment decisions suggests that the effects of background variables are *indirect* by influencing the accumulation of human capital.

In part, this is a semantic question, concerned with the definition of human capital, which it does not seem profitable to pursue. But there seem good reasons for examining the earnings of people with similar identifiable characteristics to see if family background still conveys any advantage. Do people with the same educational experience, qualifications, access to apprenticeships, etc. have, on average, the same earnings? If Robin Parks and George Banks had both been to the same school, both left with the same number of O levels, both entered accountancy, would Robin still have enjoyed some advantage?

In the last part of this chapter, we present a statistical analysis of the earnings evidence. This brings together the education and labour-market variables and attempts to measure the indirect association with father's earnings which is induced by these links. Among other things, this analysis allows us to relate our findings to those in the literature on earnings determination.

Education

Years of full-time education

The dimension of education which has received most attention is the number of years of full-time education, which we have defined to be the age of leaving school or further education minus five years. This is not always an accurate indicator, since attendance may have been affected by illness, etc., and for some cases the information was not obtained, but it provides a useful starting-point.

The educational experience of the sons in our follow-up study (no information is available on the education of the fathers) is very varied. Of the 366 cases for which we have information (all figures are grossed), 81 had nine years of education (see Table 7.1): that is, they had left school at the age of 14 (in one case at the age of 13). A further 148 had left at the age of 15 and 74 at the age of 16. Fewer than one in five had received twelve or more years of full-time education, but of these a number had degrees and one, at least, a Ph.D.

Over the course of the century, the length of time spent in education has tended to increase. Most importantly, the school-leaving age was raised from 14 to 15 in 1947, and again from 15 to 16 in 1972. In Table 7.1, we show the number of years in education for three age cohorts, with the divisions corresponding broadly to the dates at which the

Table 7.1   Length of full-time education: sons

Years of education	(Age at which left school)	A1 (35 and older)	A2 (46–44)	A3 (34 or younger)	Total
9 or fewer	14 or younger	77	3	1	81
10	15	17	55	76	148
11	16	13	15	46	74
12	17	2	1	16	19
13	18	0	0	7	7
14–16	19–21	12	1	7	20
17 or more	22 or older	1	3	13	17
Total		122	78	166	366

Note: Age cohorts are defined by the son's age at interview.

minimum leaving-age changed. A large fraction of the oldest age cohort, A1, left at the age of 14, although it is noticeable that a significant minority (about 10 per cent) were in further education. (Apprenticeships are not included.) Of the middle age cohort, three-quarters left at the age of 15 or under, whereas in the youngest cohort the proportion had fallen to under half. This shift over time raises problems of interpretation. John Richards, for example, stayed on at school for two years after the minimum leaving-age, which was then 14; his brother left at the minimum leaving-age of 15 a decade later. Does John have one or two years advantage over his younger brother?

Whether the Rowntree son stayed on at school beyond the minimum leaving-age may have been a choice based on considerations of the value of the qualifications that would have resulted, or it may simply have reflected the constraints that we faced. For many children, the constraints are likely to have been important. Staying on typically imposes a financial cost, in that the son could have been earning; and the income of the family is one of the factors likely to have influenced whether or not he was able to continue in education. In low-income families, there is probably greater pressure on children to leave at the earliest opportunity. Conversely, children from better-off families may find it difficult to leave before the age of 18, if they want to: the son of a white-collar father may be strongly discouraged from leaving at 15 to take an apprenticeship. Even where the constraints allow room for choice, the decision may be influenced by the family background. Most importantly, the perception of the benefits from education may well be related to the father's occupation and earnings. As it has been put by Phelps Brown (1977, pp. 246–7):

young people do not see themselves in parts that they have not grown up to regard as naturally theirs. It is the influence of the home that predominates – the occupations of parents, relatives, friends and neighbours . . . manual workers who are concerned for their children's advancement look towards the occupations that they judge most promising among those that are known to them and that are readily accessible.

From the information in our follow-up survey, we can examine the relation between the earnings of the father and the length of education of the son. In interpreting the evidence, we must bear in mind that our survey is a 'snapshot' at a particular date, and that the recorded earnings may not have been those received at the relevant date. The man who was a struggling self-employed builder in 1950 may have been a business success by the time his sons reached the age of 15 in the mid-1960s. In using the data, we have taken earnings adjusted for the common age profile, but changes of the kind just described cannot be taken into account.

Table 7.2 shows the pattern of education for different ranges of

Table 7.2 Length of schooling and father's earnings

Father's age-adjusted earnings (in relation to national distribution)	Number of cases	Years of education									Sons staying on beyond school-leaving age (number)	Percentage
		9 or under	10	11	12	13	14–16	17 or more	Median	Mean		
Second 20%	25	3	13	5	0	1	1	2	10	11.2	9	36.0
Middle 20%	48	10	15	15	1	1	3	3	10	11.0	25	52.1
Fourth 20%	156	35	57	33	4	3	14	10	10	11.1	72	46.2
Bottom 20%	134	33	63	18	14	2	2	2	10	10.4	39	29.1
Total	363	81	148	71	19	7	20	17	10	10.9	145	39.9

fathers' earnings (the top 20 per cent is not included, since only three cases occur in this range). The median number of years of full-time education is 10 for the sample as a whole and for each of the income-groups. The median, however, is slightly misleading in this context, and we may note that the proportion with *more than* 10 years is 28 per cent for those in the bottom 20 per cent, compared with 41 per cent and 48 per cent in the two ranges above. The proportion for the top of the groups considered here, the second 20 per cent, is between these figures, but the results for this group need to be treated with caution in view of the much smaller number involved – only 25 compared with five or six times as many in the bottom two ranges. The mean number of years of education shows a similar picture, with the bottom 20 per cent being 10.4 years, compared with 11 years in the two ranges above.

As we have seen, educational experience is likely to be affected by age, and eleven years of education may have a different meaning for different cohorts. In the right-hand part of Table 7.2, we show the proportion staying on beyond the minimum school-leaving age. Of 134 sons whose fathers were in the bottom 20 per cent, only 39 (or 29 per cent) stayed on at school, whereas the group in the next higher income-range had 46 per cent staying on at school. If we ask how many continued in education beyond the age of 18, we see that only 4 of the 134 sons did so, compared with 24 out of 156 in the range above, and a rather similar percentage from the middle 20 per cent.

An alternative way of summarising the evidence from our survey about the relation between length of education and father's earnings is in terms of a least squares regression, where we take the logarithm of father's earnings as an explanatory variable. We also introduce variables to allow for the age-cohort effects noted earlier; and the latter indicate that on average the youngest age cohort, those aged 34 or under, received two more years of education, and that the middle cohort received three-quarters of a year more education, than those aged 45 or over. The father's earnings variable proved to have a coefficient of 1.983. The implications of this estimated coefficient may be seen by considering once again the position of Robin Parks and George Banks. The predicted difference in the length of full-time education is almost exactly one year. That is, we would expect someone whose father earned £8.50 a week to spend, on average, one year more at school than someone whose father was on £5 a week in 1950.

Qualifications

Only a minority of the sons had educational qualifications (where we are not including apprenticeships). Of the 366, 16 had degrees or equivalent qualifications, a further 11 had A levels (or equivalent), and 63 more had some O levels or CSE awards. Taken together, they make up a quarter of the sample. But it is interesting to ask how the acquisition of qualifications may be related to father's earnings. Here considerations will centre not just on length of education but also on the quality of schooling provided, the extent of parental support and the perceived benefit from passing examinations.

The left-hand part of Table 7.3 classifies the sons according to their educational attainment and their father's earnings. For the three main groups, the percentage with no qualifications tends to rise quite noticeably as we move down the income scale. Where the father was in the middle 20 per cent, 65 per cent of the sons left without qualifications, but this percentage was as high as 80 per cent for the children of those from the bottom 20 per cent. Of the 134 sons in the bottom 20 per cent, only four had qualifications beyond O level (or equivalent), but of the 156 in the next 20 per cent, fifteen had such qualifications and seven had degrees.

The general level of qualifications attained has been tending to rise over time. In a more detailed statistical analysis, using a logit model of discrete events, we have estimated how the probability of leaving with qualifications varied both with father's earnings and with the different age cohorts. This suggested again that those aged 34 and under had a significantly higher chance of securing qualifications. For George Banks, aged 32 when interviewed, the predicted probability is 30 per cent, but for someone twenty years older, and otherwise identically placed, it would have been 16 per cent. In this respect, our findings resemble those of other studies, such as the recent investigation by Halsey *et al.* (1980), who show 14 per cent of the age cohort born in 1923–32 obtaining the equivalent of O level, but 34 per cent of the age cohort 1943–52, which includes George Banks. We also found a significant influence of the number of children in the family. If George Banks had been an only child, rather than having a brother and a sister, then the predicted probability would have been 40 per cent rather than 30 per cent.

The same analysis examined the effect of father's earnings. If we compare Robin Parks with George Banks, then Robin had a predicted probability of acquiring qualifications of 57 per cent, which is substantially higher than the predicted 30 per cent for George Banks. At this point we should note that our results go beyond those obtained in studies such as Halsey *et al.* (1980), which are based on father's occupation. Even if occupational status and earnings were synonymous, the groupings by occupational class tend to produce a large number in the lower class. Halsey *et al.* have 14 per cent in the professional ('service') class, 31 per cent in the intermediate class, and no fewer than 55 per cent in the working class. It is a weakness of our data that we can say nothing about the professional or top class, but it is a strength that we

Table 7.3 Educational attainment and type of institution last attended by father's earnings

Father's age-adjusted earnings (in relation to national distribution)	Total	Educational attainment[a]						Type of educational institution last attended full-time							'Selective'	
		No qualifications[b]		1-4 O levels	5+ O levels	A levels	Degree	Primary or Elementary	Secondary Modern	Technical	Grammar	College of Education	University	Other/not known		
		Number	Percentage												Number	Percentage[c]
Second 20%	25	17	(68.0)	1	4	0	2	1	15	2	3	1	2	1	6	(25.0)
Middle 20%	48	31	(64.6)	3	8	1	5	9	15	5	10	1	5	3	16	(35.6)
Fourth 20%	156	119	(76.3)	10	12	8	7	26	60	21	24	14	7	4	45	(29.6)
Bottom 20%	134	108	(80.6)	8	14	2	2	16	78	13	22	1	1	3	24	(18.3)
Total	363	275	(75.8)	22	38	11	16	52	168	41	59	17	15	11	91	(25.9)

Notes: [a] Including those with apprenticeships.
[b] There is one case where qualifications not known.
[c] Expressed as a percentage of total known categories.

can examine the position in detail within the working class. Both Mr Parks, an electrician, and Mr Banks, a builders' labourer, would have appeared in the working class, but we have seen that the predicted educational experience of their children is quite different.

Type of school attended

The type of school attended is obviously important. A year spent at Park Grove Secondary Modern School cannot necessarily be regarded as equivalent to a year spent at Archbishop Holgate's Grammar School, even if the same qualifications were obtained at the end. The types of school attended by our respondents reflect the educational history of the period. A sizeable number, 52, of the total of 366 last attended a primary or elementary school; nearly half, 168, left after secondary modern or comprehensive school; 41 attended technical school; and 94 were at grammar school or went on to colleges of education or university. Those whose last school was a comprehensive were the youngest. There were, in fact, relatively few in the latter category, since the city of York retained the grammar school/secondary modern system.

Particular interest attaches to the role of 'selective' schools. Our information relates to last full-time education, so that our definition includes selection at the stage of further education as well as at the age of 11, but if we take those attending grammar schools, colleges of education or university, then there were 91 out of 363 (excluding the three cases from the top 20 per cent). Overall, a quarter enjoyed selective education. But from the right-hand part of Table 7.3, we can see that there is a clear gradient with father's earnings. In the bottom 20 per cent only 22 out of 134 went to grammar school (and two went on to higher education), which makes 18 per cent. For the next income-range, the proportion rises to 30 per cent and for the middle 20 per cent the proportion with selective education is 36 per cent.

The association indicated by Table 7.3 may be the result of age differences, with the children from the bottom 20 per cent being older, and older children being less likely to attend selective schools. On the other hand, it is not so obvious that there has been a secular increase in the chance of attending selective schools: the evidence of Halsey *et al.* (1980) suggests that the proportion rose between the birth cohorts 1923–32 and 1933–42, but *fell* between 1933–42 and 1943–52. We carried out a logit analysis of the probability of attending selective school, which showed no significant cohort effect, but did find a negative influence of the number of siblings and a positive effect of father's earnings. For George Banks, the chance of attending a selective school was predicted to be 21 per cent, whereas for Robin Parks the predicted probability was 41 per cent.

Summary

Three main conclusions may be drawn. First, we have seen that different age cohorts tended to have a rather different educational experience. This applied to the length of full-time education, where, on average, those aged 34 or under had two years more education than those aged 45 and over. It applied to the probability of acquiring qualifications, where for a person in the position of George Banks the predicted probability was 14 per cent for the oldest age cohort, but 34 per cent for the youngest. On the other hand, no such effect appeared to be operative for attendance at selective schools.

The effect of age is well documented in other studies. Where our data are particularly valuable is in illuminating the influence of family background, not least because the information on earnings allows us to consider differences *within* the working class. Here our results indicate a significant relationship with all three aspects of education. Taking Robin Parks and George Banks to illustrate this (where Mr Parks earned £8.50 as an electrician in 1950 and Mr Banks earned £5 as a labourer), Robin received on average one year more education, he had a 57 per cent change of acquiring qualifications compared with 30 per cent for George, and he had a 41 per cent chance of attending a selective school, compared with 21 per cent.

Thirdly, there is some indication from the analysis by income-ranges that the bottom 20 per cent were especially poorly placed. Sons from the bottom 20 per cent had an average length of education of 10.4 years, whereas the next 20 per cent were above the overall average (10.9 years); only 18 per cent attended selective schools, whereas 30 per cent did in the next 20 per cent income-range.

Labour-Market Experience

In this section, we examine the entry into apprenticeships, the local labour-market and geographical mobility, and the differing experience of different cohorts in the labour force.

Apprenticeships

A large proportion of our respondents had no educational qualifications; however, more than half of these had completed apprenticeships in trades including instrument-making, printing, stone-masonry, watch-making, etc. Particularly important for those living in York were apprenticeships with British Rail, including trades such as coach-building.

The mechanism by which school-leavers enter apprenticeships may be similar in part to the acquisition of examination qualifications, this being an indicator of 'success' in the same way as the O-level criterion used above. It is also possible that the father's role may be more direct.

In the case of professions such as medicine, the direct 'inheritance' of occupational status has been extensively documented; family connections facilitate entry into training for preferred occupations. The same may apply for skilled trades. The evidence from our interviews did indeed suggest that this happened where the father was employed by British Rail. Several of our respondents said that their fathers 'put their name down' for a British Rail apprenticeship when they were still at school (in one case at birth!), and that it was generally accepted that this was a way to obtain access to skilled trades.

For our respondents as a whole, 275 had no educational qualifications, and of these 156 (or 57 per cent) had completed apprenticeships. It should be noted that we are concerned with *completion*; the factors causing early school-leaving may also put pressure on apprentices to leave for jobs which – in the short term – pay better. If the proportion of those without qualifications who complete apprenticeships is related to father's earnings, then we find that for the bottom 20 per cent income-range it is 43 per cent, or well below the average. In contrast for the next 20 per cent income-range, it is 66 per cent. There appears therefore to be a marked difference between the bottom 20 per cent and those higher up the earnings ladder.

Local labour-market and geographical mobility

The reference to British Rail brings out the special nature of the labour-market faced by many of our respondents – a labour-market dominated by two industries. About two-thirds of our respondents (that is, the sons) were still in York, and we have already seen that a large proportion of the York labour force is employed in confectionery and by British Rail (British Railways before Dr. Beeching).

In Table 7.4, we show the structure of male employment in the city of York, as recorded at successive censuses. In 1951 more than one in three (37.5 per cent) of male employees were working in the food, drink, tobacco sector, or for British Rail (either on the railways or in the carriage and wagon works). Over time there has been some decline in the latter. The wagon shops were closed in 1965, and although there was some expansion in carriage maintenance work at that time, a subsequent reorganisation led to a reduction, leaving total employment significantly lower than in 1951. At the same time, the railway side, with the headquarters of Eastern Region in York, has remained important. Taken together with a small expansion in the food, etc. sector, the two industries still accounted for more than a third of employment in 1971.

There have, of course, been changes in the employment structure over the generation. Table 7.4 shows the reduction in public administration and defence (for example, as a result of the amalgamation of two

Table 7.4   Employment by industry in York, 1951–71

Industry	Male employment		
	1951 %	1961 %	1971 %
1. Agriculture	0.8	0.5	0.6
2. Mining, engineering, metals, etc.	4.0	3.3	3.7
3. Food, drink and tobacco	15.2	16.4	16.3
4. Textiles, clothing, wool, etc.	2.2	1.2	1.5
5. Ceramics, glass and cement	1.5	2.1	2.6
6. Paper and printing	2.2	3.1	2.3
7. Construction	8.7	9.7	10.7
8. Gas, electricity and water	2.6	2.5	2.1
9. Transport and communication	5.8	6.1	6.7
10. Distributive trades	10.5	11.8	10.7
11. Insurance, etc.	1.8	2.1	3.1
12. Professional services	4.3	5.4	6.9
13. Miscellaneous services	7.1	7.2	7.3
14. Public administration and defence	11.2	7.6	6.6
15. British Rail	22.1	21.0	18.8
Total	100.0	100.0	100.0

Note: The industry categories shown above differ from the minimum list headings employed in the census tables, in that we have combined a number of headings where there were relatively few employees in York (for example industry 4 above includes headings 10, 11, 12, 14 and 16) and that we have constructed a special British Rail category. The latter is formed by taking those engaged in coach and carriage-building (who would otherwise have appeared in industry 2) and those employed on the railways (who would otherwise have appeared in industry 9). Changes in classification between censuses have been taken into account as far as possible: for example, motor repairers are shown in miscellaneous services throughout (whereas the 1951 census included them under 'vehicles').

Sources: 1951 GB Census: England and Wales, Industry Tables, table 2.
1961 GB Census: England and Wales, Occupation Industry Socioeconomic Groups, Yorkshire, W. Riding, table 3.
1971 GB Census: England and Wales, Economic Activity county leaflet, Yorkshire, W. Riding, table 3.

Yorkshire regiments and the partial closure of Fulford barracks). The figures for ceramics, glass, etc. reflect the expansion of the Redfearn National Glass Ltd. Other developments are not easily detected from the statistics, including, for instance, the growth of F. Shepherd and Son Ltd, the building firm which has branched out into the production of the 'Portakabin' temporary accommodation units. There is the arrival of the University of York, and the growth of tourism. The overall picture, however, is more one of stability than of rapid structural change.

If the Rowntree sons stayed in York, therefore, they would have entered a labour-market with certain special features and which resembled that in which their father was employed in 1950. To this extent, observed continuities may reflect the characteristics of York, rather than transmitted advantage or disadvantage. On the other hand, there is the possibility of moving. The association between geographical mobility and occupational mobility has been noted in earlier studies. In the United States, Duncan, Featherman and Duncan (1972) find that, excluding those with farm backgrounds, migrants have consistently higher occupational status. In the UK, Rutter and Madge note that 'mobility in work and in place of residence is characteristic of people in scientific, technical and administrative professions where promotion and upward social mobility is dependent in part on a willingness to move house in order to obtain a more responsible job' (1976, p. 156).

In our context, the evidence about geographical mobility needs to be interpreted with care. Not only may our snapshot picture be unrepresentative (for example, where a son has gone to London for training, but expects to return later in his career to York), but also the mobility may occur in either generation. Mr Hughes, living in York in 1950, moved soon after the interview to Stoke-on-Trent; his son Richard grew up in Stoke and went to work in a local firm. In contrast, Mr Hanson stayed in York and his son David went to Park Grove School. David moved, however, to Ipswich for career advancement. In both cases we classify the sons as 'mobile', but the situation is quite different.

This means that an association between father's earnings and mobility may arise because of the father's career history or because higher family income facilitates mobility by the children. From the upper part of Table 7.5, we can see that the rate of mobility out of York is indeed lower for the bottom 20 per cent earning range. (The sample here is somewhat larger, because we include a number of cases not covered in earlier tables since we lacked information on the length of education.) The proportion leaving York is only 22.5 per cent for the bottom 20 per cent earning range, compared with more than 40 per cent for the other ranges; and the proportion leaving Yorkshire and Humberside altogether is similarly about half. Again, there appears to be a noticeable difference between the bottom 20 per cent and the rest of the sample.

The observed association may arise indirectly because of the role of education. Those with qualifications may find it easier to move; and the pursuit of qualifications, particularly in the case of higher education,

Table 7.5 *Migration, father's earnings and education*

| | Total | Number migrating | | | |
| | | From York | | From Yorkshire and Humberside | |
		Number	Percentage	Number	Percentage
Father's earnings ranges					
Second 20%	26	11	(42.3)	7	(26.9)
Middle 20%	54	26	(48.1)	10	(18.5)
Fourth 20%	180	75	(41.7)	36	(20.0)
Bottom 20%	142	32	(22.5)	12	(8.5)
Total	402	144	(35.8)	65	(16.2)
Educational qualifications					
No qualification or apprenticeship	119	35	(29.4)	17	(14.3)
Apprenticeship	156	39	(25.0)	9	(5.8)
O levels or School Certificate	63	28	(44.4)	12	(19.0)
A levels or degree	28	22	(78.6)	16	(57.1)
Not known	39	21	(53.8)	12	(30.8)
Total	405	145	(35.8)	66	(16.3)

Note: The figures for those migrating 'from York' include those leaving Yorkshire and Humberside altogether.

may mean leaving York. In the lower part of Table 7.5, we show the proportions leaving York with different levels of qualifications. There is a marked difference between those with no qualifications or an apprenticeship and those with O levels or beyond. Not surprisingly, 16 of the 28 with A levels or a degree are living outside Yorkshire and Humberside. When one looks at the kind of jobs involved – for example, electronics engineer, planner, academic, commodity dealer – it is clear that the York labour-market offers limited opportunities.

We have carried out a logit analysis of the probability of leaving Yorkshire and Humberside, introducing father's earnings, years of education and age-cohort effects. The results show a positive relation with father's earnings, but this is not particularly well determined and not much weight can be placed on this finding. The education variable, however, is significant, and indicates, for example, that if George Banks receives $12\frac{1}{2}$ rather than $11\frac{1}{2}$ years education, then the probability of leaving Yorkshire and Humberside increases by a third. This difference of one year is that predicted earlier from the analysis of the association between father's earnings and length of education. Taking the indirect effect via education with the – debatable – direct effect, the predicted probability of migration for Robin Parks is 24 per cent, compared with 9.5 per cent for George Banks.

Differing experience of different cohorts

When we interviewed the sons, they had been in the labour force for very different periods. Some were recent entrants, born perhaps in the baby boom of the late 1940s; others were near to retirement, having started work in the 1930s. There will therefore be differences not just of age, but also in the kind of labour-market conditions which they have experienced. As a result, although we have evidence about earnings at a broadly similar calendar date – so that in this sense the macroeconomic climate is the same for everyone – there may be enduring effects of past events.

One important example is provided by the extent of training. From the point of view of both employee and employer, training is likely to be most relevant in the early stages of a person's work career. This may mean that a person's earning capacity is particularly influenced by labour-market conditions when he enters the labour force. The availability of apprenticeships, or of 'on the job' training more generally, is likely to vary with the level of unemployment. The prospects for acquiring training for someone entering the labour force in 1950 must have been considerably brighter than twenty years earlier or thirty years later.

A second, and often overlooked, factor is the size of different cohorts. In the United States, attention has been drawn to the importance of being 'demographically lucky', and the process has been described by Easterlin (1980, pp. 147–8):

The story of the past forty years is in part one of the impact of major swings in generation size on the economy and society. From World War II to around 1960, the small generations born chiefly in the low birth rate era of the 1930s were entering the labor market. Younger workers were in increasingly short supply . . . their personal economic fortunes improved, and the general state of social and economic health was good. But in the last decade or so, the labor market has been increasingly flooded with the offspring of the 1950s baby boom . . . This large generation has had difficulty supporting its economic aspirations.

The same pattern does not necessarily apply in the UK, but there are some reasons for supposing that our respondents entering the labour force in the period from the Second World War to 1970 faced better prospects than those who preceded them and those who came after.

It is clearly difficult to separate the cohort effect from those of age. Part at least of the hump-shaped relation of earnings with age may reflect the cohort effect rather than the life-cycle profile for an individual. In what follows, we simply treat the combined effect, assuming that there is a quadratic relationship between earnings and length of time in the labour force. But it needs to be remembered that we cannot attribute this factor solely to age; in the same way, the use of age-adjusted earnings in the previous chapter means that we were, in effect, expressing earnings *relative* to those of the age cohort (and not just a pure age effect).

Earnings
In this section we draw together the different elements discussed earlier and examine the association between family background, education, labour-market experience and the earnings of the Rowntree children. The determinants of earnings have been the subject of extensive literature (see for a recent review, Phelps Brown, 1977). This literature has in part been eclectic, seeking simply to 'explain' earnings, typically in a multiple regression framework, by the introduction of relevant characteristics. Thus, the earnings equations estimated by Taubman (1975) in the United States include more than thirty variables, among them education, ability, religion, family background, how time was spent when growing up, location, age, weight, etc. Other writers have developed the analysis from an explicit theoretical model, notably the human-capital approach of Mincer (1958) and Becker (1964). Thus, Mincer (for example, 1976) estimates a relationship between the logarithm of earnings and years of education, years of work experience, and weeks worked in the year. The logarithmic specification is derived from the human-capital model, although it has been the subject of debate (Blinder, 1976).

Our approach may be seen as midway between these. We do not simply include all the variables at our disposal in the hope of finding some that are statistically significant. Rather, we seek to incorporate the mechanisms discussed earlier in the chapter, and which we have argued may be expected to influence economic success. There is a clear rationale in each case for their inclusion. At the same time, we do not limit ourselves to the relatively small range of factors considered by the human-capital school. In particular, we pay more attention to the role of family background. This aspect tends to be played down by the American writers in the human-capital tradition.

Mincer, for instance, notes that 'most of the studies which include family background variables in the earnings equations report small effects, net of the human capital variables such as schooling and experience' (1976, p. 172). In what follows, we distinguish between the 'indirect' effect via education and the 'direct' effect. The latter may, of course, reflect other variables not included in our analysis, but this treatment allows us to distinguish education, and in places migration, from other variables.

Earnings: a multiple regression approach

In order to allow comparison of our results with those of earlier investigations, we make use of a multiple regression approach, but we provide in the text an interpretation of the results which we hope can be understood without reference to the statistical details.

The results are set out in Table 7.6, where we have taken in each case the logarithm of hourly earnings of the son as the variable to be 'explained'. The analysis of the previous chapter may be seen in this context as an attempt to relate the son's earnings solely to the father's earnings, whereas here we are introducing other explanatory variables. This is not entirely correct, since one of the 'new' variables, length of education, we have seen to be related to father's earnings, and the work-experience variables are related to the age adjustment used in Chapter 6.

Let us begin with the work experience variables, where we have defined Exp to be present age minus age at leaving full-time education, and both Exp and its square, denoted by (Exp)^2, appear in all the equations. So for George Banks, who left school at 15 years of age and was interviewed at the age of 32, the work experience is 17 years. From the estimated coefficients in the first column of Table 7.6, we can see that the logarithm of his predicted earnings is:

$$0.044 \times 17 - 0.0008 \times 17^2 = 0.52$$

higher than if he had just started to work. Or his predicted earnings are 68 per cent higher. It should be noted that the work-experience variable is different from age. For Bill James, who went to university, the work-experience variable is eleven years, even though he is the same age as George Banks. The effect may therefore be different from the use of the age adjustment as in Chapter 6. The profile by work experience is plotted in Figure 7.1. It rises sharply in the initial range, with earnings after ten years some 45 per cent higher than at the outset; reaches a peak at twenty-eight years (for example, at age 43, if one leaves school at age 15), where earnings are 86 per cent higher; and then falls to 27 per cent at work experience of fifty years.

The second major variable in equation 1 in Table 7.6 is the length of education. In Chapter 1, we referred to the findings of Psacharopoulos and Layard with regard to the private return to an additional year of schooling in Britain. The coefficient on the length of schooling in Table 7.6, equation 1, indicates that, other things being equal, an extra year is associated with a gain in earnings of about 7 per cent (calculated as $e^{0.066}$

Table 7.6 Multiple regression equations for earnings

| | Dependent variable: logarithm of son's hourly earnings | | | |
	(1)	(2)	(3)	(4)
Constant	−1.327	−0.610	−0.412	−1.107
Years of education	0.066 (0.009)	—	—	0.051 (0.010)
Exp	0.044 (0.006)	0.038 (0.006)	0.042 (0.006)	0.042 (0.006)
$(Exp)^2$	−0.0008 (0.0001)	−0.0007 (0.0001)	−0.0009 (0.0001)	−0.0008 (0.0001)
Logarithm of father's earnings	0.308 (0.104)	0.264 (0.103)	0.301 (0.103)	0.276 (0.103)
Highest attainment:[a]				
apprenticeship	—	0.197 (0.042)	—	—
1–4 O levels or CSE	—	0.098 (0.071)	—	—
5+ O levels or School Certificate	—	0.322 (0.059)	—	—
A levels	—	0.407 (0.100)	—	—
Degree or higher	—	0.688 (0.086)	—	—
Education type:[b]				
secondary or comprehensive	—	—	−0.216 (0.054)	—
grammar or public	—	—	0.038 (0.061)	—
technical	—	—	−0.075 (0.073)	—
college of education	—	—	0.259 (0.116)	—
university	—	—	0.380 (0.095)	—
selective school	—	—	—	0.137 (0.048)
Standard error of estimate	0.285	0.272	0.277	0.281

Notes: The regressions are based on 252 father/son pairs, not grossed. Neither father's earnings nor the earnings of the son are age-adjusted. The logarithms are to base e.
[a] The excluded category consists of those with no qualifications and those for whom qualifications are not known.
[b] The excluded category consists of those last attending primary/elementary or whose school type is not known.

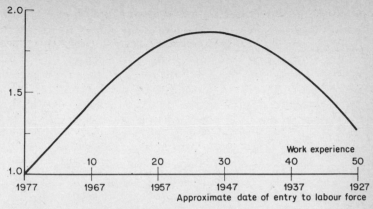

Figure 7.1   Variations of earnings with length of work experience

− 1). The 'other things being equal' includes work experience, so that if we compare George Banks, with 10 years' education, and Bill James, with 16 years' education, then we have:

advantage to Bill because of education   48.6 per cent
'advantage' to George because of work experience   14.2 per cent

The net advantage to Bill is therefore some 30 per cent. On the other hand, we have put 'advantage' in inverted commas in the case of work experience, since this disappears with time, and by his late forties Bill will have caught up in terms of the benefit from work experience, enjoying an overall advantage in excess of 48.6 per cent.

Years of education is only one dimension of the acquisition of 'human capital', and the other equations in Table 7.6 show alternative treatments. Looking first at column 4, we can see that the addition of a selective-school variable to the equation just discussed appears to contribute to the explanation. The positive coefficient indicates that those who had the benefit of selective education, via grammar school or higher education, receive on average 15 per cent higher earnings. On this basis, the educational advantage of Bill James over George Banks is predicted to be 35.8 per cent on account of his longer period of full-time education (the coefficient on years of education is smaller than in column 1) and 15 per cent on account of the selectivity variable, making a total advantage of 56 per cent (calculated as $(1.358 \times 1.15) - 1$).

The relation with the type of full-time education last received is shown in equation 3, where we replace the length of education variable by a categorical variable. This shows the predicted earnings advantage *relative* to the excluded category, which is those who last attended a primary or elementary school or those for whom the type of schooling was not known. This is a rather mixed group. It is therefore on the *differences* in these coefficients that attention is focused. As may be seen, a person attending a grammar/public school, but not going on to higher education, has an advantage compared to a person at a secondary modern of some 29 per cent, and relative to a person at a technical school of some 12 per cent. A person going to a college of education has an advantage of over 60 per cent over the person at a secondary modern, and attending university is associated with a further 13 per cent.

The final dimension of education considered here is the acquisition of qualifications. In equation 2, we show the highest educational attainment, with the excluded category being those with neither qualifications nor apprenticeship or from whom the information is missing. The advantage associated with five or more O levels, or the School Certificate, appears considerable – more than would be indicated by simply considering the additional length of time involved. With A levels and a degree the earnings differential rises steadily. On this basis, Bill James is predicted to earn, with his degree, virtually double the pay of George Banks, who left without qualifications and did not take an apprenticeship.

With the introduction of apprenticeships, we are moving into the variables discussed under the heading of 'labour-market experience'. The coefficient for apprenticeships suggests that the earnings are higher by about 20 per cent, holding other variables constant. This difference is less than that associated with 'good' O levels, but is none the less sizeable. In terms of the return to extra years of education, indicated by equation 1, an apprenticeship is equivalent to about three years.

Finally, in equations not reported here we have examined the effect of leaving York. These suggest that those who have left the city have, on average, earnings which are 17 per cent higher than for those who have stayed; for those who have left Yorkshire and Humberside the effect is slightly larger.

Earnings and family background

For the group of fathers and sons that we are considering, the regression coefficient in a simple regression of the logarithm of son's earnings on father's earnings (again, a logarithm) is around 0.42. From equation 1 in Table 7.6, we can see that the introduction of years of education causes this to fall to around 0.30. This indicates that the indirect relation via education is of importance. In the same way, the equation with the more elaborate qualifications variable, including apprenticeships, shows the coefficient as falling somewhat further, to around 0.26, and the same happens with the introduction of the migration variable (capturing the effect of leaving Yorkshire and

Humberside). At the same time, the coefficient is in all cases more than half the 0.42 from which we began.

Robin Parks and George Banks may again be used to illustrate the magnitude of the relationship. Suppose we take equation 1 first. We have seen that Robin is predicted to receive, on average, one year more education. From the estimated coefficient in Table 7.6, this is associated with an earnings advantage, at the same number of years experience, of 6.8 per cent. The part of the association not related to education, the 'direct' effect, is given by:

$$\left\{\frac{8.50}{5.00}\right\}^{0.308} = 1.178$$

or 17.8 per cent advantage. Taken together, the predicted advantage is 25.8 per cent, with the direct link accounting for the greater part (the total effect is calculated as $(1.178 \times 1.068) - 1$).

Suppose we now include attendance at a selective school. The earlier analysis suggested that the probability of going to a grammar school or higher education was 20 per cent higher for Robin Parks than for George Banks. Taken with the estimated earnings coefficient in Table 7.6, this implies an average advantage of 20 per cent × 15 per cent = 3 per cent. Their differential chances may be summarised (from equation 4) as follows:

one year difference in education	5.2 per cent
selective school	3.0 per cent
'direct' relation with father's earnings	15.8 per cent

The balance has shifted in the direction of the indirect association, but the direct association remains more than half of the total. Moreover, the same is found when one considers other treatments of the links: for example, when earnings are related to qualifications and we make use of the earlier discussion of the probability of acquiring qualifications, or earnings are related to geographical mobility.

As in the analysis of earlier chapters, we need to take account of the measurement error. In addition to the possible error in father's earnings, it is conceivable that the education variables, for example, may be measured with error. Griliches comments that 'one doesn't usually think that such a well defined variable as "years of school completed" could be subject to much recording or recall error. But in cross-sectional household interview data all of the variables are subject to some error' (1977, p. 12). Error may be introduced, for example, where we have failed to allow adequately for gaps in education. Unfortunately, unlike the two-variable case, the multiple regression case where

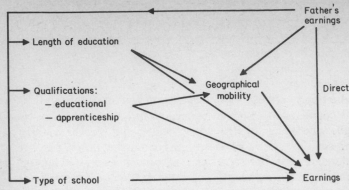

Figure 7.2   The association of earnings from father to son

more than one variable is measured with error does not yield any simple expression for the bias like that given earlier (see p. 86). Moreover, the range of possible assumptions about the measurement errors, and their correlation, becomes considerably wider. This aspect is not pursued here, but it warrants further attention.

Summary
In Figure 7.2 we have summarised the main mechanisms considered in this chapter. In each case we have seen that there appears to be an association – that these are possible links by which earnings advantage or disadvantage may be transmitted from father to son. There remains, however, a great deal to be investigated. We have seen suggestions from our data that the bottom 20 per cent of the earnings range are particularly poorly placed. The role of labour-market opportunities, one vehicle by which the direct effect may operate, needs to be explored. These are among the subjects discussed in the next two chapters.

8 Education and Family Background

Introduction
In this chapter we explore in more detail three aspects of education: selective schooling, staying on at school beyond the minimum school-leaving age, and the level of academic qualifications. These were all considered in the statistical analysis of the previous chapter from fathers and sons, where both were in work when interviewed. Here we take a much larger group. We require that both parents and children be below the retirement age when interviewed (in order to eliminate the most important life-cycle differences), but not that they be in employment. We are including therefore Mrs Hardy, a widow of 45 in 1950, and her sons Norman and John. We also include daughters as well as sons. The resulting sample of 317 sons and 303 daughters is therefore considerably larger than that discussed in Chapter 7. These are ungrossed figures; we shall be referring throughout this chapter to ungrossed numbers, since we are making extensive use of case-study material, where grossing makes little sense.

Family living standards
Our principal concern is with the relation between educational performance and family living standards. In Chapter 7, we took the father's earnings as an indicator, but this cannot be applied to the wider sample considered here. Mrs Hardy, for example, had only her widow's pension and family allowance. The index we use of family income is therefore the National Assistance ratio described in Chapter 5, that is, the ratio of net income minus housing outlay to the National Assistance scale of 'requirements' for a family of that size. We refer to this as the NA ratio.

In Table 8.1 we show the distribution of the 620 families considered in this chapter by ranges of the NA ratio, where each 1950 family appears as many times as they have children in the sample. As is to be expected, the exclusion of the retired reduces the proportion in the lowest ranges: 16 per cent of the 620 are below 140 per cent of NA, compared with 24 per cent in the full sample. From Chapter 5 it may be recalled that Mr and Mrs Parks had a NA ratio of 217, which is somewhat above the median for our sample. We have earlier contrasted them with the Banks family, where 1950 earnings were £5 a week. Adding family allowances, subtracting National Insurance contributions and rent, this gives a NA ratio of 120. One in ten of our sample were in fact below 120 per cent of the NA scale, and this group will receive particular attention (the Banks family being just above the cut-off).

Use of the NA ratio is open to the valid objection that it is influenced by the stage of the life cycle. For this reason, we have also calculated a 'predicted' NA ratio, taking account of the variation with family composition and age. Thus the Parks family, with three children and aged 35, are predicted to have a below-average NA ratio (some 80 per cent of the mean), because of the number of dependants. Seen this way, their actual position is rather more favourable than indicated by a score of 217. The same applies to the Banks family. (Comparisons of the Parks and Banks families are not affected, but life-cycle differences are important where the parents are older or younger or have different commitments, as with Mrs Hardy.) In what follows, we use both the recorded NA ratio and the comparison with the predicted value.

Table 8.1   Living standards of parents in sample considered in Chapter 8

Living standards in 1950	Parents in 1950	
	Number	Percentage
Below National Assistance	33	5.3
100–119%	29	4.7
120–139%	34	5.5
140–159%	51	8.2
160–199%	157	25.3
200–299%	237	38.3
300% or more	79	12.7
Total	620	100.0

Selective Schooling

Out of the 620 sons and daughters considered here, 158, or just over one in four, attended selective education, defined to be grammar school (in one case public school) or full-time higher education. The 158 were split exactly equally between sons and daughters.

Selection and parental living standards

The association between family background and attendance at selective schools, found in Chapter 7 for father's earnings, is also shown when we classify parents according to the NA ratio. From Table 8.2, it may be seen that out of 79 children whose parents were at 300 per cent of the NA scale or above, 27 attended selective schools, or just over a third. The proportion then tends to fall as we move down the income-range.

All those ranges below 200 per cent of the NA scale have a percentage less than the overall average (25.4 per cent). For the bottom group, out of 62 children only 10 enjoyed selective education, or 16.1 per cent. Interestingly, although this group consisted equally of sons and daughters, the latter accounted for seven of the ten with selective education.

Table 8.2   *Attendance at selective schools by parents' NA ratio*

Parents' living standards in 1950 in relation to NA scale (%)	Sons		Daughters		Total	
	Total number	Number (and percentage) attending selective schools	Total number	Number (and percentage) attending selective schools	Total number	Number (and percentage) attending selective schools
less than 120%	31	3 (9.7)	31	7 (22.6)	62	10 (16.1)
120–159%	35	8 (22.9)	50	9 (18.0)	85	17 (20.0)
160–179%	49	13 (26.5)	38	7 (18.4)	87	20 (23.0)
180–199%	40	6 (15.0)	30	6 (20.0)	70	12 (17.1)
200–239%	63	15 (23.8)	54	16 (29.6)	117	31 (26.5)
240–299%	65	19 (29.2)	55	22 (40.0)	120	41 (34.2)
300% or more	34	15 (44.1)	45	12 (26.7)	79	27 (34.2)
Total Percentage	317	79 (24.9)	303	79 (26.1)	620	158 (25.4)

The evidence in Table 8.2 suggests a definite association between parental income and selective education; it does not, however, indicate that the lowest income-group faced particular disadvantage. Those below 120 per cent of the NA scale are not unique in having a lower proportion. This may be illustrated by taking the 95 per cent confidence interval for the overall proportion, which is 22.0–28.8 per cent. For the two lowest ranges (less than 120 per cent and 120–159 per cent) and for the range 180–199 per cent, the percentage attending selective schools is below the lower end of the 95 per cent confidence interval, and for the upper two ranges the percentage attending selective schools is clearly above the upper end of the confidence interval.

The classification in Table 8.2 does not allow for life-cycle differences, but a similar pattern emerges when we consider the NA ratio in relation to that 'predicted', allowing for age and family composition. In the 33 cases where the parents' living standards were 60 per cent or more *below* that predicted, five children went to a selective school, whereas in the 18 cases where parents' living standards were 60 per cent or more *above* the predicted NA value, eight children went to a selective school. For the 569 parents whose living standards differed by less than 60 per cent from the predicted value, 145 children (25.5 per cent) went to a selective school. These results show that for the extreme deviations the correlation is even more marked than with the unadjusted figures.

The consequences of adjusting for differences in age and household composition are brought out when we look in detail at the *type* of school or institution last attended. In Table 8.3 we show the classification into the six types which were discussed in Chapter 7. At first sight, there is little apparent association between the type of school/higher education and parents' living standards. The living standards of the parents of those last attending elementary schools are higher than of those attending colleges of education and are a little below those of people attending grammar schools. When we consider the deviation of the actual NA

Table 8.3 Type of schooling by National Assistance ratio and predicted National Assistance ratio

Type of schooling	Number of children	Mean actual National Assistance ratio	Deviation in National Assistance ratio (mean actual − predicted)	Average age
Elementary	130	223	−12.3	51
Secondary modern	299	201	−1.8	36
Technical	37	198	−2.3	33
Grammar	114	235	12.6	42
College of education	21	216	12.7	34
University	19	245	22.9	35
Total	620	213	−0.14	40

Notes: 1. In four cases a respondent attended a technical school after a grammar school; they are classified as having received selective education, but appear in the 'technical' category above.

   2. The predicted values are estimated from a more extensive sample, so that the mean is different from that of the present sample.

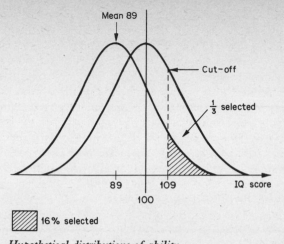

Figure 8.1 *Hypothetical distributions of ability*
Note: To generate a selected proportion of 16 per cent, the distribution (with the same
standard deviation) would have to be 11 points to the left or the overall mean (100).

ratio from that predicted, then the overall gradient is much clearer,
with those attending elementary or secondary modern schools coming
from less well-off backgrounds than those at grammar schools or higher
education. The reason for this change can be found, for instance, in the
greater concentration of the elementary group in the older age-ranges
(see the final column in Table 8.3), where there are higher predicted
NA ratios (which peak at age 47), and amongst those with fewer
children.

Differences in ability
The differing proportions attending selective schools may be a reflection of differential intellectual abilities. This is an aspect on which
we were not able to obtain information, but a hypothetical calculation
may be helpful in forming a view about the effect this could have. (Here
we are drawing on the work of Halsey *et al.*, 1980.)

Suppose that selective schools admitted about a third of the population – a figure based broadly on national proportions – and that
admission was based solely on ability, as measured in a standard
intelligence test. With normally distributed scores on an ability test, a
mean of 100 and a standard deviation of 20, this implies a cut-off score
of 109. Suppose that the same cut-off was applied to the low-income
group. For this to yield a percentage of 16 per cent being selected, the
mean of the ability distribution for this group must be quite a long way
to the left (see Figure 8.1), and we can calculate the mean (if the
standard deviation is the same) as 89. This, in turn, would imply that 17

per cent had a score below 70, which is typically taken as a definition of retardation. Although it is conceivable that the distribution of IQ is so different for the children of low-income families from that for the population as a whole, it is hard to believe. It does not therefore seem likely that ability differences alone could account for observed differences in the proportions attending selective schools.

Low-income families

We now look in more detail at the position of the 62 children whose parents were below 120 per cent of the NA scale in 1950. These children come from 25 families, and in Table 8.4 we summarise some of their main characteristics. The names are of course fictitious. The families are ordered by the number of children covered by our data (in some cases there are other siblings not covered because of non-response, etc.), and within these groups in order of increasing NA ratio.

The first point concerns the relation between the NA scale, used to classify the families, and the predicted value. As may be seen, a large proportion are substantially below the predicted values, indicating that they have relatively low incomes, even when allowance is made for age and family composition. In 17 out of 25 cases, the discrepancy is £1 or more. The main case which would have been classified differently is the large family of the Yves.

The second feature which the table brings out is the preponderance of elderly families at the lowest NA levels (both unadjusted and in terms of deviation from the predicted values). In six cases the head of household was aged 60 or over when interviewed by Rowntree in 1950, and in a further nine cases the household head was aged 50–59. The recorded living standard may differ considerably from that which ruled when the Rowntree child was at school. This is particularly likely to be the case when the effects of the Second World War are taken into account. As may be noted, 26 of the 62 children reached the age of 11 before 1940. We must bear this consideration in mind when drawing conclusions from the earlier statistical analyses.

In terms of individual case-studies, the age differences suggest that we should concentrate on those where the parents were under 50 at the time of the Rowntree interview. Thus we begin by considering the Edwards family, where the son, who was an only child, did not attend a selective school. At the time of the Rowntree interview, he was 2 years old and his mother was a widow (they lived with her mother). Their main source of income was a widow's pension (no National Assistance), and the NA assessment appears a reasonable reflection of the family living standards when he was young. The son went to a secondary modern school, which he left at 15 to enter an apprenticeship.

The second family we consider is that of the Keiths, where the

Table 8.4   Families below 120 per cent of National Assistance scale

Attend selective school?[a]	Family and number and sex of children	Additional details about family circumstances
	1-child families	
	Albert	NA scale 38. £1.77 below predicted.
√	D	No father. Mother aged 58.
	Reached 11 in 1932	Attended GS; left at 16.
	Barry	NA scale 51. £1.58 below predicted.
x	D	No father. Mother aged 59.
	Reached 11 in 1934	Left at 14.
	Charles	NA scale 65. £1.46 below predicted.
√	D	No father. Mother aged 56.
	Reached 11 in 1931	Attended GS; left at 15.
	David	NA scale 66. £5.05 below predicted.
x	D	Father 63. Mother 50.
	Reached 11 in 1953	Left at 15.
	Evans	NA scale 71. £0.78 below predicted.
x	S	No father. Mother aged 28.
	Reached 11 in 1959	Left at 15.
	Fredericks	NA scale 83. £1.30 below predicted.
√	D	No father. Mother aged 50.
	Reached 11 in 1931	Left at 16.
	Grayam	NA scale 86. £3.67 below predicted.
x	D	Father and mother aged 60.
	Reached 11 in 1930	Left at 14.
	Henry	NA scale 87. £3.65 below predicted.
x	S	Father 60. Mother 59.
	Reached 11 in 1939	Left at 15.
	Ivor	NA scale 105. £0.90 below predicted.
x	D	No father. Mother aged 58.
	Reached 11 in 1929	Left at 14.
	Janes	NA scale 112. £0.93 below predicted.
√	S	No father. Mother aged 45.
	Reached 11 in 1932	Attended GS; left at 15.
	2-children families	
	Keith	NA scale 48. £4.08 below predicted.
x√	DD	Father aged 27. Mother's age not known.
	Reached 11 in 1960 and 1968	Left at 15, 16.
	Lance	NA scale 68. £1.44 below predicted.
xx	DS	No father. Mother aged 55.
	Reached 11 in 1931 and 1936	Left at 14, 14.
	Malcolm	NA scale 73. £3.81 below predicted.

Table 8.4   (contd.)

Attend selective school?[a]	Family and number and sex of children	Additional details about family circumstances
xx	SD	Father aged 63. Mother aged 60.
	Reached 11 in 1932	
	and 1933	Left at 14, 14.
	Neville	NA scale 80. £1.46 below predicted.
xx	SS	No father. Mother aged 47.
	Reached 11 in 1934	
	and 1937	Left at 14, 14.
	Oliver	NA scale 86. £0.96 below predicted.
x√	SD	No father. Mother aged 54.
	Reached 11 in 1947	
	and 1953	Left at 15, 16.
	Patrick	NA scale 97. £3.34 below predicted.
xx	SS	Father 62. Mother 60.
	Reached 11 in 1931	
	and 1941	Left at 14, 14.
	Quentin	NA scale 111. £0.50 below predicted.
x√	SD	Father aged 34. Mother aged 29.
	Reached 11 in 1960	
	and 1963	Left at 15, 21[b].
	3-children families	
	Rowland	NA scale 83. £3.85 below predicted.
xxx	SDD	Father aged 45. No mother.
	Reached 11 in 1933,	
	1935 and 1945	Left at 14, 14, 15.
	4-children families	
	Stephens	NA scale 59. £1.50 below predicted.
xxxx	DDDD	No father. Mother aged 58.
	Reached 11 in 1927,	
	1928, 1931, 1933	Left at 14, 14, 14, 14.
	Thomas	NA scale 116. £2.92 below predicted.
xxxx	SDSS	Father aged 62. Mother's age not known.
	Reached 11 in 1928,	
	1933, 1940, 1943	Left at 14, 14, 14, 14.
	Urwin	NA scale 119. £2.83 below predicted.
xxxx	SDDS	Father aged 42. Mother aged 37.
	Reached 11 in 1946,	
	1948, 1952, 1958	Left at 15, 15, 15, 15.
	5-children families	
	Victor	NA scale 115. £0.89 below predicted.
xxxxx	DSSDS	No father. Mother aged 47.
	Reached 11 in 1936,	

Table 8.4 (contd.)

Attend selective school?[a]	Family and number and sex of children	Additional details about family circumstances
	1940, 1942, 1943, 1945	Left at 14, 14, 14, 14, 14.
	Williams	NA scale 118. £1.71 below predicted.
x√√x√	SSSSD	Father aged 43. Mother aged 35.
	Reached 11 in 1949, 1952, 1954, 1957, 1965	Left at 15, 25[b], 23[b], 16, 16.
	6-children family	
	Xavier	NA scale 95. £0.75 below predicted.
xxxxxx	SSSDSD	No father. Mother aged 55.
	Reached 11 in 1930, 1933, 1941, 1945, 1948, 1952	Left at 14, 14, 14, 15, 16, 15.
	7-chilren family	
	Yves	NA scale 113. £0.52 above predicted.
xxxxxxx	SDSDSDD	Father aged 41. Mother aged 36.
	Reached 11 in 1942, 1945, 1947, 1950, 1954, 1956, 1958	Left at 14, 15, 15, 15, 15, 15, 15.

Notes: [a] √ Attended selected school.
  x Did not attend selected school.
  Where there is more than one child in the family, the symbols are listed according to birth order.
  [b] Partook of higher education.
  S = son, D = daughter.
  (All names are fictitious.)

youngest of the three daughters (Pauline) attended a grammar school, but the middle one went to a secondary modern. (The eldest child did not respond to the survey.) In 1950, Mr Keith was out of work, and receiving National Insurance sickness benefit. This means that the NA assessment may not have been representative, but the schedule records a history of ill health. Around 1955 he obtained a job at Rowntrees and worked there steadily for fourteen years, and then worked at the glassworks from 1969 (information from daughter). This may have been relevant to the differential experience of Patricia (aged 6 in 1955) compared with Pauline, who was born in 1957 and who went to grammar school in 1968.

Thirdly, there is the Urwin family where none of the four children attended a selective school. In 1950 Mr Urwin was working as a coal-filler, earning £5.44 a week, and this, together with family allowances, was the sole source of income. The children were then aged 15, 13, 9 and 3. The eldest child attended secondary modern school and reported long periods of interruption due to bronchitis. The others also attended secondary modern schools.

The Williams family, with five children, had no fewer than three at selective schools. In 1950, the father was off work as a result of a war injury, and received a war pension and National Assistance; there were four children, aged 12, 9, 7 and 4 (the other was born after 1950). At that time the father had not worked for seven years, so that the National Assistance assessment may be taken as a reasonable guide to the standard of living over a longish period. One child attended a secondary modern school. The fact that three attended selective schools is striking, but possibly rather special in that they were religious schools.

Finally, there is the Yves family, with seven children covered by our sample, and nine children in all. In 1950, Mr Yves was working at Rowntrees for £6.20 a week, and supporting six children under the age of 16. The third eldest child was at work (the other two had left home already). Of the nine children, not one went to a selective school. The older two went to elementary school, the others to secondary modern, and all left at the minimum school-leaving age. The children of this family appear to have derived the minimum benefit from the educational system.

Summary

The results of the previous chapter suggested a definite association between father's earnings and the proportion attending selective education; the bottom 20 per cent of the earning range were especially disadvantaged (the percentage being 18 per cent). The findings in this section, using the National Assistance ratio as an indicator of family position, bear out the existence of an association, although there does not appear to be a marked difference between the low-income group (those below 120 per cent) and those immediately above. Of the 62 families below 120 per cent of the NA scale, only 10 (or 16 per cent) attended selective schools, and the percentage does not rise much above 20 per cent until we reach families with 200 per cent of the NA scale or more. In families above 240 per cent of the NA scale, over a third of the children attended selective schools. Put another way, the average NA ratio for those attending selective schools is some 13 percentage points above that predicted, given their age and family composition. It is conceivable that these differences could be accounted for solely by differences in performance on IQ tests, but the implied distribution of scores is not a plausible one. Ability undoubtedly has a role in the explanation, but it cannot be the only factor at work.

In this chapter we are also considering the position of daughters, and we noted that the proportion attending selective schools was similar. For those below 120 per cent of the NA scale, the daughters at selective schools outnumbered the sons (seven to three), but the case-studies did not suggest any obvious reason for this. The details of the low-income families (those below 120 per cent) did, however, point to the role of ill health and interruption of school attendance, and to the possibility that disadvantage may run in families.

Staying on at School

For most of our respondents, the effective minimum school-leaving age was 14 or 15, and only 31.6 per cent stayed on at school beyond the age of 15. In contrast to attendance at selective schools, the proportion for sons (37 per cent) is substantially higher than that for daughters (26 per cent). Out of the 620, only 56 (9.0 per cent) stayed on to the age of 18 and/or went on to higher education. Again, the proportion is higher for sons: 35 out of the 56 were sons.

Staying on and parental living standards

The relation between age of leaving full-time education and parental income is shown in Table 8.5. If we consider the proportion leaving at 15 or younger, then we see a definite difference between the bottom two groups (less than 120 per cent and 120–159 per cent of NA scale) and the remainder. The 95 per cent confidence interval for the overall proportion is 64.7–72.1 per cent, and those below 160 per cent of the NA scale are well outside this interval. Of the low-income group (below 120 per cent), only 10 out of 62 stayed on at school until the age of 16 or older, and 83.9 per cent left at 15 or younger. Above 160 per cent of the NA scale, there is no evident pattern. The position may therefore be summarised as indicating a difference between the lowest income-groups and the rest of the respondents, rather than a steady progression with income.

Of the 147 children from the bottom two ranges (below 160 per cent of the NA scale), only four stayed on to age 18 or went on to higher education. If they had had the same experience as the average for our sample, then this number would have been 13; the difference is a measure of the disadvantage. Above 160 per cent of the NA scale, the percentage leaving at 18 or older does not seem to be related to parental income.

As we have seen, the proportion of sons staying on beyond 15 is higher than that for daughters, and this is true for all except the lowest income-group. The same applies to staying on to 18 +.

Allowing for the effect of age and family composition and making use of the predicted NA ratio, as in the previous section, we can divide the

Table 8.5 Family background and length of schooling

Parents' living standards in 1950 in relation to NA scale (%)	Sons						Daughters						Total					
	Leaving at 15 or less		Leaving at 16 or 17		Leaving at 18+		Leaving at 15 or less		Leaving at 16 or 17		Leaving at 18+		Leaving at 15 or less		Leaving at 16 or 17		Leaving at 18+	
	No.	(%)	No.	(%)	No.	(%)	No.	(%)	No.	(%)	No.	(%)	No.	(%)	No.	(%)	No.	(%)
Less than 120%	27	(87.1)	2	(6.5)	2	(6.5)	25	(80.6)	5	(16.1)	1	(3.2)	52	(83.9)	7	(11.3)	3	(4.8)
120–159%	23	(65.7)	12	(34.3)	0	(0)	41	(82.0)	8	(16.0)	1	(2.0)	64	(75.3)	20	(23.5)	1	(1.2)
160–179%	31	(63.3)	14	(28.6)	4	(8.2)	28	(73.7)	6	(15.8)	4	(10.5)	59	(67.8)	20	(23.0)	8	(9.2)
180–199%	20	(50.0)	14	(35.0)	6	(15.0)	23	(76.7)	5	(16.7)	2	(6.7)	43	(61.4)	19	(27.1)	8	(11.4)
200–239%	39	(61.9)	12	(19.0)	12	(19.0)	37	(68.5)	13	(24.1)	4	(7.4)	76	(65.0)	25	(21.4)	16	(13.7)
240–299%	41	(63.1)	16	(24.6)	8	(12.3)	35	(63.6)	16	(29.1)	4	(7.3)	76	(63.3)	32	(26.7)	12	(10.0)
300% or more	19	(55.9)	12	(35.3)	3	(8.9)	35	(77.8)	5	(11.1)	5	(11.1)	54	(68.4)	17	(21.5)	8	(10.1)
Total	200	(63.1)	82	(25.9)	35	(11.0)	224	(73.9)	58	(19.1)	21	(6.9)	424	(68.4)	140	(22.6)	56	(9.0)

Note: The percentages are the ratio of the number in that cell to the total in that range of living standards (given in Table 8.2).

Table 8.6   Length of education and predicted NA ratio

| | Children leaving school aged | | | | | Total |
| | 15 or less | | 16–17 | 18+ | | |
	No.	(%)		No.	(%)	
75p or more *below* predicted	147	(74.6)	36	14	(7.1)	197
within 75p of predicted	181	(67.0)	66	23	(8.5)	270
75p or more *above* predicted	96	(62.7)	38	19	(12.4)	153
Total	424	(68.4)	140	56	(9.0)	620

respondents into three groups according to the deviation from the 'predicted' level, as shown in Table 8.6. We have taken those who are 75 pence or more above or below the predicted level, where 75 pence represents some 60 per cent of the single person's NA scale. Again, there is a clear difference between the 'low' group and the sample as a whole; and the 'high' group appear in this case to do noticeably better than the average. The proportion leaving school aged 15 or younger in the case of the 'high' group is outside the 95 per cent confidence interval for the overall proportion (and that for the 'low' group is similarly above the upper end of the confidence interval). It may be that the association between length of education and age means that the unadjusted NA ratios used in Table 8.5 fail to bring out the gradient with parental income. The lack of any apparent relationship with the NA ratio above 160 per cent in Table 8.5 may be due to the fact that those with higher NA ratios tend to be older and, other things being equal, their children are likely to have had a shorter education.

Staying on and type of school
The proportion of children staying on at school is much higher at selective schools. Of the 158 at selective schools, according to the definition we are using, 132 stayed on beyond the age of 15 and 47 stayed on to age 18 or older. This means that 83.5 per cent of those at selective schools stayed on beyond 15, compared with 13.9 per cent for those at non-selective schools.

This – scarcely surprising – difference leads one to ask whether the shorter duration of education for children from low-income backgrounds is a reflection of the smaller proportion attending selective schools, or whether they suffer additional disadvantage within each type of school. In the mid-1950s, the Central Advisory Council for

Education, in its report *Early Leaving* (1954), drew attention to the high rate of academic failure among the children from unskilled manual workers' homes who did enter grammar schools: 'of about 4360 children from unskilled workers' homes who entered grammer schools, only about 1500 obtained the benefit that the grammar school is specifically designed to give'. The authors went on to note the influence of physical conditions (particularly housing), attitudes of parents and teachers, and incentives for the children, and the differences between boys and girls. Similarly, Floud, Halsey and Martin wrote that when 'we consider those [unskilled manual workers'] children who in fact succeed in reaching the grammar schools, we see that what differentiates them most sharply from other children is the shortness of their school careers' (1956, p. 207).

In order to explore this, we can carry out some simple arithmetic. Let us divide the respondents by ranges of parental income, and assume that the proportion staying on beyond the age of 15 was determined solely by type of school (selective or non-selective) and not related to parental income. This gives a hypothetical 'income-independent' number staying on. For example, of the 62 below 120 per cent of the NA scale, 10 attended selective schools. The 'income-independent' number staying on is then:

$$83.5\% \times 10 + 13.9\% \times 52 = 15.6$$

The actual number staying on, from Table 8.5, is 10, or only about two-thirds.

The results of this calculation are shown in Table 8.7. From this it does appear that the children of low-income families had a disadvantage at selective schools. The families with the lowest incomes have a smaller

Table 8.7   Staying on and type of school

Parents' living standards in 1950 in relation to NA scale (%)	Number of children staying on at school beyond the age of 15			
	'Income-independent' number	Actual number	Non-selective schools	Selective schools
less than 120%	15.6	10	2 out of 52	8 out of 10
120–159%	23.6	21	5 out of 68	16 out of 17
160% and above	156.8	165	57 out of 342	108 out of 131
Total	196.0	196	64 out of 462	132 out of 158

proportion staying on than would be predicted on an 'income in-dependent' basis. From the group below 160 per cent of the NA scale, there is a 'loss' of some eight children who could have been expected to stay on and who did not do so. It is, however, interesting to note from the right-hand part of Table 8.7 that the disadvantage seems to be within the non-selective sector. Of the 120 children from below 160 per cent of the NA scale attending non-selective schools, only 7 stayed on beyond the age of 15, whereas 57 out of 342 stayed on from families above 160 per cent of NA – or exactly one in six. This suggests that better-off families may have been able to compensate, at least in part, for the disadvantage of their children's failure at the age of 11 to enter a selective school, by allowing them to stay on or to take further edu-cation.

Low-income families

We now look in more detail at the position of the families at the bottom of the income scale. The case-studies set out in Table 8.4 provide some information about the educational experience of children whose parents were below 120 per cent of the NA scale. As we have seen, they derived limited benefit from the educational system. Indeed only 13 out of 62 stayed on beyond the minimum school-leaving age (this was 14 years of age in the early part of the period and 16 years at the end, so that it is not the same as leaving beyond the age of 15). These cases are indicated in Table 8.4 by printing the school-leaving age in italic. One of the six Xavier children and none of the Yves children, for example, stayed on beyond the minimum leaving-age. It is also interesting to note the comments recorded in one case by Rowntree and Lavers (1951, p. 63):

Husband complains of having to keep children at school until age of 15. He says that not only ought they to be earning, but that in their last year at school they demand pocket money.

Of the ten children attending selective schools, two left at the age of 15, five left at age 16 and three stayed on to 18 or went into higher education. In order to explore further the position of low-income families attending selective schools, we provide brief descriptions of three case-studies from this group and from those in the range 120–149 per cent of the NA scale. The latter brought in a further fifteen children (from ten families). The parents of the latter tended to be younger; all the heads of household were in fact under 50 years of age and seven were aged 40 or younger. It seems reasonable to suppose therefore that the living standards recorded in the 1950 survey were close, at least in time, to those ruling when the children were at school. These children as a whole exhibited the pattern we have described: 22 of the 25 stayed on until the age of 16, but the majority left at that age; only four stayed on until the age of 18.

The first family is the Olivers from Table 8.4, who in fact had seven children (only two provided sufficient details to be included in the sample used in this chapter). Three at least of the daughters attended grammar school. One left at 14, having missed a substantial period of schooling at the age of 10 because of scarlet fever. Another, the daughter included in Table 8.4, also missed 18 months' schooling because of illness. This meant that she would have had to stay on at school until she was 17 years old to take O levels. She decided not to, and left at 16 without any qualifications.

Ill health and absence from school was mentioned by a number of families. The Ambleside family consisted of five children and had a 1950 NA assessment of 132 (at that time four of the children had been born and were aged between 1 and 11 years). One of the children attended grammar school, but reported several months' absence at the age of 11 due to pneumonia. He, like his brothers and sisters at secondary modern school, left at the age of 15. One of the sisters missed a few months as a result of an accident. Another reported that her schooling had been adversely affected by frequent changes of school (for example, she was moved to a new secondary modern which had just been opened).

For the Ambleside family, leaving school at 15 years of age meant the end of formal education. A rather different pattern is illustrated by the Quentin family. In 1950 Mr Quentin was relatively low paid, and had six children to support (one was born subsequently). After that he was promoted and reached a senior position in his firm, so that the family's standard of living no doubt improved considerably in relative terms. Of the six surviving children (we only have the information required for Table 8.4 in two cases), five attended secondary modern schools. However, of these four went on to the York School of Commerce or to Technical College and stayed until age 18, acquiring qualifications. One went on to university, and her qualifications are in fact greater than those of the youngest daughter, who went to grammar school and teaching training college. For this family, with 24 O levels, two teaching qualifications, and a degree, between them, the fact that five out of six went to secondary modern schools does not appear to have been a major bar. This brings us to the question of educational qualifications, which is the subject of the next section.

Summary
The evidence in this section reinforces the findings in Chapter 7 that children from low-income families are likely to spend a shorter time in full-time education. The straightforward analysis in terms of the

parents' NA ratios indicated a marked difference between those below 160 per cent and the remainder in terms of the proportions staying on at school. This needs to be interpreted carefully in the light of the tendency for the length of schooling to rise over time, but the evidence – from a comparison of the NA ratio with the predicted value, allowing for differences in age and family composition – suggests that the percentage staying on at school increases steadily with income.

The tendency for children from low-income families to leave school early was related to school type. Interestingly, we found that the children of low-income families at selective schools were just as likely to stay on to age 16 or later. There appeared, for this group, to be no additional disadvantage – in contrast to the findings quoted earlier. However, among those at non-selective schools, the proportion staying on appeared definitely to be associated with income. As was brought out in one of the case-studies, the opportunity existed to recover from failure of the eleven-plus – either by staying on, or by attending commercial college, etc. – but the extent to which advantage was taken of this opportunity appeared to be related to family background. A further feature which may have influenced staying on, and school performance generally, was ill health; in some cases this led to protracted absences.

Academic Qualifications
The vast majority of our respondents had no academic qualifications (we are not including apprenticeships): 231 sons and 241 daughters. Of the remainder, 105 (57 sons and 48 daughters) had CSE awards or some O levels, and 42 had A levels or higher qualifications. (In one case, the qualifications are not known, and the analysis in this section relates to 619 cases.)

Qualifications and parental living standards
In Table 8.8, we show the relationship between parental incomes and academic qualifications, distinguishing between three categories. The higher group clearly covers a wide range, from Mr Lloyd with one A level to Dr Needham with a Ph.D. Later, we consider specifically those with degrees.

The association with family income is brought out clearly by the proportion with no qualifications, which is more than 85 per cent for those whose parents were below 160 per cent of the NA scale, and around 70 per cent for the upper ranges. If we take as a yardstick the 95 per cent confidence interval for the overall proportion, then this is 72.9–79.6 per cent. The lowest two ranges are clearly above this; and in broad terms the upper three groups are either at the lower value or below it. In the case of sons and daughters, the proportions are more or

Table 8.8 Family background and academic qualifications

Parents' living standards in 1950 in relation to NA scale (%)	Sons				Daughters				Total			
	No qualifications		CSE or O levels	A levels or higher	No qualifications		CSE or O levels	A levels or higher	No qualifications		CSE or O levels	A levels or higher
	No.	(%)			No.	(%)			No.	(%)		
Less than 120%	29	(93.5)	0	2	27	(87.1)	4	0	56	(90.3)	4	2
120–159%	28	(80.0)	6	1	45	(90.0)	4	1	73	(85.9)	10	2
160–179%	36	(73.5)	10	3	30	(78.9)	6	2	66	(75.9)	16	5
180–199%	25	(62.5)	10	5	27	(90.0)	2	1	52	(74.3)	12	6
200–239%	44	(69.8)	8	11	39	(72.2)	13	2	83	(70.9)	21	13
240–299%	48	(75.0)	11	5	39	(70.9)	13	3	87	(73.1)	24	8
300 or more	21	(61.8)	12	1	34	(75.6)	6	5	55	(69.6)	18	6
Total	231	(73.1)	57	28	241	(79.5)	48	14	472	(76.3)	105	42

less at the lower and upper limits of this interval. For five of the seven income-ranges, the proportion with no qualifications is lower for sons than for daughters.

As with length of education, there has been a rise over time in the proportion acquiring qualifications, and the evidence needs to be interpreted with this in mind. Suppose that we consider the 316 sons, and divide them into the three age cohorts used in earlier analyses. Further, let us consider those at or above 160 per cent of the NA scale and those below. The latter group we have seen to have a much higher overall proportion with no qualifications: 86.4 per cent against 69.6 per cent for the remainder. If we now consider the age cohorts separately, then we obtain the following figures:

	Percentage with no qualifications		
	aged less than 35	*aged over 35–44*	*aged 35–44*
Parents' NA ratio less than 160%	81.0	78.3	100.0
Parents' NA ratio 160% or above	59.6	76.9	75.6
Total number	120	88	108

For the middle age-group, there is no effective difference, but – interestingly – the relative differential is virtually the same for the other two cohorts. The proportion with no qualifications is a third higher for those whose parents were below 160 per cent of the NA scale.

Qualifications and type of school

The proportion with no qualifications is very much lower at selective schools. Of the 158 at such schools, only 41 (or 25.9 per cent) had no qualifications, whereas at non-selective schools 431 out of 461 (or 93.5 per cent) were in this position. A quarter of those at selective schools went on to study for A levels or higher qualifications, compared with only 1 per cent of those at non-selective schools.

Of the 30 who did finish non-selective education with some academic qualifications, only one came from a family where the parents' income was below 160 per cent of the NA scale, and 13 came from families above 200 per cent of the NA scale. Put another way, of the 120 families from below 160 per cent of the NA scale with children at non-selective school, only one acquired O levels or CSE qualifications; whereas of the 216 families with children at the same type of school, but with incomes of 200 per cent of the NA scale or higher, 15 acquired qualifications. This again brings out the ability of better-off families to 'recover' from the disadvantage of failing the eleven-plus. In terms of our case-studies, it is illustrated by the Quentin family. Mr Quentin's economic standing undoubtedly improved after the 1950 interview, and his children – in contrast, say, to those of the Ambleside family – were able to obtain a variety of qualifications, despite the fact that five out of six went to secondary modern schools.

What about the experience of low-income families at selective schools? In terms of staying at school until the age of 16, we found no apparent disadvantage, but this does not seem to apply to the acquisition of qualifications. There were 27 children from families below 160 per cent of the NA scale at selective schools, and of these 10 failed to obtain qualifications: that is, 37 per cent rather than 26 per cent. In effect, three of the ten missed out on the qualifications which they would have got, if their experience of selective education had been the same as the overall average.

Higher education and degrees

Of the 62 respondents from the families below 120 per cent of the NA scale, whose educational histories we have summarised in Table 8.4, only three went on to higher education. Rachel Quentin and two of the sons from the Williams family went to teacher training college, and are qualified teachers. This has, of course, traditionally been an avenue for upward mobility, although in the case of the Quentin family we have noted that their financial circumstances appear to have improved after 1950, so that they may be more appropriately classified higher up the scale.

None of these children acquired degrees. In the present sample of 619 there are in fact 19 with degrees, from universities, polytechnics and teacher training colleges (B.Ed.). In the follow-up study as a whole, there are 25, with sons predominating (21 sons, compared with 4 daughters). Those with degrees are mostly young. Of the 25 in the whole study, nine are aged 20–29, ten are 30–39 and only six are aged 40 and over. This is a reflection of the trend towards higher qualifications, and it should be borne in mind that a number obtained their qualifications after the normal age, either returning to full-time study or via the Open University. Mr Rotheram, for example, had trained as a draughtsman, but at the time of the interview was close to completing an Open University degree course. His wife, too, had taken a degree, in this case a full-time course, some twenty years after she left school.

For the Rotherams, parental income is not likely to have been a relevant factor, but for those going on to higher education straight from school, the ability to finance further study may well have been affected. For the 19 respondents with degrees in our sample, the NA ratios of their parents were (in increasing order): 138, 167, 171, 180, 185, 203,

206, 209, 210, 217, 226, 244 (brother and sister), 265, 276, 290, 293, 322 and 350. It is the case therefore that only one came from a family below 160 per cent of NA. This was the Griffiths family, where Mr Griffiths earned £4.50 a week in 1950, on which he had to support his wife and two children; this gave an NA ratio of 138, when allowance was made for National Insurance contributions and his mortgage. The majority of those with degrees came from families over 200 per cent of the NA scale. For example, the James family, where the father earned £8.50 as a skilled craftsman in 1950 (their NA ratio was 217), are more typical than the Griffiths.

Summary

The results of this chapter have, in part, reinforced those of Chapter 7. Using a wider sample, and a different indicator of economic status, we have again shown the association between family background and education. The case-studies, focusing in particular on families below 120 per cent of the NA scale, have – we hope – provided a useful complement to the statistical analyses. They have also illuminated certain aspects not covered in the earlier treatment, including the influence of ill health and the extent to which children from the same family have common educational experience.

The findings in part, take us further in our knowledge about the links and the degree of association. Chapter 7 was concerned exclusively with sons; here we have considered both sons and daughters. From the families in our sample, it appears that the proportions attending selective schools are similar; but when it comes to staying on at school

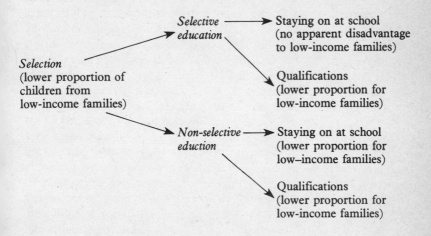

Figure 8.2 Disadvantage to children from low-income families of selective education

or to the acquisition of qualifications, then sons come out better. The proportion staying on beyond the age of 15 is 37 per cent for sons compared with 26 per cent for daughters. Of the nineteen with degrees, sixteen are sons and three daughters. These patterns are reproduced fairly broadly across ranges of parental income; the main noticeable exception is that daughters outnumber sons among children from low-income families attending selective schools.

One of the most interesting findings concerns the stages at which the relation with family income appears to arise. The conclusions about the disadvantage to the children from low-income families can only be tentative, since there are a number of other factors which may be at work, but they may be summarised as in Figure 8.2. If disadvantage is indeed transmitted in this way, then it evidently has implications for educational policy.

9 The York Labour-Market And Employment Opportunities

Introduction

The majority of our respondents left school at 16 years old or younger, with the minimum of academic qualifications. How did their subsequent earnings depend on the labour-market they entered and the employment opportunities open to them in the early stages of their working lives? Their labour-market experience will have differed considerably. Some will have entered in the 1930s, in conditions like those described in Walter Greenwood's *Love on the Dole*; some will have started out in the 1950s of John Braine's *Room at the Top*; and still others will have first looked for jobs in the less confident 1970s of David Lodge's *Changing Places*. The local labour-market, too, will have been different. For the majority, it was York, or at least Yorkshire and Humberside. But for some it was Kent, Surrey, Sussex or London (not California, since the overseas respondents are excluded).

In this chapter, we concentrate on a group for whom the age differences are not so marked: those aged 25–44 at the time of interview. This excludes all those who entered the labour-market before 1945 and all those who were too young when interviewed to have had any substantial labour-market experience. We also pay particular attention to those still resident in York, although we do not concentrate exclusively on this group. Finally, we consider solely the position of men, taking the sons and sons-in-law of the original families. By choosing a relatively more homogeneous subsample for study in this chapter, we hope to bring out some of the ways in which features of the labour-market are related to economic success.

The 'labour-market sample'

The sample analysed in this chapter consists of all second-generation families with a male head of household aged between 25 and 44 at the date of interview. Given the method of selection, we should expect to find more sons than sons-in-law (since unmarried daughters are excluded). There are in fact 263 sons and 215 sons-in-law, making a total of 478. Of these, 70 per cent were included in the families discussed in the previous chapter, and 286 (60 per cent) appeared in both Chapters 7 and 8. There is therefore considerable overlap between the samples, but there are still a sizeable number whose experiences have not so far entered the anlysis: 70 of the 478 were covered neither by Chapter 7 nor

Chapter 8. (All these figures are ungrossed, as are all those given below unless otherwise specified.)

The labour-market sample is, by definition, younger than the full set of respondents, and may be expected to differ in a number of characteristics. Comparison with the full sample shows that those considered in this chapter are more likely to have dependent children. Most heads of household are employed, with a standard of living likely to be in the middle ranges. They are more likely to have moved away from York than the sample as a whole. The parents of the sample, by virtue of its method of selection, are also more likely to have been in the middle earnings and income ranges in 1950, and the 1950 household is likely to have composed a married couple with the head of household in work and young children at home. At the same time, despite the fact that both generations are at a relatively favourable stage of the life cycle (compared at least with retirement), there are significant numbers with low standards of living.

Apprenticeships

The fact that the labour-market sample is younger means that they are more likely to leave full-time education with academic qualifications. For the 478 sons and sons-in-law, we have information on qualifications for 450. Of these, 17 had qualifications from higher education, 21 had A levels as their highest qualification, and 83 had O levels. As we have seen in Chapter 7, these academic qualifications are associated, other things being equal, with a higher expected level of earnings. Our main concern here, however, is with the 329 who left school without qualifications of O-level standard or higher.

Possibly the most important distinction is between those school-leavers who enter an apprenticeship and those who do not benefit from such training. Of course, it would be wrong to draw a rigid dividing line between jobs that offer a formal apprenticeship and those that provide substantial on-the-job training. But we have seen that the formal completion of an apprenticeship is associated with an estimated average earnings advantage of 20 per cent more than those without this formal qualification. In Chapter 7, we saw that the proportion with an apprenticeship was considerably lower where the father was in the bottom 20 per cent of the earnings distribution. We now explore in more detail the relation with parental income.

Apprenticeships and family income

Of the 329 without O levels or better, 92 had completed an apprenticeship. If we consider how this was related to the family income as measured by the NA ratio, then we find some tendency for families below 160 per cent of the NA scale to be less likely to have apprenticed their children. On the basis of the overall proportion (28.8 per cent), we would have expected that out of 95 families below this level, 27 of the sons and sons-in-law would have served apprenticeships, whereas the actual number was 19.

By considering sons and sons-in-law together, however, we are quite possibly confounding two separate aspects of the intergenerational transmission process: the access to training based on family background and the pattern of marriage. It may therefore be helpful to consider the position of sons on their own. To begin with those whose parents were below 120 per cent of the NA scale, there were 11 families with 25 sons (see Table 9.1). Some of these families have been included in the discussion of the previous chapter, but the restriction of the sample to those aged 25–44 means that some are excluded, and families with only daughters do not appear. As the case-studies show, the experience is rather varied. The Yves family had three sons included and none completed an apprenticeship (nor had other qualifications); the Aston family typified the average for the group, with one of the five sons serving an apprenticeship; but the Williams family show that the outcome can be very different, since two of the four sons completed apprenticeships and two secured A levels. The history of the Williams family illustrates a further point – that in some cases an apprenticeship may act as a constraint rather than as an opportunity. Harold Williams, the eldest son, had felt parental pressure to leave school and take up an apprenticeship, whereas two of his brothers had been able to stay on at school. As a result, when he was interviewed Harold earned only about two-thirds as much as his brother who had become a schoolteacher.

Excluding the six sons who had academic qualifications, or for whom information is missing, there are 19 in the first part of Table 9.1, of whom six had served apprenticeships. This is, in fact, slightly higher than would have been expected on the basis of the overall proportion. The same is true of those between 120 per cent and 160 per cent of the NA scale, shown in the second part of Table 9.1. Excluding the nine sons where the information is missing, and the eight with educational qualifications, there were 29 sons, of whom twelve served apprenticeships.

A second aspect on which the case-studies cast some light is the pattern *within* families. To the extent that families convey an advantage in securing training, this may benefit all sons equally or it may be confined to one or two of them. As with the transmission of wealth, we may find a pattern of equal division or there may be a system of primogeniture, with the family estate passing to one child, typically the eldest son. The evidence in Table 9.1 is mixed. The Nottingham and Quarmby families provided support for the view that access to apprenticeships runs in families and is shared; and the four Williams sons all

Family	Industry of head of household (1950)	Qualifications (birth order)	Total sons in sub-sample
Families below 120 per cent of NA scale			
Evans		App (1)	1
Bedford		None (2), None (3)	2
Cromer		Educ (2)	1
Oliver		None (6)	1
Aston		None (8), None (10), None (11), App (12), None (13)	5
Xavier		DK (5), App (7)	2
Quentin	Confectionery	Educ (1), Educ (2), App (4)	3
Yves	Confectionery	None (4), None (6), None (8)	3
Victor		None (5)	1
Williams		App (1), Educ (2), Educ (3), App (4)	4
Urwin	Distribution	None (1), None (4)	2
Total			25 (of which 1 DK)
Families 120–159 per cent of NA scale			
Derby		None (2)	1
Exeter	Distribution	Educ (2)	1
Fulham	Misc. services	DK (2)	1
Gillingham		Educ (1)	1
Hertford	Railways	None (2), None (5)	2
Imber	Construction	None (2)	1
Johnston		Educ (2)	1
Keighley	Railways	DK (2), None (3)	2
Lancaster	Construction	DK (1), DK (2)	2
Manchester	Misc services	None (3)	1
Nottingham	Glass	App (1), App (2)	2
Oundle	Construction	None (1), Educ (2), App (4)	3
Petersfield	Printing	DK (1), DK (2), DK (3)	3
Quarmby	Confectionery	App (1), App (4)	2
Russell	Confectionery	Educ (3), None (4)	2
Salford	Railways	None (1), App (2), App (3)	3
Tyne	Confectionery	App (1)	1
Upham	Professional services	App (1)	1
Vancouver	Public admin.	App (1)	1
Westfield		None (2)	1
Aberdeen	Confectionery	None (1), App (2), None (3)	3
Ball	Confectionery	None (1)	1
Canvey		Educ (1), Educ (3)	2

Table 9.1 (contd.)

Family	Industry of head of household (1950)	Qualifications (birth order)	Total sons in sub-sample
Dorset	Distribution	App (3)	1
Essex	Public admin.	DK (1), DK (2)	2
France	Misc. services	None (4), None (5)	2
Grattan	Professional services	Educ (1), None (2), None (3)	3
Total			46 (of which 9 DK)

Note: None = No qualification.
      Educ = O level or higher academic qualification.
      App = Apprenticeship.
      DK = Information not available (i.e. don't know).
(All names are fictitious.)

seem to have derived some advantage. However, in the case of the Salfords, only two of the three sons served apprenticeships, and it was the eldest that missed out. Similarly, in the Oundle and Aberdeen families, the eldest son did not serve an apprenticeship, but a younger brother had that advantage.

Apprenticeships and father's employment

Any advantage transmitted to the children in terms of securing access to training may result from the general effect of higher economic status or it may be a specific influence via the father's place of employment. Is it easier for a son to enter a firm or trade in which his father is employed? In order to explore this possibility, we consider the pattern by the industry in which the father was employed in 1950 (which is not, of course, necessarily the industry in which he was working when his son entered the labour force).

Given the nature of employment in York in 1951, it is scarcely surprising that there is considerable concentration. Taking the 'distinct' fathers in work in 1950, we find that of the 248 in total, no fewer than 76 were employed by British Rail, either by the railway itself or in the wagon and coach works. A further 41 were employed in food, drink and tobacco. This industrial category includes British Sugar's processing plant, but it was dominated by the confectionery firms of Rowntrees, Terrys and Cravens. It is on these two industries, which account for nearly half of the employment for the labour-market sample, that we concentrate.

In the case-studies in Table 9.1, we have shown the industry in which the father worked (in a sizeable number of cases the father was not in work or there was no father). The numbers involved, however, are not sufficient to allow us to draw any conclusion. Therefore in Table 9.2 we have summarised the position for the sons in the entire labour-market sample where the father was employed in British Rail (BR) or the confectionery industry.

In their report on the 1950 survey, Rowntree and Lavers claim that there is little apparent association between employment and economic status. Their examples of the jobs done by people in the three classes above the poverty line (1951, p. 69) show British Rail employees in all three classes. There are hints in the case-studies, however, that families where the father worked on the railways were often better placed. In the case of Mr Bootham, who earned £9.26 a week, Rowntree and Lavers commented that the 'family circumstances [were] very good. Parents hope it may be possible for both children to go to university' (1951, p. 77). In the event, this ambition was not realised, and indeed the results in Table 9.2 suggest that the proportion with educational qualifications was not especially high (for all sons and sons-in-law, it was 29 per cent). What is noticeable is that a higher percentage of those without educational qualifications served an apprenticeship: 28 out of 50. The Salfords in Table 9.1 are not atypical. The father's role in securing British Rail apprenticeships was noted earlier in Chapter 7, and was a subject brought out by respondents during the interviews.

The position in confectionery may be contrasted with that on the railways. The qualitative impressions from the interviews did not suggest that the same mechanism was in operation, and the figures in Table 9.2 indicate that the proportion with apprenticeships was rather lower (although that with educational qualifications was higher). There are some reasons to believe that the labour force is structured in a rather different way in the two industries, an aspect which we develop below.

Earnings and Success

To this point, we have built up a picture of some of the factors influencing the acquisition of educational qualifications and securing apprenticeships. We now wish to look at the reasons why people with similar qualifications have more or less success in terms of earnings, and whether family background continues to play any role.

In order to do this, we look at the position of those who do noticeably better or worse than would be expected, *given their qualifications*. (It should be emphasised that it is not absolute success or failure which is at

Table 9.2 Apprenticeships by industry of father: British Rail and confectionery

	Number of sons	Percentage of total (excluding cases where no information)
British Rail		
No qualifications	22	32.4
Apprenticeship	28	41.2
Educational qualification: O level or higher	18	26.5
No information	7	
Total	75	100.1
Confectionery		
No qualifications	12	35.3
Apprenticeship	11	32.4
Educational qualification: O level or higher	11	32.4
No information	8	
Total	42	100.0

stake.) The analysis is based on a multiple regression equation of the type described in Chapter 7, relating the logarithm of hourly earnings to work experience and its square, to educational qualifications, and to whether or not the person has taken an apprenticeship. It should be noted that the father's earnings are not included; we are interested in investigating the possible operation of a direct effect of family background. We then consider those sons whose actual earnings depart from the predicted level by more than 30 per cent (which is one standard error of the regression equation).

An example may help. John Keighley, with no qualifications and without an apprenticeship, has predicted hourly earnings after 18 years' work experience of £1.42. His actual earnings when interviewed were £1.16. This is below that predicted, but only by some 20 per cent, so that we do not single him out for special attention. There are in fact 35 cases (drawn from those who are both in the labour-market sample and have the information required to compare actual and predicted earnings) which are more than one standard error (30 per cent) from the predicted value. These cases, referred to collectively as 'outliers' are distributed as follows:

	Below predicted earnings	Above predicted earnings
More than 2 standard errors	2	2
1.5–2 standard errors	3	3
1–1.5 standard errors	12	13

It may be noted that they fall more or less equally above and below the predicted earnings.

Family background
The earlier regression analysis indicated that there was a significant relationship between son's earnings and father's earnings, in addition to that occurring through qualifications; this indication is borne out by the outliers identified above. Of the 17 cases where the son's earnings fell below the predicted level, only five had fathers earning more than £7 a week, and in five cases the father earned £6 a week or less. Of the 18 cases where the son's earnings were above the predicted level, eleven had fathers earnings more than £7 and only three earned £6 or less.

Our particular focus here is on the role of the father's employment. Of the 35 outliers, eleven had fathers working for British Rail and four for Rowntrees. These numbers are not particularly different from those which might be expected, on the basis of the overall proportions. What is striking, however, is that eight of the eleven whose fathers worked for British Rail are in the group whose earnings are above the predicted level, compared with only one of four whose fathers worked for Rowntrees. An example from the eight is given by the Robertson family. In 1950 Mr Robertson was a coach-builder in the British Rail works; in 1975–8 his son was a project engineer with the Electricity Board, having done an apprenticeship as a scientific instrument-maker and taken an HNC. Another example is Mr Burns, who was a shunter with British Rail; his son is now a graphic designer, having been to grammar school and art college. Moreover, of the three whose fathers worked for British Rail in 1950 and whose earnings are below the predicted level, two are not typical examples of low pay, and the sons would more typically be thought of as upwardly mobile. Mr Shilton in 1950 was a crane-driver employed by British Rail. His son left school at 15, worked as a panel-beater until 24, then went to evening classes and finally theological college. He is now a curate with a low salary and long hours, and this puts him way below the predicted value. Dr Needham, whose father was in the carriage works, has a Ph.D., and his low hourly wage appears to be due to the long hours which he works as a research officer.

These case-studies suggest a further aspect: that employment in British Rail may be more of a springboard for upward mobility than employment at Rowntrees. Mr Bowyer, whose father was a Rowntrees foreman, left school with no qualifications and is a lorry driver with a food wholesaler on very low pay. Mr Clark is a packer at Rowntrees, like his father, and is 1.5 standard deviations below the predicted value. He, like other Rowntree employees in the sample, has had a variety of jobs. At the same time, one cannot read too much into these examples. There is also Mr McGovern, who worked in the cream-toffee department of Rowntrees and whose son is now a top planning engineer.

Work history of the sons

In Fig. 9.3, we show the current jobs of the sons who are outliers – in the sense of being unusually 'successful' or 'unsuccessful' relative to their qualifications – together with the available information about their past employment.

This list suggests several possible hypotheses. The first concerns job mobility. Of the 17 'unsuccessful', nine had changed the *kind* of job they did (excluding the one who did different jobs in Rowntrees), in some cases on several occasions: for example, Mr Clark had been in the army, in the merchant navy, a chef and in pub management, before he went to work in Rowntrees in his thirties. Of the 18 'successful' sons, there had been a change in the kind of job in only three or four cases, and the number of job changes recorded was smaller: for example, Mr Francis, now working as a glass sorter, had started as a shop assistant, worked his way up to manager of a supermarket, before switching to Redfearns Glass Works.

In referring to job mobility, we have in mind mobility *between* different types of job, or what may be referred to as 'horizontal' mobility. Such mobility appears to be associated with the 'unsuccessful' group. The concept of a 'job' is, of course, ill defined; some of the job changes may simply mean that a person is a few years behind on the experience/earnings profile (for example, the assistant pub manager expects to earn more when he gets his own pub). We have also to remember that the information on job histories is not always complete. None the less, it seems worth considering the hypothesis that movement between jobs, with little attachment to a particular career, is associated with a lower level of earnings than would be expected with a given level of qualifications.

In contrast, 'vertical' mobility (or promotion within a firm or profession) tends to be associated with earnings above the predicted level. For example, Mr Anderson had served a technical apprenticeship with a large building firm, moved around the country with promotion, and left to join a smaller firm in order to obtain a senior position. His earnings are more than one standard error above the predicted level.

Such vertical mobility often involves geographical movement. The

Table 9.3 Work careers

Below predicted earnings level (more than one standard error)	Above predicted earnings level (more than one standard error)
Curate (panel-beater 9 years)	Lithographer (always)
Lorry driver (always)	Planner (always)
Rowntrees (always, although different jobs)	Paint-sprayer (always)
Boilerman (RAF, fitter, coach-builder)	Computing (always)
Assistant pub manager (printer 14 years)	Teacher (always)
Rowntrees (army, merchant navy, pub management, chef)	Computing (always)
Watchmaker (always)	Engineer (scientific instrument-maker)
Printer (always)	Process worker (Shepherds 'Portakabin', previously house-painter)
British Rail (only worked 1 year, fork-lift truck driver)	Designer (always)
Assistant accountant (3 years part-time bookmaker)	Planning engineer (always)
Bricklayer (always)	Rowntrees (always, different jobs)
British Rail (always)	British Rail (draughtsman)
British Rail (always)	Teacher (always)
Wood machinist (cleaner, milkman)	Building engineer (apprentice engineer)
Civil Service (left army after 27 years)	Accountant (always)
Economist (always)	Construction manager (joiner)
Clerk (trainee manager of building society 5 years)	Glass (shop assistant, manager)
	Commodity dealer (always, started at Rowntrees)

equation used to predict earnings did not include a location variable, which we have earlier seen to be significant. The role of geographical mobility, however, can be seen for the groups of outliers. The great majority of those with less than predicted earnings are living in York or the locality. In contrast, the locations of those above the predicted value by more than one standard deviation include Hampshire (two instances), Bedfordshire, Cardiff, Norwich, Cambridgeshire and Hertfordshire. This movement may reflect, in part, the lack of improved employment prospects in York (for example, the absence of electronics firms) or, in part, promotion within a firm or industry with national connections.

Intergenerational Continuities in Employment

The influence of a job history, which we identified in the previous section, brings our attention back to the kind of labour-market in which people find themselves. In the final section of this chapter, we examine this further by approaching the evidence from a different direction.

Transition between industries

If access to employment is governed by the nature of a father's industry, and if a steady job history is a significant factor, then particular interest attaches to those cases where both father and son, or son-in-law, are employed in the same industry. In considering this, we confine attention to those cases where the second-generation respondent was in York, although we recognise that this excludes some genuine cases of continuity.

In Table 9.4, we show the transition matrix between industries for the 177 father/son pairs for whom the information was available, where the industry categories are a reduced version of those used earlier in Table 7.4. As a result of the small numbers involved in certain cases, we have combined several industries, although we are careful to bear in mind, when assessing the degree of continuity, that the resulting classes are far from homogeneous. It is immediately apparent from Table 9.4, however, that the main diagonal entries with a sizeable number of fathers and sons are those for food, drink and tobacco and for British Rail. The numbers in these cells are about double those expected on a purely random basis, and this remains true when account is taken of the changes in employment between 1950 and 1975–8. Interestingly, there is a symmetrical relationship between food and British Rail, where in both cases substantially fewer sons are recruited from the other industry than would be expected on a random basis. We would expect some 6.5 sons with fathers in food to enter British Rail, compared with the three actually observed; and we would expect around seven sons,

Table 9.4 *Transition matrix for industry of fathers and sons in York*

Fathers		Sons										
		1 & 2	3	4 & 6	5	7	8 & 9	10	11–13	14	15	Total
1–2	Agriculture, etc.	0	2	1	0	1	2	1	1	0	0	8
3	Food, drink and tobacco	0	8	1	3	4	1	4	5	1	3	30
4 & 6	Textiles etc.	1	0	3	0	0	1	0	3	1	2	11
5	Glass	0	0	1	0	1	0	1	0	0	0	3
7	Construction	0	3	0	3	2	0	1	1	1	2	13
8 & 9	Gas, transport etc.	1	1	2	0	0	1	0	1	0	3	9
10	Distribution	0	2	1	0	4	2	1	1	0	0	11
11–13	Insurance, etc.	1	3	0	1	7	0	0	1	2	3	18
14	Public administration	0	1	2	3	3	1	1	2	0	3	16
15	British Rail	2	4	4	4	5	8	4	6	1	20	58
	Total	5	24	15	14	27	16	13	21	6	36	177

Note: Definition of industry categories: (1 & 2) agriculture, mining, engineering, metals, etc.; (4 & 6) textiles, clothing, wool, paper and printing, etc.; (8 & 9) gas, electricity, water, transport and communication; (11–13) insurance, professional services, miscellaneous services.

whose fathers work for British Rail, to work for the food industry, compared with the four actually observed.

There is therefore some tendency for sons to follow their fathers' employment: for example, the total on the diagonal of Table 9.4 is 36 compared with an expected number of a random basis of 22. On the other hand, in some cases the cells are too broad for the comparison to be meaningful: for example, if the father was employed in textiles and the son in printing. On these grounds, we have excluded five cases where the industry of father and son was effectively quite different, although it was classified the same in Table 9.4. In the case of sons-in-law, a similar analysis shows that there is no apparent tendency for concentration on the diagonal, with fewer cases (16) than expected (20) on a random basis; in particular, the number in the British Rail diagonal cell is six, compared with seven on a random basis, and the number for food is similar to that expected. Moreover, in two of the sixteen cases, the industry was effectively different, and these are excluded.

In what follows we consider in more detail the 45 diagonal cases (31 sons and 14 sons-in-law). First, we compare their characteristics with those of the entire labour-market sample. They may have characteristics in common which are different from those of the group as a whole and which may help us to understand why they are employed in the same industries as their fathers/fathers-in-law (for this purpose, we take the 340 sons and sons-in-law in York, for whom we have information on the employer in each generation). Given the small numbers involved, too much weight cannot be attached to the observed differences, but the following points seem to emerge. The 'continuity' group work mainly in British Rail and the food industry, the proportions in other industries being in the same relationship as in the labour-market sample as a whole. The continuity group tend to be rather older. This is possibly surprising, if we are expecting continuity to arise due to the point of entry into the labour-market, and it suggests that the family connection may continue to operate or become more important. Alternatively, there may have been a decline over time in the influence of the father's employment. In the case of sons, the continuity group contains rather more first and second-born children than in the sample as a whole (the information is not available for sons-in-law).

Employment in British Rail

In the continuity group there are twenty sons, including two pairs of brothers, and six sons-in-law who work for British Rail. We have already commented on the apparent tendency for fathers to be able to secure access to apprenticeships in British Rail for their sons. The twenty sons can be classified according to their level of skill (on a rather approximate basis, but one which is probably sufficiently accurate for our purpose) into fourteen skilled, three semi-skilled and two clerical. This leaves only one unskilled worker, and suggests that the acquisition of skills, or equivalent training (for example, as a booking clerk), is a significant part of the story.

Eleven of the fourteen skilled sons began and completed their apprenticeships at British Rail, including all seven of those with skilled fathers. None of the eleven have left the company of their own accord during their employment there, although some had breaks for National Service and four – all of whom worked in the carriage shops – were made redundant during the early or mid-1960s (one was made redundant twice). All returned after spells of not more than two years working elsewhere. Of the three who started their apprenticeships elsewhere, one transferred to British Rail in the middle of his apprenticeship and the other two moved there after ten or more years working elsewhere. Of the six sons who are not classified as skilled, four started work at British Rail, one had worked at numerous semi-skilled jobs before being employed at British Rail and one (the unskilled son) gave no details of his job history.

It seems from this evidence that there is some direct 'inheritance' of skilled jobs at British Rail. On this basis, we should expect a less strong relationship between the employment of fathers and sons-in-law there, and this actually is the case. Not only are there fewer father/son-in-law pairs in the continuity group, but also there is less similarity in their experience. The one skilled son-in-law, for example, did not serve an apprenticeship, but worked his way up to become a train driver. It may be noted, however, that two of the sons-in-law in British Rail had fathers who had also worked there in the past.

Employment in the confectionery industry
There are six father/son pairs in the continuity group, where both were employed in the confectionery trade (five from Rowntrees and one from Cravens). Three were doing unskilled process work, as were their fathers in 1950. Two of these sons (brothers) had not been working at Rowntrees long and had done a large range of unskilled and semi-skilled jobs before. The other son had worked all his life at Rowntrees, apart from time spent on National Service and 6 weeks' unemployment when demobilised. Of the remaining three sons, one had completed a printing apprenticeship outside York, had had a variety of printing jobs and at the time of interview was working as a skilled printer with Rowntrees. His father had been a process worker there. The other two sons were non-manual workers. One, whose father had been a charge-hand at Rowntrees, had done a variety of jobs after leaving school, but had worked at Cravens as a clerk for the last 18 years. The remaining

son was a salaried computer controller with 3 O levels. His father, although a production assistant in 1950, had become a general manager at Rowntrees.

The four sons-in-law in this group consist of two pairs of brothers-in-law. One father-in-law was a process worker at Rowntrees in 1950, although in fact he had spent most of his life employed by York Council. Both sons-in-law had worked for several York employers. One, whose wife (the daughter of the 1950 respondent) also worked at Rowntrees, was a process worker; the other, whose wife and father had both worked at Rowntrees in the past, had a senior clerical job when interviewed. The other father-in-law had been a charge-hand at Rowntrees. One of his sons-in-law had started work there as an unskilled process worker and was a fitter's mate when interviewed. The other son-in-law was a clerk, and had worked at Rowntrees for ten years, after being a clerk in several other York firms.

The reasons behind continuity of industry between generations appear rather different in the case of confectionery than in the case of British Rail. In confectionery, the nature of the work done by the respondents is less skilled and there does not appear to be a tradition of putting down the names of sons to work there. Rowntree employees appear to have changed their employer more often than British Rail employees, and in this sense there is less attachment to employment in that particular firm. On the other hand, employment in Rowntrees does seem to run in the families or extended families. Indeed, several respondents said that there was a family tradition of working for one or other of the confectionery firms. This is brought out by the links with sons-in-law, which was not evident with British Rail.

These family connections are illustrated by the Yves family, where the father was a process worker in 1950 at Rowntrees. He had five daughters and four sons who were all married by 1975–8. Two of the sons had worked at Rowntrees in the past. Three of the daughters worked or had worked at Rowntrees and the other two had worked at Cravens. Of their husbands (the respondent's sons-in-law), two were working at Rowntrees, one had in the past and the father of one of them had worked there. Similarly, there is Mr Russell, who had been a charge-hand at Rowntrees in 1950. Of his two sons, one worked at Cravens, together with his wife, and the wife of the other son worked at Rowntrees. He had seven daughters, two of whom had worked at Rowntrees. Two of their husbands worked there and another had done so in the past. One father-in-law had also worked at Rowntrees.

Comparison between British Rail and the confectionery industry
From the experience of the small number of families we have studied, it

Table 9.5 *Earnings position of fathers and sons where both are employed by British Rail (B) or the confectionery industry (C)*

Income range for father	Income range for sons				
	Top 20%	Second 20%	Middle 20%	Fourth 20%	Bottom 20%
Second 20%					
Middle 20%	B		B	B B B B B	
Fourth 20%	B	B B	B B B	B	
	C				C C C C
Bottom 20%	B		B		
	C				C

Notes: The C entries include one where father and son are both employed in the sugar plant. Earnings are not known for three cases in British Rail.

appears that the continuities in employment in the two major employers arise in rather different ways. In British Rail, the continuity appears to be due to the recruitment of sons (not sons-in-law) into skilled jobs and due to a relatively high degree of continuity in employment (over the period we are investigating). In contrast, in the confectionery trade, the continuity appears to be associated with a family tradition of working for one or other firm. This tradition extends to sons-in-law, and indeed seems to involve women as much as men. We have also seen that the attachment to the firm is weaker in this case, in that people may switch to other sectors, usually doing work of a similarly unskilled or semi-skilled kind.

This characterisation of the York labour-market leads us to go further and speculate that there may be a degree of segmentation in the labour-market. The labour forces of British Rail and the confectionery firms do not appear significantly to 'intersect'; and we have noted earlier that there is substantially less recruitment into the railway industry than expected of sons whose fathers were in the food, drink and tobacco industry, and vice versa. There are clearly exceptions, particularly among unskilled workers and clerical workers, but the overall impression is that the working experience of those employed by British Rail is different from that of those working in confectionery.

Moreover, British Rail has a number of the features of a 'primary' labour-market, with well-defined points of entry, internal promotion, and relative stability of employment; the confectionery firms, on the other hand, appear closer to the 'secondary' model, with a more rapid turnover, less training on the job, etc.

Finally, we may examine the relation with economic 'success' measured in terms of earnings and the NA/SB ratios. The reader may have noted that two of the continuity groups have already featured in our discussion of low-income families – the Russells and the Yves. Mr Russell was in the 140–159 per cent range of the NA scale in 1950, and the family of one of his daughters was rather similarly placed in 1975–8, with an SB ratio of 132. However, the other daughter was better off, with an SB ratio of nearly 200. The same applied to the Yves family, where one daughter was in the range just above her father, but the other was comfortably above 200 per cent of the SB scale. It would therefore be a mistake to equate continuity of employment with continuity of economic status. This is illustrated in Table 9.5, where we show the earnings range of fathers and sons included in the continuity group, (B denotes British Rail and C denotes confectionery.) The data are adjusted for age differences and are comparable to those shown in Table 6.3b. There is no indication that the continuity group are clustered closer to the diagonal than the sample as a whole. We therefore end this chapter by emphasising that we regard labour-market position as useful in understanding the process of earnings determination, but not as a fully adequate indicator of economic status.

10 Summary

Our Study

At the start of this research project, virtually nothing was known about continuities in economic status between generations in Britain. There had been a series of major investigations of occupational mobility, but intergenerational evidence on earnings and income had not been collected (see the review in Chapter 2). Our purpose has therefore been to try to fill this gap. We have aimed to provide evidence about the extent of economic mobility across generations and to throw light on mechanisms which lead to mobility or immobility.

The method adopted in the investigation has been to follow up the children of families interviewed approximately a generation ago by Seebohm Rowntree in York in 1950. This approach of linking to an earlier study was selected in preference to the two other possibilities (discussed in Chapter 2) of a prospective longitudinal study or a retrospective study. The former would have been more expensive to conduct and much longer in duration, and we felt that the latter would not have yielded sufficiently reliable information on earnings and income.

The choice of the Rowntree 1950 survey as the basis for the follow-up study was largely dictated by our requirements that (1) the parents were interviewed approximately a generation earlier, so that they would be at broadly the same stage in the life cycle; (2) it contain information on earnings and incomes; and (3) that the names and addresses of the respondents be available to permit the tracing of the children. The first requirement precluded, for example, use of Townsend's 1968–9 survey of poverty in the United Kingdom (Townsend, 1979). The second requirement rules out the longitudinal studies of Douglas and the National Children's Bureau, which did not ask questions about parental income or earnings. The third requirement meant that we could not use official surveys, such as the 1953–4 Household Expenditure Enquiry, where the names are not revealed. Rowntree's survey, however, did satisfy all three requirements, and we were able to obtain access to approximately two-thirds of the original survey returns.

The Rowntree survey is not of course ideal. It relates to only one city and, despite Rowntree's claims, York cannot be regarded as a microcosm of Great Britain. In particular, employment is dominated by British Rail and the confectionery firms. The survey covered only the 'working-class' population. The design of the survey, and its execution, do not measure up to modern standards. Not all the original returns are available to us. These aspects, discussed in Chapter 3, mean that any conclusions must be qualified. But we felt that in view of the limited alternatives available, and the definite strengths of the Rowntree survey, a follow-up survey was worthwhile.

The use of the follow-up approach depended critically on our success in tracing the children of the original Rowntree respondents. In this there was little previous work to guide us. The techniques we had to use were therefore very much of our own creation, and there is little doubt that they could with hindsight be improved. As explained in Chapter 3, we first employed a relatively straightforward approach, based on street directories and other records. This allowed us to locate the children of 37 per cent of the original Rowntree families (500 of those covered by the 1363 schedules available to us) and to establish in a further 5 per cent of cases that there were no surviving children. The remaining 'difficult to trace' cases required more intensive methods, and in view of our limited resources we took a random 10 per cent subsample and concentrated on achieving a high success rate for this smaller group. Through a great deal of detective work, we located the children in 45 per cent of the cases from this subsample and established for a further 15 per cent that there were no surviving children. Grossing these figures up (to allow for the 10 per cent sampling fraction), we had accounted in all for:

830 families in which children were found
221 families in which there were no surviving children

that is, a total of 1051 (76 per cent of the grossed total of schedules)
In assessing the success of this tracing exercise, one needs to bear in mind the very restricted information from which we had to work. For example, many of the children were not recorded on the 1950 schedules, because they were not yet born or because they had already grown up and left home. Given this, and the long time which had elapsed, the 'success' rate of 76 per cent seems to us relatively satisfactory. At the same time, the consequences of attrition from the original sample need to be borne in mind.

We then proceeded to interview the children of the original Rowntree families. The 1975–8 survey, described in Chapter 4, contained a variety of detailed questions on employment, income, education, family circumstances, housing and other topics. In the interviewing we attached a great deal of importance to obtaining a high response rate. The response achieved from personal interviews was 81 per cent in terms of complete replies, which is high by the standards of surveys which contain questions on income. Unfortunately, our resources did not allow us to interview in person all the children traced, and we had to rely on a postal questionnaire for a number of families, including 53 overseas, and those of the 10 per cent subsample living away from York. The response here was considerably lower, and reduced the overall response rate to 70 per cent in terms of complete replies.

The final results of our survey cover 1716 respondents in the United Kingdom (and 39 from overseas). The main characteristics of these 'Rowntree children' are described in Chapter 4. Some two-thirds live in York and a further fifth in Yorkshire and Humberside. The proportion of the 'Rowntree children' over retirement age is relatively small (17 per cent) and 36 per cent have children under the minimum school-leaving age. The corresponding proportions in 1950 were 17 per cent and 44 per cent; this suggests that the timing had been fairly successful in securing data at the interval of a generation. Further encouraging evidence in this respect is provided by the fact that the ages of 73 per cent of the children were within 10 years of the ages of their parents when the latter had been interviewed in 1950.

Evidence about Mobility

At the beginning of Chapter 1, we outlined the questions which led to us embarking on this research study. It will be clear to the reader that the answers given must be qualified ones. The special features of the 1950 Rowntree survey, and its relatively small sample size, the failure to trace all the children, and the incomplete response to our own 1975–8 survey, all mean that the findings may be unrepresentative in crucial respects. For both parents and children, we have only a snapshot at one date in their lives; and even this may be blurred by measurement and other error. Throughout the text, we have tried to draw attention to the limitations of our material, and to explore the implications of correcting for important shortcomings.

Even with perfect data, the complexity of the questions is such that they can be addressed in a variety of different ways. The factual question as to the extent of mobility across generations may appear at first sight straightforward, but closer examination indicates that a great deal lies behind any answer. Thus we began in Chapter 5 with an analysis in terms of incomes, expressed relative to the National Assistance (1950) or Supplementary Benefit (1975–8) scale, but it is not clear that *income*, rather than *earnings*, is the appropriate indicator. After all, the studies of occupational mobility typically focus on those in work.

In the same way, the *presentation* of the extent of mobility is an issue of considerable significance. We cannot normally present the full data, but the choice of a summary measure can affect the impressions drawn by the reader. In Chapter 5, we estimate, for example, that the regression coefficient relating the living standards of parents and children was around 0.15–0.20 (the latter making allowance for possible measurement error). This is a lot smaller than the value of 0.5 discussed for heights of fathers and sons, and suggests that family background conveys relatively little advantage. On the other hand, the transition matrix shows that a child whose parents were below the National Assistance level in 1950 is 1.5 times as likely to be below the SB level in 1975–8 than if there were perfect mobility. Or if we define low-income families as those below 140 per cent of the National Assistance/ Supplementary Benefit scale, then 48 per cent of the children of low-income parents themselves have low incomes, compared with 25 per cent of the children whose parents did not have low incomes. These calculations of differential odds from the same data may give the impression of a more marked relationship with family background.

The complexity of the questions we are addressing is further illustrated by the need to adjust for *life-cycle differences*. The pattern of transitions just described may largely be a function of age, with those below 140 per cent being in both generations pensioners whose incomes are low for life-cycle reasons. Although life-cycle differences arise in the study of variables such as intelligence or height, they are of considerably greater significance in the case of economic variables. The life-cycle picture is examined in Chapter 5, which presents a modern version of the celebrated Rowntree diagram of the variation with age of incomes relative to need, and shows how substantial the variation still is.

Extent of Earnings Mobility

Consideration of the findings for incomes led us to conclude that, although the results are of considerable interest, it is the degree of *earnings* mobility which should be our primary concern. The life-cycle element, for example, is more easily handled, if attention is limited to those in work. There is the further important advantage that we can relate the observed earnings more easily to the national picture, and in Chapter 6 we express the earnings categories in terms of the estimated national distribution.

The regression analysis in Chapter 6 suggests that the coefficient relating the earnings of fathers and sons (adjusted for age) is of the order of 0.4–0.5 (the latter making an allowance for possible measurement error). In this case, it is close to that found for heights and other physical characteristics, but whether it is large or small is a matter for the reader to judge. Those who approach the issue with the prior view that Britain is a highly rigid, immobile society may find this regression coefficient surprisingly small. Those whose starting-point is the case of perfect mobility may find it surprisingly high. The same may also apply to those whose standard of reference is the degree of correlation expected for the *same person* on a 25-year time-span. Suppose that the process determining earnings is such that the correlation is reduced by a factor of 0.98 for each year's distance, then the correlation between earnings at the ages of 25 and 50 would be only 0.6.

The estimated regression coefficient may be interpreted in terms of the implied advantage to the children from better-off families. To illustrate this, we may compare the prospects of Robin Parks, whose father earned £8.50 a week in 1950 as a welder, with those of George Banks, whose father earned £5.00 a week as a labourer. Mr Parkes was comfortably above median earnings in 1950, according to the estimated national distribution, but Mr Banks was at the bottom decile. Taking the estimated regression coefficient, we can see that the predicted advantage for Robin Parks over George Banks is some 24–30 per cent. Even allowing for regression towards the mean, George can expect to be quite a long way below the median. We can also consider the probability of children remaining low paid. With a regression coefficient of 0.5, the probability of a person being in the bottom 20 per cent of the earnings distribution is 45 per cent if his father was also in the bottom 20 per cent of the range, but only 4 per cent if his father was in the top 20 per cent.

The predictions from the regression coefficient may be compared with the transition matrices in Chapter 6. These show, for example, that if we take the bottom 20 per cent of the earnings distribution of Rowntree fathers, then 45 per cent of their sons are also in the bottom 20 per cent of the distribution for age-adjusted hourly earnings, which is exactly what is to be expected with a regression coefficient of 0.5. The transition matrices also bring out aspects which are not revealed by a single summary indicator such as the regression coefficient, as noted above. Thus, we suggested that there might be an asymmetric pattern of mobility, with long-range movements being more common in an upward direction and the trickling down process more gradual, some 40 per cent of those in the bottom 20 per cent of the earnings distribution of sons rose by more than one range, but only 12 per cent of those in the top 20 per cent of the distribution were estimated to fall by this distance.

Determinants of Earnings

There are many factors which could be responsible for the observed association of earnings across generations. In Chapters 7–9, we examine a selection of these, paying particular attention to the relationship between family background and education and to labour-market experience. In this, we are not attempting to demonstrate causal links, but to describe the quantitative strength of different associations. Given the fact that no evidence has to date been available on parental income – as opposed to proxy measures such as occupation – the establishment of the quantitative picture is itself a major step forward. Moreover, we have sought to couple this with the rich qualitative information recorded by our interviewers.

The statistical investigation of earnings in Chapter 7 starts from earlier analyses, which have related earnings to length of education and work experience. For these variables, our data yield similar results: for example, an extra year of education appears to be associated with additional earnings of 7 per cent. It is in the introduction of father's earnings that we have broken new ground. Here we find a coefficient of around 0.3, which indicates that the children from better-off families still have a sizeable advantage, even when allowance is made for the effect of education. Expressed another way, the introduction of education and other explanatory variables into the regression equation reduces the coefficient on father's earnings, from 0.4–0.5 to 0.3, but still leaves it at a quite substantial value. As we bring in other variables, such as the type of school, educational qualifications and migration from York, the coefficient of fathers' earnings is reduced somewhat further, but remains at about 0.25. On this basis there is a large association remaining with family background, in addition to the indirect effect working through the education or migration variables.

The indirect effect via education is explored in more detail in terms of the length of schooling, the probability of leaving with qualifications and the probability of attending a selective school. The statistical findings may again be illustrated by the Parks family, where Robin's father earned £8.50 a week in 1950, and the Banks family, where George's father earned £5.00 a week. Robin Parks is predicted to receive an extra year of full-time education more than George Banks. The probability of Robin's acquiring academic qualifications is 57 per cent, compared with 30 per cent for George. The chance of Robin attending a selective school is 41 per cent, compared with 21 per cent for George.

The relationship between family background and education, developed further in Chapter 8, has been extensively analysed in studies where the father's occupation is used to measure family advantage. In an important sense, our research complements this earlier work. Whereas we can say nothing about the differential experience of the professional/managerial classes, compared with the working class, our evidence does allow us to consider differences within the range of working-class earnings, where occupational data do not typically allow fine discrimination. Moreover, our analysis suggests a number of findings which do not appear to have received much prominence in earlier work. The examination of the proportions staying on at school until the age of 16 or older reveals that low-income Rowntree families suffered no apparent disadvantage where the children were attending selective schools, but that there was a definite disadvantage in the case of non-selective schools. It seems that the children from better-off homes were able to offset the disadvantage of having failed to secure entry to a selective school by remaining longer at school or entering further education. In contrast, when it came to academic qualifications, the children of low-income families appeared to be at a disadvantage in both selective and non-selective schools, and the same applied to higher education.

Our concern with education extends beyond school and further education to the role of apprenticeships, which we found to be positively associated with earnings. In Chapter 9, this is related to family background and to the industrial pattern of employment. In this respect, the special features of the York labour-market prove to be a strength rather than a weakness, in that they allow us to probe the differences between two major employers in York – British Rail and the confectionery industry. In both cases, there is a definite tendency for sons to follow fathers. In the case of British Rail, there is good reason to believe that this is linked with apprenticeships. For example, it applies to sons and not sons-in-law, and in a number of cases there is direct evidence that fathers 'put their son's name down' on the waiting list for an apprenticeship. In contrast, the continuities in Rowntrees seem to be of a rather different nature, less closely linked to job entry and with a less structured labour-market. In this case, the pattern extends to sons-in-law. More generally, the nature of the labour-market appears to be of importance. Although the evidence is largely qualitative, there is some tendency for workers to be divided into those with a relatively weak attachment to particular jobs, often moving 'horizontally' and those who had a clear perception of an internal labour-market and who moved largely 'vertically' (again, apprenticeships appear to play a positive role).

The Research in Context

The difficulties of extrapolating from our research findings to conclusions for the design of policy will be evident. The reader will scarcely need reminding that the conclusions are based on a small, and quite possibly unrepresentative, group of parents and children. Or that the period of much of the educational and labour-market experience is that of Churchill, Eden and Macmillan rather than that of Callaghan and Thatcher.

We should, however, end by stressing a theme which is more easily forgotten – that the research has concentrated on certain elements of the social and economic system and viewed them in a particular way. This reflects both the conventional demarcation lines of academic disciplines and the genuine difficulties in taking a wider view of the subject. Yet, the fact that we have only a partial picture must be in the forefront of our minds when considering policy implications.

One example may serve to underline this important point. Our analysis suggests that one means by which family background conveys an advantage is by allowing the children at non-selective schools to stay on at school and by helping them attain academic qualifications. For this, and other reasons, it may be judged desirable to provide maintenance grants for those staying on at school beyond the age of 16. On the face of it, this may help to raise the earnings of the low paid. On the human-capital view, if we narrow differences in education, then earnings differences will correspondingly lessen. But, the impact of changes in educational policy depends on repercussions elsewhere, particularly the response of earnings differentials. There are good reasons to imagine that the 'return' to education may alter, and this is indeed one explanation of what has been observed with the expansion of higher education. If we take the opposite view from that of human capital, and assume that the structure of jobs and associated earnings is fixed, and all that the educational process does is to determine the allocation to these jobs, then allowing children to stay on at school will do nothing to alter the structure of earnings. And, although the link with family background via education may be weakened, the mechanism by which people secure good jobs may be modified to give greater weight to other aspects. The family-background effect may show up in other ways, rather than via education.

As this example illustrates, we cannot view individual behaviour in isolation, and we must consider the social and economic structure in which individuals or families are positioned. In the same way, we should note that much research on incomes and earnings is concerned with the responses of individuals, typically drawn from a random sample of a large population, rather than with their interdependence. Our Rowntree families are somewhat different, in that the 1950 respondents showed a number of common features and represented a sizeable fraction of the community in question, and we have tried to examine some aspects of their common environment, notably in terms of employment. But it is only a timid step in the direction of a wider treatment of behaviour. We need to go further in considering why families, apparently identical with respect to the characteristics we have considered, have enjoyed different life experiences. We need to investigate how the behaviour of employers, unions, education authorities and other institutions has influenced earnings and employment opportunities.

In assessing the policy implications, our findings must therefore be considered in a broader context. At the same time, we believe that the history of the Rowntree families and their children provides a valuable glimpse of some of the processes determining the transmission of economic advantage and disadvantage.

Statistical Terms: An Explanatory Note

In this book, we employ a variety of statistical techniques. The aim of this note is to provide a brief explanation. For further details, the reader is referred to basic statistics texts such as Blalock (1972), Hodges and Lehmann (1970), Hoel and Jessen (1971), and Kazmier (1979), or to introductory texts on econometrics, such as Duncan (1975), Hanushek and Jackson (1977), Johnston (1972), Theil (1978), Kane (1969), Kmenta (1971), Maddala (1977), Wonnacott and Wonnacott (1970).

The terms which the reader may encounter in the text are set in italic when they are first mentioned below.

Distributions and their Descriptions

In much of the text we are concerned with distributions – of incomes, earnings or other variables. In describing these, it is convenient to use a variety of summary statistics. The most widely used is the *mean*, or arithmetic average. Suppose we observe the following ten figures for income:

$$60, 65, 70, 70, 75, 75, 80, 85, 90, 150$$

The mean, formed by summing and dividing by 10, is 82. It may be noted that this is greater than the *median*, which is the value at the middle of the group: that is, the income level such that half the group are below and half above. In the example given, the median is between the fifth and sixth incomes, which are both 75. It is typically the case with income and earnings distributions that the median is below the mean.

The mean and the median are indicators of the location of the distribution; in order to give a measure of the spread of the distribution, we may use the *variance*, or the *standard deviation* (which is the positive square root of the variance). The variance is the arithmetic average of the squared differences from the mean. In the example given earlier, this is formed by adding $(60-82)^2$, $(65-82)^2$, and so on up to $(150-82)^2$, and then dividing by 10. Alternatively, we may use the *quantiles*, which are the levels of income which divide the population into groups of an equal (specified) size. Among those used in the text are *quintiles*, which divide the population into fifths, and *deciles*, which divide the population into tenths. The top quintile is the value of income such that 20 per cent of the population are at or above this level. In the example given above, the top quntile is between 85 and 90, and the bottom quintile is between 65 and 70. (In any actual example, with many more observations, there will not usually be such a wide interval, and the quantiles are quoted as single numbers.)

On occasion, we have referred to particular distributions. The best-known is the *normal* distribution; this has a frequency distribution (showing the relative number of occurrences) which is a bell-shaped curve, symmetric about the mean, and is drawn in all books on statistics. In the case of incomes or earnings, it is more commonly assumed that they can be approximated by the *lognormal distribution*, where the logarithm of income follows the normal distribution. The frequency distribution for income is then skewed, with a longer upper tail, and a mean in excess of the median.

At various points we are concerned with the relation between two distributions. This may be conveniently described in terms of the *covariance*, or of the *correlation coefficient*. Suppose that we have two variables, X and Y, with means denoted by $\bar{X}$ and $\bar{Y}$, respectively. Then the covariance is defined in terms of the product of deviations from the means $[(X - \bar{X})(Y - \bar{Y})]$ averaged over all observations. As may be seen, this average will be positive where larger values of X tend to go together with larger values of Y – there is a positive association – see, for example, Figure 1.1. In this case there is a tendency for X and Y to vary together *linearly*: that is, along the (broken) straight line. The correlation coefficient, which is 0.5 for these data, is defined as:

$$R = \frac{(\text{covariance } X, Y)}{(\text{standard deviation } X) \times (\text{standard deviation } Y)} \quad (1)$$

The coefficient in general lies between -1 and $+1$, and gives a measure of the extent to which X and Y vary together linearly.

Estimation and Confidence Intervals

In our analysis of the evidence from our sample we are, in effect, using it to draw conclusions about a wider population. We are making estimates of the characteristics of the population from our sample data. Thus we take the mean income of the sample as an estimate of the mean income in the population as a whole, or the proportion leaving York in the sample as an estimate of the population propensity to migrate. We are also interested in the reliability of the estimate, and may for this purpose construct *confidence intervals*. Denoting the sample size by N, the formula used to calculate a 95 per cent confidence interval for the mean is $\pm 1.96 \, S/\sqrt{N}$, where S is the sample estimate of the standard deviation. For the proportion p, the 95 per cent confidence interval is

$\pm \ 1.96\sqrt{[p \ (1-p)/N]}$. (The 95 per cent confidence interval is such that there is a 95 per cent probability that the true value lies in that interval.) So that for a sample of 400 and a proportion of 0.5, the 95 per cent confidence interval is $\pm \ 1.96 \div 40 = \pm \ 4.9$ per cent.

Linear Regression Model
The term *regression*:

was introduced by [Sir Francis] Galton in connection with the inheritance of stature. Galton found that the sons of fathers who deviate *x* inches from the mean height of all fathers themselves deviate from the mean height of all sons by less than *x* inches: i.e. there is what Galton called a 'regression to mediocrity'. (Yule and Kendall, 1950, p. 213)

Our usage in Chapter 1 corresponds therefore to the original use of the term 'regression'.

The *linear regression model* involves, in effect, fitting a straight line to the data, such as the broken line shown in Figure 1.1. The *ordinary least squares* procedure for fitting such a line is to minimise the sum of the square of the vertical deviations from the fitted line (the deviations are referred to as *residuals*). In what follows, we concentrate on the two-variable case. That is, if *Y* denotes the *dependent* variable (height of son) and *X* the *independent*, or *explanatory*, variable (height of father), then the linear regression model is:

$$Y_t = \alpha + \beta X_t + \epsilon_t \qquad (2)$$

where the subscript *t* denotes the observations ($t = 1, \ldots N$) and ϵ_t is a random variable. (Alternatively, *Y* and *X* could be the logarithms of heights.)

The standard assumptions of the linear regression model are that the X_t variable is fixed in repeated samples and that ϵ_t has zero mean, constant variance, and is uncorrelated across observations. These assumptions may well not be satisfied in any actual application, and we refer to some of the implications below. Under the assumptions described above, the 'best linear unbiased estimators' of the coefficients α and β are given by the least squares estimators. (The term 'unbiased' refers to the requirement that the expected value, across varying samples, equals the true value; the term 'best' refers to the fact that the variance about this value is the minimum among possible estimators of this type.) In the two-variable case, the least squares estimator of β is given by:

$$\hat{\beta} \equiv \frac{\text{sample covariance of } X \text{ and } Y}{\text{sample variance of } X} \qquad (3)$$

$\hat{\beta}$ is referred to as the estimated *regression coefficient*. In the case where the variance of Y is equal to that of X (for example, the variance of heights is the same for fathers and sons) then comparison of equations (1) and (3) shows that the regression coefficient $\hat{\beta}$ is equal to the correlation coefficient. Where the variance of Y exceeds that of X, the regression coefficient is larger than the correlation coefficient. The estimate of α, denoted by $\hat{\alpha}$, is obtained from the fact that the fitted line is constrained to pass through the point given by the mean sample values, $\bar{X}$ and $\bar{Y}$.

There are a variety of ways in which the goodness of fit can be assessed. We may obtain an estimate of the variance of the unexplained (random) element ϵ_i, which is referred to as the *standard error of estimate*. This is used in the calculation of the estimated *standard errors* of the estimated regression coefficients, $\hat{\alpha}$ and $\hat{\beta}$, which, in turn, together with the assumption that ϵ_i follows a normal distribution, provide a basis for calculating confidence intervals for the coefficients. For samples of the size with which we are dealing, the 95 per cent confidence interval can be taken to be $\pm 1.96 \times$ standard error of the regression coefficient. The overall goodness of fit may also be measured in terms of the proportion of the variance of Y which is 'accounted for' by the variation in X; this proportion is given by R^2.

The description given above relates to the two-variable regression; the *multiple regression model* used in Chapters 7 and 8 is similar in essential respects. The reader is referred to Johnston (1972, ch. 5), Theil (1978, chs. 7–9), Kane (1969, ch. 11), Kmenta (1971, ch. 10), Maddala (1977, ch. 8), and Wonnacott and Wonnacott (1970, ch. 3).

The assumptions underlying the linear regression model may well not be satisfied in practice. The assumptions about the random term may break down. For example, the variance of ϵ may vary systematically across observations: that is, there may be *heteroscedasticity*. One important implication is that the estimation of the standard errors of the regression coefficients may be affected. We have therefore applied the test of White (1980), based on the squared estimated residuals. The assumptions may break down because ϵ_i is correlated across observations as a result of a common 'family' component (where there is more than one child in the sample). This is an aspect which warrants further attention (for a review of siblings models, see Griliches, 1979).

The assumption that X is fixed in repeated samples is not applicable to most empirical studies in the social sciences. One particular reason for it to break down is that of *measurement error*. This means that the X used in the regression (for example, measured heights) is now correlated with the random term. This leads to estimates of β which are inconsistent. That is, if in the two-variable regression X denotes the measured value, x the true value, and u the measurement error (assumed uncorrelated with the true value of x), then the probability limit (that is, as the sample size approaches infinity) of the least squares estimator is:

$$\beta \div 1 + \left[\frac{\text{variance of } u}{\text{variance of } x} \right] = \beta \times \left[\frac{\text{variance of } x}{\text{variance of } X} \right]$$

It may be noted that the measurement error in Y does not affect this expression, but that, from equation (1), the value of R^2 will be lower, and this is one reason for the divergence of $\hat{\beta}$ and R. On measurement error, see Johnston (1972, ch. 9), Kmenta (1971, ch. 9), Maddala (1977, ch. 13), Theil (1978, ch. 17), and Bowles (1972). It should be noted that in the multiple regression case, with more than one explanatory variable measured with error, no straightforward statements can be made about the direction of bias.

Logit Model

In the regression model, the dependent variable is assumed to vary continuously; in some applications, it may take on a limited number of values. Of particular interest is the case where it is the dichotomous (0, 1) variable: for example, a person either attends a selective school ($Y = 1$) or does not ($Y = 0$).

A variety of models have been advanced. That used in the text is the *logit model*, where the probability, P, that the dependent variable takes on the value 1 is represented by:

$$\log_e \frac{P}{(1-P)} = \alpha + \beta_1 X_1 + \beta_2 X_2 \tag{5}$$

(where X_1, X_2 denote different explanatory variables). The parameters α, β_1 and β_2 are estimated by the method of maximum likelihood; and the reader is referred to Hanushek and Jackson (1977, ch. 7), Maddala (1977, ch. 9), and Andersen (1980, ch. 8). It may be noted that:

$$\frac{\partial P}{\partial X_1} = \beta_1 P(1-P) \tag{6}$$

provides an indication of the effect of changes in the explanatory variable on the predicted probability.

Notes on Sources

General
The aim of these notes is to provide a guide to the many different
sources on which we have drawn and to help the reader trace further
material. No attempt is made to survey the relevant literature in each of
the different fields. An excellent survey of research up to 1975 is given
by Rutter and Madge (1976). More recent research findings are covered
in the final report of the transmitted deprivation programme (Brown
and Madge, 1982).

Chapter 1   Intergenerational Income Mobility – the Issues
The overall pattern of income distribution in Britain is described in
Atkinson (1975) and in the reports of the Royal Commission on the
Distribution of Income and Wealth (1975, 1978, 1979a and 1979b). A
more theoretical approach to the determination of the distribution of
income is that of Conlisk (1977) and Meade (1974). The distribution of
earnings is discussed in Lydall (1968 and 1976) and Phelps Brown
(1977), who, together with Becker (1964), Taubman (1978) and
Thurow (1976), provide a good introduction to the topic. The problem
of deprivation and poverty is discussed, from a variety of perspectives,
by Berthoud (1976), Coffield, Robinson and Sarsby (1980), Jordan
(1974 and 1981) and Townsend (1979).

The relationship between income mobility and inequality of opportunity is discussed in Atkinson (1979 and 1980b), the latter being
reprinted in Atkinson (1982). The paper by Klappholz (1972) provides
a valuable assessment from the standpoint of an economist and includes
references to the philosophical literature. See also Gordon (1980),
Joseph and Sumption (1979), Lloyd Thomas (1977), Nozick (1974) and
Okun (1975), which are just some of the many references in this field.

Chapter 2   Incomes and Mobility: a Survey
When we began work on this investigation in 1974, we surveyed the
material available. The results, which showed how little was known,
are summarised briefly in Atkinson and Trinder (1976) and Atkinson
(1979). Since that time, more has been written on particular aspects,
but there remain relatively few reliable sources of evidence on intergenerational income or earnings mobility.

The use of longitudinal, or panel, data has attracted a great deal of
attention in recent years, notably on account of the University of

Michigan Panel Study of Income Dynamics, covering the incomes of individual households (Morgan *et al.*, 1974). The data used by Lillard and Willis (1978), for example, cover 1144 male heads of households from 1967 to 1973 (see also the papers in Juster, 1977). In Britain, the closest parallels are the New Earnings Survey matched samples, used in a series of papers by Hart (for example, 1976b) and Creedy and Hart (for example, 1979), and the National Training Survey, giving data on occupation but not earnings, used by Metcalf and Nickell (1981) and Nickell (1982).

These data relate to mobility *within* a person's lifetime, not across generations. The best-known *inter*generational studies in Britain are those of Douglas (1964; and Douglas *et al.*, 1968), and the National Child Development study (see Pringle, 1980; and Wedge and Prosser, 1973). The potential of the longitudinal approach, and a review of research up to 1967, is outlined in the SSRC report on *Longitudinal Studies and the Social Sciences* (Wall and Williams, 1970). Different methods of collecting data have been extensively discussed in the United States, and particular reference should be made to the work of Hauser and colleagues at the University of Wisconsin (see, for example, Featherman and Hauser, 1975 and 1977).

The very large literature on the extent on intergenerational occupational mobility is well covered in the recent books by Goldthorpe (1980) and Heath (1981). The former contains the main results of the Oxford mobility survey, which was a development of the pioneering study by Glass (1954) and colleagues (see the reassessment by Ridge, 1973). The Hope–Goldthorpe scale, developed for the Oxford survey, is described in Goldthorpe and Hope (1974) and Heath (1981). Other references on mobility in Britain are Hope (1972 and 1981), Hopper (1981), Payne *et al.* (1977) and Richardson (1977). In the United States, much recent research stems from Blau and Duncan (1967), and subsequently Duncan *et al.* (1972). The replication and development by Featherman and Hauser (1975 and 1978) is of considerable interest, as is the study of Australia by Broom *et al.* (1980). The volume of readings edited by Coxon and Jones (1975) is a most useful source, as is the text by Matras (1975). The measurement of mobility is discussed by Prais (1955), Bartholomew (1973), Boudon (1973), Bibby (1975), Shorrocks (1978), Atkinson (1980–1 and 1981a), and others.

Chapter 3 The Rowntree Survey and Tracing the Children
The basic references to the Rowntree surveys are Rowntree (1901) on the 1899 survey of York, Rowntree (1941) on the 1936 survey, and Rowntree and Lavers (1951) on the 1950 survey. Further discussion of Rowntree's work is contained in the biography by Briggs (1961), and in Jenkins and Maynard (1981a). We have obtained considerable help

from contemporary criticism of Rowntree's survey, especially the article by Townsend (1952) and an unpublished paper by Professor P. Kaim-Caudle, which he kindly allowed us to see.

In two articles (Atkinson, Corlyon *et al.*, 1981; and Atkinson, Maynard *et al.*, 1981), we have re-examined the evidence from the 1950 survey, and argued that it could have been used to throw light on a number of questions not posed by Rowntree, including the number living below the National Assistance level and the number who were entitled to, but did not claim, National Assistance. These articles go some way towards explaining the differences between the findings of Rowntree and Lavers and those of Abel-Smith and Townsend (1965) using the 1953–4 Household Expenditure Enquiry.

The published account of the 1950 Rowntree survey provides limited details of the methods employed. We have drawn on a variety of sources in order to fill out the picture. The most important are the Rowntree papers, deposited at the University of York, but these have been supplemented by discussions with those involved with the survey (see Jenkins and Maynard, 1981a).

The methods adopted in our own investigation for tracing the children are described in Chapter 4 of the unpublished report to the DHSS/SSRC Joint Working Party. Reference may also be made to Atkinson, Maynard and Trinder (1976, 1977 and 1978), and Atkinson and Trinder (1975 and 1976).

Chapter 4   The Follow-up Survey in 1975–8
The design of the questionnaire and the procedure for interviewing is described in Chapter 5 of the unpublished report, which contains a more detailed discussion of the representativeness of the respondents. The questionnaires used are reproduced in the unpublished report; these include the separate questionnaires for the personal interviews, the UK postal inquiry, and the overseas inquiry. The characteristics of the respondents are examined in Chapter 6 of the unpublished report. The intergenerational continuities in housing status are considered in Jenkins and Maynard (1981b) and multiple deprivation in Atkinson and Sutherland (1980).

Chapter 5   Income Continuities across Generations
This chapter uses the National Assistance/Supplementary Benefit standard to assess living standards. Details of the Supplementary Benefit scheme in recent years are contained in the official *Supplementary Benefits Handbook*, published by the Department of Health and Social Security (the issue most used in our research is that for February 1977). The unofficial guides by the Child Poverty Action Group *National Welfare Benefits Handbook* (published approximately annual-

ly) and Lynes (1981) are a very useful source. The National Assistance assessment is described in Atkinson, Corlyon *et al*. (1981), Atkinson, Maynard *et al*. (1981) and in the references given there; see also Abel-Smith and Townsend (1965), and Fiegehen, Lansley and Smith (1977).

There appears to be very limited information about the distribution of income in the early 1950s – see Atkinson, Jenkins and Trinder (1981). In particular, the Blue Book series constructed by the Central Statistical Office (see Royal Commission on the Distribution of Income and Wealth, 1975) groups almost half the population in the lowest income-range, so that little can be said about the shape of the lower part of the distribution. Background material on economic conditions in the early 1950s is given in Carr-Saunders, Jones and Moser (1958), Toland (1980), Upton (1980) and Zweig (1975).

The construction and interpretation of transition matrices is described in Heath (1981) and other texts on occupational mobility. The more technical issues involved in the measurement of mobility are discussed in Bartholomew (1973), Boudon (1973), Matras (1975), Prais (1955), Pullum (1975). The measurement of mobility in the context of incomes is examined in Atkinson (1981a and b), Hart (1976a and b), Markandya (1980), and Shorrocks (1978).

The regression analysis, and problems such as measurement error, are described in the Explanatory Note on Statistical Terms.

Chapter 6   Earnings in Two Generations
The available data on earnings in Britain, including those from the New Earnings Surveys, are described in the reports on the Royal Commission (1975 and 1979). A great deal of historical information is contained in the historical abstract produced by the Department of Employment (1971 and subsequent volumes).

The definition and extent of low pay is extensively discussed in the publications of the Low Pay Unit. See also Atkinson (1975), Brown (1981), Layard, Piachaud and Stewart (1978), Metcalf (1981), and Townsend (1979).

The role of family size and birth order has been discussed in the literature on the measurement of intelligence – see, for example, Belmont and Marolla (1973), and Zajonc, Markus and Markus (1979). For an analysis of the relationship with earnings, see Lindert (1977).

Some aspects of the evidence on the intergenerational pattern of earnings are discussed further in Atkinson (1980–1 and 1981a).

Chapter 7   Earnings: from Father to Son?
A great deal has been written on the determinants of earnings. Among the books covering the general area are Becker (1964), Jencks (1972),

Jencks *et al.* (1979), Lydall (1976), Phelps Brown (1977) and Taubman (1975). In the United States, the literature has tended to be dominated by the 'human-capital' theory developed by Becker (1964) and Mincer (1958, 1976 and 1979). This has been extended in the direction of family investments in children: for example, by Becker (1981), Becker and Tomes (1976), Hill and Stafford (1974 and 1977) and Leibowitz (1974). Others have treated the role of family background in different ways, and reference should be made to Ben-Porath (1980), Bowles (1972), Brittain (1977), Gustafsson (1981), Morgenstern (1973), Parsons (1975), Taubman (1979b) and Treiman and Hauser (1977). A valuable survey of empirical work in general is given by Rosen (1977); there are surveys of the effects of family background by Corcoran *et al.* (1976) and Leibowitz (1977).

The use of familial data has attracted a lot of attention in the United States in recent years, stimulated particularly by the work of Chamberlain and Griliches on brothers (see chapter 4 in the volume on kinometrics edited by Taubman, 1977a), and by Taubman on twins (see Taubman 1979 and Behrman *et al.*, 1980). A recent survey of siblings models in economics is given by Griliches (1979).

In the United Kingdom, the human-capital approach has been adopted by Psacharopolous and Layard (1979), and Papanicolaou and Psacharopolous (1979) examine the effect of family background.

The statistical techniques used in the chapter are described in the section entitled Statistical Terms: an Explanatory Note. The rationale for the particular form of the earnings equation is given by Mincer (for example, 1979), but see also Blinder (1976). The econometric problems in estimating earnings functions are discussed in an illuminating way by Griliches (1977). Some of the conceptual problems arising in the analysis of intergenerational earnings data are discussed in Atkinson (1981b) and Jenkins (1982).

Chapter 8   Education and Family Background
There are many studies covering the general field of education and family background, and here reference is only made to a small selection. Among the works on which we have drawn are Boudon (1974), Bowles and Gintis (1976), Brown, Cooper and Johnson (1981), Floud *et al.* (1956), Musgrove (1979) and Rutter *et al.*, (1979). Particular reference should be made to Halsey *et al.* (1980).

Chapter 9   The York Labour-Market and Employment Opportunities
The role of labour-market structure, long emphasised by more institutional writers, has recently began to receive more prominence. Among the recent studies are those by Berg (1981), Wilkinson (1981)

and Wright (1979). Particular reference should be made to the internal and segmented labour-market theories: Doeringer and Piore (1971), Edwards, Reich and Gordon (1975), Loveridge and Mok (1979) and – for a critique – Cain (1976).

References

Abel-Smith, B. and Townsend, P. (1965), *The Poor and the Poorest*, London: G. Bell.

Andersen, E. B. (1980), *Discrete Statistical Models*, Amsterdam: North-Holland.

Atkinson, A. B. (1975), *The Economics of Inequality*, Oxford: Oxford University Press.

Atkinson, A. B. (1979), 'Intergenerational income mobility', *IHS Journal* (Zeitschrift des Instituts für Höhere Studien, Wien), vol. 3, pp. 61–73.

Atkinson, A. B. (ed.) (1980a), *Wealth, Income and Inequality*, Oxford: Oxford University Press.

Atkinson, A. B. (1980b), 'Income distribution and inequality of opportunity', *IHS Journal*, vol. 4, pp. 65–80.

Atkinson, A. B. (1980–1), 'On intergenerational income mobility in Britain', *Journal of Post-Keynesian Economics*, vol. 3, pp. 194–218.

Atkinson, A. B. (1981a), 'The measurement of economic mobility', in P. J. Eijgelshoven and L. J. van Gemerden (eds.), *Festschrift in honour of Professor J Pen*, Utrecht: Het Spectrum.

Atkinson, A. B. (1981b), 'Intergenerational earnings mobility in Britain', paper presented at Free University of Berlin, May 1981.

Atkinson, A. B. (1982), *Social Justice and Economic Policy*, Brighton: Harvester Press, and Cambridge, Mass.: MIT Press.

Atkinson, A. B., Corlyon, J., Maynard, A. K., Sutherland, H. and Trinder, C. G. (1981), 'Poverty in York: a re-analysis of Rowntree's 1950 survey', *Bulletin of Economic Research*, vol. 33, pp. 59–71.

Atkinson, A. B., Jenkins, S. P. and Trinder, C. G. (1981), 'Intergenerational income transitions in Britain: 1950–late 1970s', unpublished paper, London School of Economics.

Atkinson, A. B., Maynard, A. K. and Trinder, C. G. (1976), 'Poverty in York: a follow-up survey based on the 1950 Rowntree–Lavers sample', unpublished paper, University of York.

Atkinson, A. B., Maynard, A. K. and Trinder, C. G. (1977), 'Intergenerational income mobility – preliminary evidence from the Rowntree data', unpublished paper, University of York.

Atkinson, A. B., Maynard, A. K. and Trinder, C. G. (1978), 'Evidence on intergenerational income mobility in Britain', *Economics Letters*, vol. 1, pp. 383–8.

Atkinson, A. B., Maynard, A. K. and Trinder, C. G. (1980), 'Evidence on intergenerational income mobility in Britain: some further results', paper presented to International Economic Association Conference, Mexico City, August 1980.

Atkinson, A. B., Maynard, A. K. and Trinder, C. G. (1981), 'National Assistance and low incomes in 1950', *Social Policy and Administration*, vol. 15, pp. 19–31.

Atkinson, A. B. and Sutherland, H. (1980), 'Indices of deprivation and intergenerational continuities', discussion paper, London School of Economics.

Atkinson, A. B. and Trinder, C. G. (1975), 'Intergenerational income mobility – preliminary results from a pilot-study', unpublished paper, University of Essex.

Atkinson, A. B. and Trinder, C. G. (1976), 'Intergenerational income mobility', in *Selected Evidence Submitted to the Royal Commission for Report No 1*, London: HMSO.

Bartholomew, D. J. (1973), *Stochastic Models for Social Processes* (2nd ed), London: Wiley.

Bauer, P. T. (1981), *Equality, the Third World and Economic Delusion*, London: Weidenfeld.

Becker, G. S. (1964), *Human Capital*, (2nd 1975), New York: NBER.

Becker, G. S. (1981), *A Treatise on the Family*, Cambridge, Mass.: Harvard University Press.

Becker, G. S. and Tomes, N. (1976), 'Child endowments and the quantity and quality of children', *Journal of Political Economy*, vol. 84, pp. S134–62.

Behrman, J. R., Hrubec, Z., Taubman, P. and Wales, J. (1980), *Socioeconomic Success*, Amsterdam: North-Holland.

Belmont, L. and Marolla, F. A. (1973), 'Birth order, family size and intelligence', *Science*, vol. 182, pp. 1096–101.

Benjamin, B. (1957), 'Intergenerational differences in occupation', *Population Studies*, vol. 11, pp. 262–8.

Ben-Porath, Y. (1980), 'The F-connection: families, friends and firms and the organisation of exchange', *Population and Development Review*, vol. 6, pp. 1–30.

Berg, I. (ed.) (1981), *Sociological Perspectives on Labor Markets*, New York: Academic Press.

Berthoud, R. (1976), *The Disadvantages of Inequality*, London: Macdonald & Jane's.

Bibby, J. (1975), 'Methods of measuring mobility', *Quality and Quantity*, vol. 9, pp. 107–36.

Bielby, W. T., Hauser, R. M. and Featherman, D. L. (1977), 'Response errors of black and non-black males in models of the intergenerational transmission of socioeconomic status', *American Journal of Sociology*, vol. 82, pp. 1242–88.

Blalock, H. M. (1972), *Social Statistics* (2nd edn), New York: McGraw-Hill.

Blau, P. M. and Duncan, O. D. (1967), *The American Occupational Structure*, New York: Wiley.

Blinder, A. S. (1976), 'On dogmatism in human capital theory', *Journal of Human Resources*, vol. 11, pp. 8–22.

Boudon, R. (1973), *Mathematical Structures of Social Mobility*, Amsterdam: Elsevier.

Boudon, R. (1974), *Education, Opportunity and Social Inequality*, New York: John Wiley.

Bowles, S. (1972), 'Schooling and inequality from generation to generation', *Journal of Political Economy*, vol. 80, pp. S219–51.

Bowles, S. and Gintis, H. (1976), *Schooling in Capitalist America*, London: Routledge & Kegan Paul.

Briggs, A. (1961), *A Study of the Work of Seebohm Rowntree*, London: Longman.

Brittain, J. A. (1977), *The Inheritance of Economic Status*, Washington, DC: Brookings Institution.

Broom, L., Jones, F. L., McDonnell, P. and Williams, T. (1980), *The Inheritance of Inequality*, London: Routledge & Kegan Paul.

Brown, J. C. (1981), *Low Pay and Poverty in the United Kingdom*, London: Policy Studies Institute.

Brown, J. C., Cooper, S. and Johnson, S. (1981), *Education and Poverty in the United Kingdom*, London: Policy Studies Institute.

Brown, M. and Madge, N. (1982), *Despite the Welfare State*, London: Heinemann Educational Books.

Cain, G. C. (1976), 'The challenge of segmented labor market theories to orthodox theory: a survey', *Journal of Economic Literature*, vol. 14, pp. 1215–57.

Carr-Saunders, A. N., Caradog Jones, D. and Moser, C. A. (1958), *A Survey of Social Conditions in England and Wales*, Oxford: Clarendon Press.

Carter, C. O. (1962), *Human Heredity*, Harmondsworth: Penguin Books.

Central Advisory Council for Education (1954), *Early Leaving*, London: HMSO.

Central Statistical Office (1979), *Social Trends*, London: HMSO.

Cherry, N. and Rodgers, B. (1979), 'Using a longitudinal study to assess the quality of retrospective data', in L. Moss and H. Goldstein (eds.), *The Recall Method in Social Surveys*, Windsor: NFER.

Clarridge, B. R., Sheehy, L. S. and Hauser, T. S. (1978), 'Tracing members of a panel: a 17 year follow-up', in K. F. Schuessler (ed.), *Sociological Methodology*, San Francisco: Jossey Bass.

Coffield, F., Robinson, P. and Sarsby, J. (1980), *A Cycle of Deprivation?*, London: Heinemann Educational Books.

Conlisk, J. (1977), 'An exploratory model of the size distribution of income', *Economic Inquiry*, vol. 15, pp. 345–66.

Corcoran, M., Jencks, C. and Olneck, M. (1976), 'The effects of family background on earnings', *American Economic Review Papers and Proceedings*, vol. 66, pp. 430–5.

Coxon, A. P. M. and Jones, C. L. (eds.) (1975), *Social Mobility*, Harmondsworth: Penguin Books.

Creedy, J. and Hart, P. E. (1979), 'Age and the distribution of earnings', *Economic Journal*, vol. 89, pp. 280–93.

Davie, R., Butler, M. and Goldstein, H. (1972), *From Birth to Seven*, London: Longman.

Department of Employment (1971), *British Labour Statistics: an Historical Abstract 1886–1968*, London: HMSO.

Department of Employment (1978), *Family Expenditure Survey 1977*, London: HMSO.

Doeringer, P. and Piore, M. (1971), *Internal Labor Markets and Manpower Analysis*, Lexington, Mass.: Lexington Books.

Douglas, J. W. B. (1964), *The Home and the School*, London: MacGibbon & Kee.

Douglas, J. W. B., Ross, J. M. and Simpson, H. R. (1968), *All Our Future*, London: Peter Davies.

Duncan, O. D. (1975), *Introduction to Structural Equation Models*, New York: Academic Press.

Duncan, O. D.,Featherman, D. L. and Duncan, B. (1972), *Socioeconomic Background and Achievement*, New York: Seminar Press.

Easterlin, R. A. (1980), *Birth and Fortune*, London: Grant McIntyre.

Edwards, R. C., Reich, M. and Gordon, D. M. (1975), *Labor Market Segmentation*, Lexington, Mass.: D. C. Heath.

Falconer, D. S. (1977), *Introduction to Quantitative Genetics*, London: Longman.

Featherman, D. L. (1980), 'Retrospective longitudinal research: methodological considerations', *Journal of Economics and Business*, vol. 32, pp. 152–69.

Featherman, D. L. and Hauser, R. M. (1975), 'Design for a replicate study of social mobility in the US', in K. C. Land and S. Spilerman, (eds.), *Social Indicator Models*, New York: Russell Sage Foundation.

Featherman, D. L. and Hauser, R. M. (1977), 'The measurement of occupation in social surveys', in R. M. Hauser and D. L. Featherman (eds.), *The Process of Stratification*, New York: Academic Press.

Featherman, D. L. and Hauser, R. M. (1978), *Opportunity and Change*, New York: Academic Press.

Feinstein, C. H. (ed.) (1981), *York 1831–1981*, York: William Sessions.

Fiegehen, G. C., Lansley, P. S. and Smith, A. D. (1977), *Poverty and Progress in Britain*, Cambridge: Cambridge University Press.

Floud, J., Halsey, A. H. and Martin, F. M. (1956), *Social Class and Educational Opportunity*, London: Heinemann.

Glass, D. V. (ed.) (1954), *Social Mobility in Britain*, London: Routledge & Kegan Paul.

Goldthorpe, J. H. (1980), *Social Mobility and Class Structure in Modern Britain*, Oxford: Oxford University Press.

Goldthrope, J. H. and Hope, K. (1974), *The Social Grading of Occupations*, Oxford: Oxford University Press.

Gordon, S. (1980), *Welfare, Justice and Freedom*, New York: Columbia University Press.

Griliches, X. (1977), 'Estimating the returns to schooling: some econometric problems', *Econometrica*, vol. 45, pp. 1–22.

Griliches, Z. (1979), 'Sibling models and data in economics: beginnings of a survey', *Journal of Political Economy*, vol. 87, pp. S37–64.

Gustafsson, B. (1981), 'Income and family background', in N. A. Klevmarken and J. A. Lybeck (eds.), *The Statics and Dynamics of Income*, Clevedon: Tieto.

Halsey, A. H., Heath, A. F. and Ridge, J. M. (1980), *Origins and Destinations*, Oxford: Oxford University Press.

Hanushek, E. A. and Jackson, J. E. (1977), *Statistical Methods for Social Scientists*, New York: Academic Press.

Harbury, C. D. and Hitchens, D. M. W. N. (1979), *Inheritance and Wealth Inequality in Britain*, London: Allen & Unwin.

Hart, P. E. (1976a), 'The comparative statics and dynamics of income distributions', *Journal of the Royal Statistical Society* (ser. A), vol. 139, pp. 198–225.

Hart, P. E. (1976b), 'The dynamics of earnings 1963–1973', *Economic Journal*, vol. 86, pp. 551–65.

Hause, J. C. (1972), 'Earnings profile: ability and schooling', *Journal of Political Economy*, vol. 80, pp. S108–38.

Hauser, R. M. and Daymont, T. N. (1977), 'Schooling, ability and earnings:

cross-sectional findings 8 to 14 years after high school graduation', *Sociology of Education*, vol. 50, pp. 182–206.

Heath, A. F. (1981), *Social Mobility*, London: Fontana.

Herrnstein, R. (1973), *IQ in the Meritocracy*, London: Allen Lane.

Hill, C. R. and Stafford, F. P. (1974), 'The allocation of time to preschool children and educational opportunity', *Journal of Human Resources*, vol. 9, pp. 323–41.

Hill, C. R. and Stafford, F. P. (1977), 'Family background and lifetime earnings', in F. T. Juster (ed.), *The Distribution of Economic Well-Being*, Cambridge, Mass.: NBER.

Hodges, J. L. and Lehmann, E. L. (1970), *Basic Concepts of Probability and Statistics*, San Francisco: Holden-Day.

Hoel, P. G. and Jessen, R. J. (1971), *Basic Statistics for Business and Economics*, New York: John Wiley.

Hope, K. (ed.) (1972) *The Analysis of Social Mobility*, Oxford: Oxford University Press.

Hope, K. (1981), 'Vertical mobility in Britain: a structured analysis', *Sociology*, vol. 15, pp. 19–55.

Hopper, E. (1981), *Social Mobility*, Oxford: Basil Blackwell.

Husen, T. (1969) 'Talent, Opportunity and Career', Stockholm: Almquist & Wiksell.

Jencks, C. (1972), *Inequality*, New York: Basic Books.

Jencks, C. (1979), *Who Gets Ahead?*, New York: Basic Books.

Jenkins, S. P. (1982), 'Life cycle bias and the measurement of intergenerational mobility', University of York Discussion Paper.

Jenkins, S. P. and Maynard, A. K. (1981a), 'The Rowntree surveys: poverty in York since 1899', in C. H. Feinstein (ed.), *York 1831–1981*, York: William Sessions.

Jenkins, S. P. and Maynard, A. K. (1981b), 'Intergenerational continuities in housing', University of York Discussion Paper 75.

Jensen, A. R. (1969), 'How much can we boost IQ and scholastic achievement?', *Harvard Educational Review*, vol. 39, pp. 1–213.

Johnson, H. G. (1973), 'Some micro-economic reflections on income and wealth inequalities', *Annals of the American Academy of Political and Social Science*, vol. 409, pp. 53–60.

Johnston, J. (1972), *Econometric Methods*, New York: McGraw-Hill.

Jordan, B. (1974), *Poor Parents*, London and Boston: Routledge & Kegan Paul.

Jordan, B. (1981), *Automatic Poverty*, London: Routledge & Kegan Paul.

Joseph, Sir K. and Sumption, J. (1979), *Equality*, London: John Murray.

Juster, F. T. (ed.) (1977), *The Distribution of Economic Well-Being*, Cambridge, Mass.: NBER.

Kaim-Caudle, P. (1953), 'Studies in poverty', University of Durham, unpublished paper.

Kane, E. J. (1969), *Economic Statistics and Econometrics*, New York: Harper Row.

Kazmier, L. H. (1979), *Basic Statistics*, New York: McGraw-Hill.

Kelsall, R. K. and Kelsall, H. M. (1974), *Stratification*, London: Longman.

Kemsley, W. F. F. (1979), 'Collecting data on economic flow variables using interviews and record keeping', in L. Moss and H. Goldstein (eds.), *The Recall Method in Social Surveys*, Windsor: NFER.

Keynes, Lord (1931), *Essays in Persuasion*, London: Macmillan.

Klappholz, K. (1972), 'Equality of opportunity, fairness and efficiency', in M. Peston and B. A. Corry (eds), *Essays in Honour of Lord Robbins*, London: Weidenfeld & Nicholson.

Kmenta, J. (1971), *Elements of Econometrics*, London: Macmillan.

Knight, F. H. (1947), *Freedom and Reform*, New York: Harper.

Layard, R., Piachaud, D. and Stewart, M. (1978), *The Causes of Poverty*, Background Paper No 5, Royal Commission on the Distribution of Income and Wealth, London: HMSO.

Leibowitz, A. (1974), 'Home investments in children', *Journal of Political Economy*, vol. 82, pp. S111–31.

Leibowitz, A. (1977), 'Family background and economic success: a review of the evidence', in P. J. Taubman (ed.), *Kinometrics*, Amsterdam: North-Holland.

Lillard, L. A. and Willis, R. J. (1978), 'Dynamic aspects of earning mobility', *Econometrica*, vol. 46, pp. 985–1012.

Lindert, P. H. (1977), 'Sibling position and achievement', *Journal of Human Resources*, vol. 12, pp. 198–209.

Lloyd Thomas, D. A. (1977), 'Competitive equality of opportunity', *Mind*, vol. 86, pp. 388–404.

Loveridge, R. and Mok, A. L. (1979), *Theories of Labour Market Segmentation*, The Hague: Martinus Nijhoff Social Sciences Division.

Lydall, H. F. (1968), *The Structure of Earnings*, Oxford: Oxford University Press.

Lydall, H. F. (1976), 'Theories of the distribution of earnings', in A. B. Atkinson (ed.), *The Personal Distribution of Incomes*, London: Allen & Unwin.

Lynes, T. (1981), *The Penguin Guide to Supplementary Benefits*, Harmondsworth: Penguin Books.

Maddala, G. S. (1977), *Econometrics*, New York: McGraw-Hill.

Markandya, A. (1980), 'Toward a theory of intergenerational economic mobility', *European Economic Review*.

Matras, J. (1975), *Social Inequality, Stratification and Mobility*, Englewood Cliffs,: Prentice Hall.

Meade, J. E. (1974), *The Inheritance of Inequalities, some Biological, Social and Economic Factors*, London: Oxford University Press.

Metcalf, D. (1981), *Low Pay, Occupational Mobility and Minimum Wage Policy in Britain*, Washington, D.C.: AEI.

Metcalf, D. and Nickell, S. (1981), 'Occupational mobility in Britain', *Research in Labour Economics*, Vol. 4, Greenwich, Conn.: JAI Press.

Mincer, J. (1958), 'Investment in human capital and personal income distribution', *Journal of Political Economy*, vol. 66, pp. 281–302.

Mincer, J. (1976), 'Progress in human capital analyses of the distribution of earnings', in A. B. Atkinson (ed.), *The Personal Distribution of Incomes*, London: Allen & Unwin.

Mincer, J. (1979), 'Human capital and earnings', in D. Windham (ed), *Economic Dimensions of Education*, Washington, DC: National Academy of Education.

Morgan, J. N. *et al.* (1974), *Five Thousand American Families*, Ann Arbor: Institute for Social Research, University of Michigan.

Morgenstern, R. D. (1973), 'Direct and indirect effects on earnings of schooling and socio-economic background', *Review of Economics and Statistics*, vol. 55, pp. 225–33.

Musgrove, F. (1979), *School and the Social Order*, Chichester: John Wiley.

Nickell, S. (1982), 'The determinants of occupational success in Britain', *Review of Economic Studies*, vol. 49, pp. 43–53.

Nozick, R. (1974), *Anarchy, State and Utopia*, Oxford: Basil Blackwell.

Okun, A. M. (1975), *Equality and Efficiency: The Big Trade-Off*, Washington, DC: Brookings Institution.

Olneck, M. (1977), 'On the use of sibling data to estimate the effects of family background, cognitive skills, and schooling', in P. Taubman (ed.), *Kinometrics*, Amsterdam: North-Holland.

Papanicolaou, J. and Psacharopoulos, G. (1979), 'Socioeconomic background and monetary rewards in the UK', *Economica*, vol. 46, pp. 435–9.

Parsons, D. O. (1975), 'Intergenerational wealth transfers and the educational decisions of male youth', *Quarterly Journal of Economics*, vol. 89, pp. 603–17.

Payne, G., Ford, G. and Robertson, C. (1977), 'A reappraisal of social mobility in Britain', *Sociology*, vol. 11, pp. 289–310.

Phelps Brown, Sir E. H. (1977), *The Inequality of Pay*, Oxford: Oxford University Press.

Porter, R. D. (1973), 'On the use of survey sample weights in the linear model', *Annals of Economic and Social Measurement*, vol. 2, pp. 141–58.

Prais, S. J. (1955), 'Measuring social mobility', *Journal of the Royal Statistical Society*, vol. 118, pp. 56–66.

Pringle, M. K. (1980), *The Needs of Children* (2nd edn), London: Hutchinson.

Psacharopoulos, G. (1977), 'Family background, education and achievement', *British Journal of Sociology*, vol. 28, pp. 321–5.

Psacharopoulos, G. and Layard, R. (1979), 'Human capital and earnings: British evidence and a critique', *Review of Economic Studies*, vol. 46, pp. 485–503.

Pullum, T. W. (1975), *Measuring Occupational Inheritance*, Amsterdam: Elsevier.

Richardson, C. J. (1977), *Contemporary Social Mobility*, London: Frances Pinter, and New York: Nichols Publishing Company.

Ridge, J. M. (ed.) (1973), *Mobility in Britain Reconsidered*, Oxford: Oxford University Press.

Rosen, S. (1977), 'Human capital: a survey of empirical research', in R. G. Ehrenberg (ed.), *Research in Labor Economics*, Greenwich, Conn.: JAI Press.

Rowntree, B. S. (1901), *Poverty: A Study of Town Life*, London and New York: Macmillan.

Rowntree, B. S. (1941), *Poverty and Progress: A Second Social Survey of York*, London, New York and Toronto: Longman Green.

Rowntree, B. S. and Lavers, G. R. (1951), *Poverty and the Welfare State*, London, New York and Toronto: Longman Green.

Royal Commission on the Distribution of Income and Wealth (1975), *Report No 1*, Cmnd 6171, London: HMSO.

Royal Commission on the Distribution of Income and Wealth (1978), *Report No 6, Lower Incomes*, Cmnd 7175, London: HMSO.

Royal Commission of the Distribution of Income and Wealth (1979a), *Report No 7*, Cmnd 7595, London: HMSO.

Royal Commission on the Distribution of Income and Wealth (1979b), *Report No 8*, Cmnd 7679, London: HMSO.

Rutter, M. L. and Madge, N. (1976), *Cycles of Disadvantage*, London: Heinemann Educational Books.

Rutter, M. L., Maughan, B., Mortimore, P. and Ouston, J. (1979), *Fifteen Thousand Hours*, London: Open Books.

Sewell, W. H. and Hauser, R. M. (1975), *Education, Occupation and Earnings*, New York: Academic Press.

Shorrocks, A. F. (1978), 'The measurement of mobility', *Econometrica*, vol. 46, pp. 1013–24.

Soltow, L. (1965), *Toward Income Inequality in Norway*, Madison: University of Wisconsin Press.

Taubman, P. (1975), *Sources of Inequality in Earnings*, Amsterdam: North-Holland.

Taubman, P. (ed.) (1977a), *Kinometrics*, Amsterdam: North-Holland.

Taubman, P. (1977b), 'Schooling, ability, nonpecuniary rewards, socio-economic background, and the lifetime distribution of income', in F.T. Juster (ed.), *The Distribution of Economic Well-Being*, Cambridge, Mass.: NBER.

Taubman, P. (1978), *Income Distribution and Redistribution*, Reading, Mass.: Addison-Wesley.

Taubman, P. (1979), 'Equality of opportunity and equality of outcome: a lesson from the studies of twins', *IHS Journal* (Zeitschrift des Instituts für Höhere Studien, Wien), vol. 3, pp. 43–60.

Tawney, R. H. (1964), *Equality* (new edn), London: Allen & Unwin.

Theil, H. (1978), *Introduction to Econometrics*, Englewood Cliffs, NJ: Prentice-Hall.

Thurow, L.C. (1976), *Generating Inequality*, London: Macmillan.

Toland, S. (1980), 'Changes in living standards since the 1950s', *Social Trends*, vol. 10, pp. 13–38.

Townsend, P. (1952), 'Poverty: ten years after Beveridge', *Political and Economic Planning*, vol. 19, no. 344.

Townsend, P. (1979), *Poverty in the United Kingdom*, London: Allen Lane.

Treiman, D. J. and Hauser, R. M. (1977), 'Intergenerational transmissions of income', in R. M. Hauser and D. L. Featherman (eds.), *The Process of Stratification*, New York: Academic Press.

Upton, M. (1980), 'Reviving Rowntree: poverty lines and the levels of social security benefits for the unemployed; 1950–1978', *Social Policy and Administration*, vol. 14, pp. 36–46.

Wall, W.D. and Williams, H. L. (1970), *Longitudinal Studies and the Social Sciences*, London: Heinemann Educational Books.

Wedge, P. and Prosser, H. (1973), *Born to Fail?*, London: Arrow Books.

White, H. (1980), 'A heteroskedasticity-consistent covariance matrix estimator and a direct test for heteroskedasticity', *Ecomometrica*, vol. 48, pp. 817–38.

Wilkinson, F. (ed.) (1981), *The Dynamics of Labour Market Segmentation*, London: Academic Press.

Williamson, J. G. (1980), 'Earnings inequality in nineteenth-century Britain', *Journal of Economic History*, vol. 40, pp. 457–76.

Wolff, P. de and van Slijpe, A. R. D. (1973), 'The relation between income, intelligence, education and social background', *European Economic Review*, vol. 4, pp. 235–64.

Wonnacott, R. J. and Wonnacott, T. H. (1970), *Econometrics*, New York: John Wiley.

Wright, E. O. (1979), *Class Structure and Income Determination*, New York: Academic Press.

Yule, G. U. and Kendall, M. G. (1950), *An Introduction to the Theory of Statistics*, (14th edn), London: Griffin.

Zajonc, R. B., Markus, H. and Markus, G. B. (1979), 'The birth order puzzle', *Journal of Personality and Social Psychology*, vol. 37, pp. 1325–41.

Zweig, F. (1975), *Labour, Life and Poverty*, East Ardley, Wakefield: EP Publishing and New York: British Book Centre.

Index